T0354819

AuthorHouse™
1663 Liberty Drive
Bloomington, IN 47403
www.authorhouse.com
Phone: 1 (800) 839-8640

Published by AuthorHouse 05/11/2015

ISBN: 978-1-5049-0500-8 (sc)
ISBN: 978-1-5049-0502-2 (hc)
ISBN: 978-1-5049-0501-5 (e)

Library of Congress Control Number: 2015905796

Print information available on the last page.

All human form imagery & likeness used are models handcrafted by the
author. Headgears & clothing styles are endeavors inspired to depict
the period called for in the chapters for illustrative purposes.

This book is printed on acid-free paper.

"Spirited Deed Revelations"

The Factual Quest for the Truth, Accuracy, Integrity in the History

of Historic Site # 06000160 – 2006 US National Register

The Spirit House

Resurreccion Dimaculangan

07/01/2011 13:36

Plate 3-5057   Nostalgia for a Loggia

Dedication

"Spirited Deed Revelations" # 06000160 The Factual Quest for the Truth is intended to be the basis of this Site's story in the pages of History.

This work is dedicated to the direct descendants of the Family that funded the procurement of the House.

To the Historians, and History Buffs that believe in truths based on facts as cornerstones of History to have Integrity, and Accuracy.

To every dreamer that hoped and labored with tenacity, yet at the end of the journey all efforts were washed away like castles in the sand,

To the winners that were able to have achieved the crossovers and lucky to also relish the fruits of their toils after long nights and days when it did all seemed so futile,

Here's to you: my sincerest gratitude, and thank you for paving the way for me and those that would follow,

Where dreams are piped and construed as fanciful flights of fancy: The Spirit of Hope lives on. Faith for the sacred cause of destiny by choice, Reliance in the God given talents imbedded in our Human DNA.

To my Family, that suffer in silence and made it possible for me to go past conventions of cultural traditions to have the privileges of chasing after my Dreams - big dreams, totally unheard of, thus could have been easily shut off. This Dream that continuously burn inside of me, and in gargantuan persistence so strong, that the only relief is to follow it's course to the end.

This book is part of the Journey, towards that Dream.

Beriopauladixiesamjavesnickmiladodiruthfelixalexmaxbeckyalvinramiljoizejomilamorjoramnikojobobernicefelizalitacora

Plate 4-5061   Amoretto

History tells the story based on facts. Data conscientiously collected, painstakingly recorded, meant to be revisited. Time, and again. The purpose: To equip the new generation with wisdom from the past. Discernment is one, a valuable instrumentation of moving forward, without the errors of our ancestors. This book, is a by - product of that collected information. The act of going over records, brought forth Discernment.

Neophyte and Barefoot Museologist Resurreccion Dimaculangan presents the multifaceted Story of her Home. A one object exhibit by itself. The Architecturally Unique Design, bespeaks of Craftsman Guild influence, yet exudes the Decorative Gothic Victorian Style for the overall visceral effect. A true Americana, of the Folk Art tradition, Tramp Art the size of a real livable structure. The Historical contexts that made this Site important, tell of status quo shattering Truth Schemed to be intentionally Ignored. That is, if one cared enough to approach the story based on factual, legally accepted evidentiary proofs, that coincide with property ownership. Information data found in Deeds, used not only here in the US, but around the globe.

An interactive story format where Readers can fact check; think analyses. The truth hurt. Yes. Not for this one. The Denial of that Distortion, hurt. A travesty of History. An affront to the Human Spirit. A blatant Disregard for Real people that lived, and died, as corroborated in the pages of these Deeds. We owe the Dead, the Truth in: The $65,000.00 question of "How do we move forward without losing their true legacy?

1. Tell the story accurately with integrity, to embody the Honesty of the American Spirit in this Spirit House.

2. Effectuate that overarching purpose to entwine Elegance, with Utility, for sustainability that endures. This is Stage One, in an attempt to make it Right.

Foreword

It is a privilege to be able to earn a Masters Degree in Museology. Especially considering what I had gone through to finish this two year Graduate Program in a year. Not only is this true for this type of academic achievement, but for all institutional, and non - traditional learning in any Scientific discipline, or field of Study. Does this make me an Expert? No. I do not go about under that pretext either. It is the application of what was learned, in the furtherance of knowledge, that makes the certificates of scholarly pursuits worth their ink in them. The conviction that there is a higher calling for this Diploma to be of better purpose. On this context was the procurement of this House had been acted upon, made possible through much effort, and deliberation to pursue that lonely avenue of making a "Positive Difference One Person at a Time".

The Structure landmarked #06000160 was captivating enough by itself; grand, and stately in bearing, even in it's rugged state, devoid of human habitation. The " For Sale" sign in front sending a message of needing someone, to breathe fresh life to it. A caress of Nostalgia. This enigmatic pull so strong was enough to incite in me, the uncontainable inspiration to switch from "renting" to "home / property ownership". The idea of securing a roof over my head, that can create for greater possibilities of a chance to provide an opportunity to carve out a career of choice, in the realm of Museology; the challenge to generate revenue to maintain / sustain the House, and myself as the initial Primary worker - are mesmerizingly too good not to take on, as a test of bravado. Not only have I the accountability for the student loans incurred, but for the investments of time, career, and moving forward. Factor property taxes. Also materials, and tools, no matter how measly cost a fortune. The responsibilities to oneself, to family, to community - the measures of productivity; to be a contributing entity to human progress. Expenditures need be covered by some revenue generation called income.

I took the leap of faith, with the gut feelings all somersaulting. It was the most inconceivable decision people around me thought they had ever known. So was the transportation system we now enjoy. Had it not been for those innovative minds, we would not just be riding horses for pleasure today; but that they would still be the primary form of mobility - I countered. Remember the electrification of the world known as harnessing Light & Energy? The fiber-optic communications; unheard of discoveries, and so forth inventions. No one believed these were possible then.

Until the unthinkable, the unexplainable, came to open an entire new wave of doing things, that made life easier, more ergonomically comfortable. All because some person dared enough to try. Thank You, to the non - conventional mindsets that made the Impossible - Possible. To those who dared; to those that made them happen: Salute!

If you're saying: "what a noble thought, thank you" to me, and this cause - I say: You're very Welcome," as I continue the journey on a mission, to answer the call for diversity in mindset, to move the Project Conservation, & Preservation of this Magnificent House, directionally forward. That meant: Back to Sustainability. Skeptics? Not new. They will always be around. Cynicism. Why not? Makes the journey more eventful than it already is.

We hear about dreamers and idealists that acted on their goals in what is called Garage start ups. Yes, realistically, they either owned their garage/s or they rented spaces, or a space for one. Well, this is my version of that. Two birds in one, and maybe more. Only this time I am not renting. A little bit more serious than that. Trying to live a life that real mature human beings aspire. The establishment of a roof over my head, a career calling, a greater chance of revenue generation source for a lifetime, at the same time give back to the cause of honoring the legacy of the generation that pioneered the life dedicated to the responsible enjoyment of the freedom that you and I now enjoy

Three years from 03 November 2011, the date of final fund transferred, and 04 November 2011 closing, What had been accomplished? Or Not? WHY? What can be done to move it forward?

Since the entire world around here made it known to me in more obtrusive ways that can be put nicely here, to have a SAY to what happens to a Privately owned House, here's the action resorted to accommodate that Need to include the Community, and the Public. The answer? The 444-a Tax exemption.

There are a few technical things to consider in putting a formal request under this tax break. Besides filing the prescribed approved request form prior to the tax cycle deadline, the law had to be in placed to be enacted; but if it is not there yet, it has to be ratified in the local town level, then the submission of the application follows.

The State & Federal levels left the adoption of the Tax Exemption 444-a, as an option for the towns not specifically named under this law. It would go to the procedural process of public hearings after a formal request should have been submitted if the Historic landmarked requirements are met, for structures used as a home, and so forth. In consonance with the landmarked registration, the formation of a Preservation Commission is necessary.

The IRS Exemption titled 444 - a for Historic Residential Dwelling is an incentive implement for enforcing RPTL 444-a for Historic Property. Here is the gist of what is this 444-a is all about, as lifted off both the IRS and the NY blue book for instant reference here.

A. Tax Exemption <u>444 - a</u> for Historic Residential Dwelling[1]. Excerpt from the §444-a.

1. "Real Property altered or rehabilitated subsequent to the effective date of a local law or resolution adopted pursuant to this section shall be exempt from taxation and special ad valorem levies as herein provided. After a public hearing, the governing body of a county, city, town or village may adopt a local law and a school district, other than a school district governed by the provisions of article fifty - two of the education law, may adopt a resolution to grant the exemption authorized pursuant to this section. A copy of such law or resolution shall be filed with the commissioner and the assessor of such county, city, town or village who prepares the assessment roll on which the taxes of such county, city, town, village or school district are levied.

2. (a) Historic property shall be exempt from taxation to the extent of any increase in value attributable to such alteration or rehabilitation pursuant to the following schedule:

Year Exemption	Percent of Exemption
1 to 5	100
6	80
7	60
8	40
9	20
10	0

(b) No such exemption shall be granted for such alterations or rehabilitation unless:

(i) Such property has been designated as a landmark, or is a property that contributes to the character of an historic district, created by a local law passed pursuant to section ninety - six - a or one hundred nineteen - dd of the general municipal law;

(ii) Alterations or rehabilitation must be made for means of historic preservation;

(iii) Such alterations or rehabilitation of historic property meet guidelines and review standards in the local preservation law;

(iv) Alterations or rehabilitation are commenced subsequent to the effective date of the local la or resolution pursuant to this section.

3. Such exemption shall be granted only by application of the owner or owners of such historic real property on a form prescribed by the commissioner. The application shall be filed with the assessor of the county, city or village having power to assess property for taxation on or before the appropriate taxable status date of such county, city, town or village." ...

---

[1] Department of taxation. www.IRS.NY.

A.1   the Formal Request was submitted

   29 February 2012 : Letter of Request, Office of the Assessor

A.11   Council Meetings, 444-a on agenda

   08 February 2012 Letter to the Council via the Town Supervisor

A.111.   Public Hearing. This was supposedly for the local town. The attendees included some council members antagonistic to the request, a professor from the next town asking all the questions, accompanied by an individual that did not identify herself as a news paper representative. None from the Historical Society. Not one to support the idea of the Project, yet every one expected to dictate what would happen to the House. See the newspaper article for yourself. Clearly, it would have been hard not to understand that the challenges ahead would be more enveloped with intrigue and excoriation.

A.IV.   Local 444-a Local Town Law Passed or so on the surface. Unto this day, the printed copy of this law, Georgetown version is yet to be seen.

A.V.   Town issued a Press Release[2] that the House Received the Tax Exemption. The title of the article was "Spirit House gets Exemption on Improvements" Madison County Courier dated 30 May 2012, Georgetown, NY. I suggest the readers go over this article on their own as this is not the focus of this book, at this point.

A. VI.   Expected: The Formation of a Preservation Commission for which I applied to Spearhead as a volunteer, and / or be a part of; Followed through with the Reply of Silence. This tax exemption was resorted to establish the legitimate relationship, and shared responsibilities of honoring, respecting, and protecting the Cultural Heritage of a Community, and of a Nation. The Flagship of the Nation I swore full Citizenship

---

[2] Madison County Courier Article

allegiance to. In a manner of speaking, this is my version of thinking globally by acting locally. This is first hand application of University learning in day to day life, within the Neighborhood, as a token of Civic Duties. This is carving a lifestyle of standing up for one's convictions of what is humanly right, and lawfully civilized.

2012, July 18 A document copy titled "Local Law Filing" to establish a Local Historic Preservation Commission was received. Though the actual 444-a law wordings, had not been seen yet. Here's a gist for the Formation of the Preservation Commission Requirements' Guidelines at a glance both from the IRS & RPTL sources:

      1   **Appointment by the Mayor, Town Supervisor**

It is of note to refer that the request for the list of the appointees, if there really was a Commission formed was never responded to. Surely, appointed officers need to have a discourse with the owner of the Historic Site, even if it is just for civility purposes. The fact that these issues were not even allowed to have as grievances brought up to the Town Council tell of a very thought provoking question of what happened to free speech, especially when the agenda, called for the allowance of airing injustice provoked by either bad recording, misreading of documents etc., by the government officers should be initiated from the local level? The situation having permeated the Social and Cultural core of the community? A case for the humanities; surely this can and should be taken by the Town council?

      2   **Professional Education of Diverse Background**
      3   **Historical Interests, Expertise, Training**
      4   **Passion, Dedication, as this may be unpaid are among the different assets to look for in convening talents for this cause.**

A.VII. Tax Exemption was Never Received by the House

A.IX. Nothing had come out of this request except the press release saying this
was received by the House.

This attempt to establish a collaborative effort toward what seemed to be everyone's goal to preserve and conserve a Historic site had shown a Silhouette to be wary of. Sad. Today, as I write this in the middle of December 2014, I begin to see the pattern of "by design". The use of the press as a tool for smear campaign to mislead the public against me, the Site and it's cause. This was part of the design to ensure that people, the populace would have a reason, a twisted reason that, since the Site received the tax exemption on paper, that: "The People" have the Right to take what they can, as reflected in the practice of holding court for Tours, educational & Recreational, paid mind you, but the proceeds never reached the House. Everybody "gets taken cared off", but not the site. None. NADA. The use of the area when they can, whenever they please, for boasting, regardless of the "Cleaning Lady" became the amusement as part of the roadside - house picture taking sprees. That was how the people saw the hyper - pigmented female that invested $65,000.00 for a shell of a House. "Boy, she must really be that Stupid"; " what do you know: She went to school for Basket weaving." Even so.

Two Social and Cultural Misperceptions, Misunderstanding?

1   Edwardian Time Museology: Are the people still thinking of Museums and History to be exclusive rights of the Elite? Just because there is Historic importance does not in any way automatically meant that a site, a story or a structure had to be owned only by an exclusive group of people?! Especially if it is for sale. This one had been in the market for three years. It had been offered to the Town, the Historical Society, even before: Hearsay Information garnered. Why was this Site not procured all these years? Now that I had financed the ownership, all hell broke loose. Just a Reminder, this is the

21st going 22nd Century, not back to the looting and barbaric acts of the Dark Ages? Modernization in mindset, tolerance, openness, acceptance, diversity in action, deeds that turn everything under the sun into positives: Where History and Museums should go hand in hand, in symbiotic, synergistic interrelationship: Where there is a direct correlation of History as presented in Museums and vice versa. These precepts are not my own invention, nor a pioneering ideal. Also, the word Museum does not in any way, shape or form starts and ends in attaching that word to any site of Historic Importance. Oh, there is everything more than meets the eye, far beyond a sentence or two that I can talk about here. I take it in the most serious importance, and so should everybody.

2   Museology of the Modern Civilization, of the Society that enjoy Democratic Freedoms: Which one of the viewpoints are the readers seeing me from? Does the dream of having one's own property reserved according to caste? Why then is owning a neglected and abused gutted house an issue when it comes to Privacy? Much more when the site and the owner are both not ready to receive paying or non - paying visitors nor guests. Can this really be so hard to understand, that this needed to be verbalized here?

Stewardship is every person's privilege if one chooses to do so. It is encouraged and incentivized by the government, yet these incentives do not mean the private owner is tied to the whim of every person that want to enjoy the merits of the site or story. This particular case had not received any grants or funds, public or otherwise. So, in the premise of Democracy; please recognize that Freedom stops when another person's Rights start. Self governance is that one thing that separates civility from barbaric dark ages. Surely there is accountability and responsibility, not destruction of one's rights to achieve a wholesome, happy life, free of unwanted intrusion at any time for every one, self - evidentiary even in the suburbs of a State, in a Country, that is a World Leader?

Why am I so important to be targeted, when I am just trying to do what any conscientious citizen would have done? There was nothing in the Constitution that said my name should be J. P. Morgan; Trump, or Zuckerberg to be able to do things; nor that one had to be of Einstein intellect to be a positive contributor to Society? Maybe I missed out something in translation? What happened to Real Property Law? Article 1 gives the definition. Article 2 titled Tenure of Real Property Section 10 Capacity to hold Real Property is excerpted here:

1   " A citizen of the United States is capable of holding real property within this state, and of taking the same by descent, device or purchase."

2   " Aliens are empowered to take, hold, transmit, and dispose of real property within the same manner as native - born citizens and their heirs and devisees take in the same manner as citizens." ...

Where do the difficulties of moving this Project forward stem from?

Ownership	:	✓ Done
Deeds	:	✓ Done
Historic Registration:		? with questionable basis and context used
Taxed Acreage Record:		? inconsistent with Deed Descriptions on Record
Assessed Tax Acreage:		? Non - consistent with Deed Descriptions on Record
Tax Map:?		Mapped Dimension Contradictory with Deed Description on Record
Commissioned Boundary Survey: ?		Contradicted everything on Record

It is noteworthy to mention that the six titled parcels were never found the way they were described. We will visit this issue in consonance with this book further on.

?Adjoining Land Deeds: Nothing showed duplicity nor negation of conveyed Deeds of Land Acreage that belong to the House.

The fact is, the parcels all use each other as monumental points of references to qualify the geo - position and the definition of the boundaries for the majority of the adjoined parcels in Lot 91. You will recognize these within the pages of this book as the dissection of these inaccuracies are attempted to be unravelled. A long arduous process, a lengthy one the complexity of which cannot be digested into one capsulized form. My apologies.

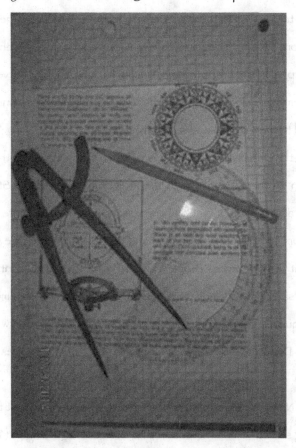

Plate 5- 0248   Measurement Implements

Backdrop picture taken from a copy of the page of a book on Forensic Historical Survey Techniques, Access courtesy of the Staley Library, DeRuyter, NY.

B. The Commissioned Boundary Survey:

A Travesty of History, Sheer Mathematical Incompetence of Gargantuan Proportion. This was the second stage of an effort tried to form a paid professional collaborative force in appropriately documenting, or should I say the act of filling in the blanks of making the documentation of this Historic site be updated.

The goal is to conform to the standards of accepted practice expected of, in any Real Property. More so for a Landmarked one. Does anybody comprehend this? This collaborative group would have started with the closing lawyer, then surveyors, to every Agency in the Community - permits, history, schools, assessors, planners, to name a few, from the local to the County, and so forth as needed.

These are the circumstances that this property is up against with. If that would have gone smooth on the initial try, then the Project move up to the State & Federal Grant Requests as needed. Grants, if necessary. Then Legitimate Paid Interns, Volunteers, Mentors can play their individual and group goals under the Cohesive Goal of Making a Positive Difference. People can visit while the work continue within an insured, secured, safer environment. Then the simultaneous commencement of the real bustle of heavy equipment type work can get underway in coordination with Engineers - Architectural & Design, and other experts in the field of Preservation, and Conservation.

Well, Good News. We were burnt to the third degree, the very first time. It was not just about getting seared. It was the notion that the wool was being put over our eyes, and as if nothing is wrong. That is the worst of all. These are signals that confirmed there is more than meets the eye, more than what goes behind the smiles. The quest begins to unravel layer upon layer of age old angst. Here are some of them.

Please do correct me if the basic acts received from these so called Professionals, and People in Office were perceived mistakenly on the negative side other than how they were intended to be understood? Maybe I missed out on the kind deeds like lawn mowing as a way to usurp taking possession of a few feet here, there; a corner, corners; then an entire land piece - by the acres, one way or another. The people feeling so entitled to walking their pets, leaving fecal and waste matter on the grounds; living off someone else's property like baiting the turkey, and the deer, dressing them there, and leaving the carcass, residues on the grounds; garbage - old and new; clambake shells by the tonnage, and the list go on. Neighborliness, is a two way street. Also, do feel free to re - educate me on how these neighborly acts of kindness cannot be mistranslated, and I thank you all in advance. Maybe then, that the possibilities of the words Honesty, Integrity, Accuracy, and the search for the Truth have never changed their meaning after all? As from my vantage view, the recipient of the run around, did these words just become suddenly "relative to"…?

History based on Facts. Fabricated data, stamped legit, passed on for popular consumption, and thus taken as History. Google or web surf the data about the site, and see for yourself. Retrace the story. This is not something lost in translation. English in every form, verbiage and usage, equals English. The official language the professed professionals use. I do not profess to be the specialist in this. I am the messenger with the unfortunate message. The errors in comprehending the Recorded Facts are widespread. Is Non comprehension deliberate, intentional? I see this travesty perpetuated as a well oiled machinery funded by tax payers dollars to obliterate the true legacy of the dead found in deeds. Example: Those four brown and white signs to denote "Historic designation" were placed along the highways, and not one agency can account for them. I know, because I had asked all different levels. Does any body know?

Let not hyper pigmentation be the driving force for the lackadaisical interest to have a look on this particular Historically Registered Landmark's first comprehensive attempts to approach this Story's History from checked facts, please.

C. The Initial Rehabilitation Stages

C.I.   Accounting for the Land Holdings that came with the title / deed

C.II.   Defining the Periphery. What Happened?

Commissioned Survey - was not able to account for the six titled parcels

C.III.   Use of Experimental Materials to promote Environmental Awareness and Responsible Use. What Happened?

Containment Barriers were ran over with a tractor. Could not do it without causing damage to his equipment, thus resorted to individually un - corkscrewed[3] them out, then transported them to the front of the site for every one to see. I am inclined to believe that this is the mindset of some in the locale, wherein this magnificent House unfortunately still stands. The aforementioned elements served as catalysts to go ahead and submit to you, dear Readers, the Story behind the Scenes.

This book aims to share the issues; the challenges, that were woven around the ignored factual story of the House as I dust myself off in it. To reach out to the people to somehow understand what conflicts, and strife lurk behind the surface; or be understood themselves. For those who do feel that the need for dialogue is obsolete, Please: Do not forget, the House is so beautiful on the outside yet was totally gutted out. The story is summed all up in that. Little by little, piece by little piece, right in front

---

3 Anodized metal picks shaped as cork screws 12' long, used as ground penetrating restraints.

of everyone, in broad - daylight, key leaders that adjoin the property complicit yet profess not to know, what happened, and why? There is nothing left but the shell. The ground will eventually disappear at the rate of how they bully me into not be able to have anything done in it. The journey to it's final resting stage of Conservation, and Preservation remain under threat. Stage One, Phase one never had a chance. No police protection[4], no government officials to look into the records. Government Agencies & Employees holding positions meant to serve the public & ensure the sanctity of the taxpayers' Constitutional Rights are either too busy or hard of hearing to pay attention to this very persistent Problem of: UNRECONCILED DIFFERENCES of RECORDS.

1   Six Deeded Acreage descriptions not Reflected in Tax Assessed Acreage,

2   Taxed, Mapped Acreage incompatible with Six Deeded Acreage descriptions;

4   Non - Consultation of Deeds on Record for the prescribed History survey prior to Registration; more so with the commissioned Boundary Survey that DO NOT reflect nor account the Six deeded descriptions; even after this inaccuracy was brought up.

5   Above all: Deeds, Assessed, Taxed, Mapped, Historical Basis & Commissioned Survey contradict one another. Not One reinforced the six Deeded descriptions. Not even any closer to 1-2-5 feet of reasonably acceptable margin of error with today's modern technology that boasts pinpoint precision and accuracy.

The rest of the real story about the real History is laid out here in an attempt to get off the ground the process of dignifying the archived facts documented, recorded - left by the very people that lived their lives and enshrined the still standing attestation epitomized by the House, that the simplest of actions using the simplest of materials can achieve timeless greatness. Read, and see for yourself.

---

4 see RPAPL 843, fences & structures, when private nuisance;RPAL853;881;861;RPAPL 311;321

Plate 6-0576   Hickory Glory

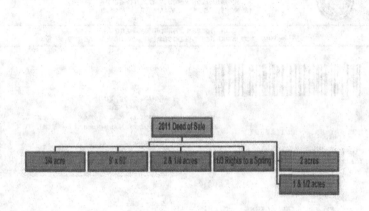

Plate 7- 2011 Deed of Sale

Resurreccion Dimaculangan

MADISON COUNTY – STATE OF NEW YORK
KENNETH J. KUNKEL JR, COUNTY CLERK
138 NORTH COURT ST, WAMPSVILLE, NY 13163

COUNTY CLERK'S RECORDING PAGE
THIS PAGE IS PART OF THE DOCUMENT – DO NOT DETACH

RECEIPT NO. : 2011165877

Clerk: TS
Instr #:   2011-6312
Rec Date: 11/04/2011 09:36:04 AM
Doc Grp: D
Descrip: DEED
Num Pgs: 5
Rec'd Frm: ALLIED LORENA

Party1: WILSON VALERIE K
Party2: RESURRECCION DIMACULANGAN
Town: GEORGETOWN

Recording:

Cover Page	5.00
Recording Fee	40.00
Cultural Ed	14.25
Records Management - Coun	1.00
Records Management - Stat	4.75
TP584	5.00
RP5217 Residential/Agricu	116.00
RP5217 - County	9.00
Sub Total:	195.00
Transfer Tax	
Transfer Tax	260.00
Sub Total:	260.00
Total:	455.00

**** NOTICE: THIS IS NOT A BILL ****

***** Transfer Tax *****

Transfer Tax# :   776

Consideration: 65000.00
Transfer Tax: 260.00

Record and Return To:

PAUL V NOYES (ALLIED)
131 SHERRILL RD
SHERRILL NY 13461

I hereby certify that the within and foregoing was recorded in the Clerk's Office for: Madison County, NY

Madison County Clerk

Plate 8-Instr#:2011-6312. 11/04/2011 P. 1

xx

An itemization of the Deeded parcels that is the True Inheritance of the House: The Provenance.

The Brown Estate: 4 Properties

1. All that tract or parcel of land, situate in the Town of Georgetown, County of Madison and State of New York, and being..... containing ¾ of an acre more or less.
2. Also that tract or parcel of land deeded by the trustees of the First Baptist Society of said town to Timothy Brown on the 15th day of August 1882, and **recorded in the clerk's office of the county of Madison on the 5th day of August,1884 at 11 o'clock a.m. in Liber 161, page 20.**
3. Also all that other piece or parcel of land deeded by Zinah J. Moseley, Milton D. Allen and Mary his wife, Isaac Fletcher and Mercy, his wife to said Sarah H. Brown on the 22nd day of March 1871 and **recorded in the Clerk's Office of the County of Madison on the 30th day of March 1871 at 11 o'clock a.m. in Book No. 123 of Deeds, page 347.**
4. ALSO THE RIGHTS AND PRIVILEGES in and to a certain spring of water which was conveyed to the said Sarah H. Brown by a deed from Hiram N. Atwood and wife and George Curtis and wife and recorded in the Clerk's Office of the County of Madison on the 14th day of May, 1885 at 9 o'clock a.m. in Liber 162 of Deeds at page 140, to which said deed reference is hereby made for a more particular description of said water rights.

NOTE: Should we not as the scholarly approach to this, open up those books and see what they have to see?

The Leemon R. Cossit Legacy Parcel 1

Parcel II

All that tract, piece or parcel of land.... Beginning at a stake on the northwest corner of the lot now or formerly owned by Mrs. Fred Currier (formerly Ross) South line; running thence eaterly along said Currier south line about 199 ½ feet to a stake; thence in a southerly direction about 276 feet to the corner of lands owned by H.H. Whitmore; thence in a westerly direction about 323 feet to a stake; thence in a northerly direction 309 feet on the eat line of the old cemetery to the northeast corner of said Cemetery; thence west about 9 feet; thence northerly about 97 feet to the place of beginning, containing about 2 acres of land, be the same more or less.

Reserving therefrom a strip of land on the northerly end 65 feet wide on the west line and tapering to 58 feet wide on the east line.

The Leemon R. Cossitt Parcel 2

Parcel III

All that tract or parcel of land lying .... Intending to convey that portion of the lands owned by the party of the first part (formerly) purchased from Gordon F. and Theresa B. Burgess on March 30, 1947 and known as the Whitmore Farm, described as follows: Said plot begins at the southeast corner of the Baptist Parsonage lot and continues easterly on the same course 241 feet to an iron post; thence in a northerly direction parallel with highway No. 26 for 267 feet to the line between the said Whitmore Farm and the properties owned by Leemon R. Cossitt. The northerly boundary of this plot is the line of property now or formerly owned by Leemon R. Cossitt and the westerly line is the Baptist Parsonage lot.

NOTE: How would these parcels wind down to three parcels wherein there are six? Do we not know how to count? What kind of scam is this? How is history served justly, if by the facts we cannot even be responsibly accurate? In this particular example of baseline counting, it can be done, it should be done - by the numbers!

EXECUTOR'S DEED

THIS INDENTURE made the 3rd day of November, Two Thousand eleven

BETWEEN

Valerie K. Wilson,
Individually, and as Executrix of the Estate
of Helen B. Kartorie, deceased
4485 E. Lake Rd.
Cazenovia, NY 13035

Grantor,

and

Resurreccion Dimaculangan
170 Kenwood Ave.
Oneida, NY 13421

Grantee,

WITNESSETH, that whereas Letters Testamentary were issued to the party of the first part by the Orphans' Court Division, Court of Common Pleas, State of Pennsylvania on October 31, 2008 and also by Ancillary Letters Testamentary on May 12, 2009 and by virtue of the power and authority given in by Article 11 of the Estate, Powers and Trusts Law, or any amendment thereof from time to time made, and in consideration of Sixty Five Thousand and 00/100 ($65,000.00) Dollars, lawful money of the United States, paid by the party of the second part, the receipt whereof is hereby acknowledged, and other good and valuable consideration paid by the Grantee, does hereby grant and release unto the Grantee, the heirs or successors and assigns of the Grantee, forever,

ALL THAT TRACT OR PARCEL OF LAND, situate in the Town of Georgetown, County of Madison and State of New York, and being all of the premises deeded to Sarah H. Brown by Timothy Brown, May 5 1885 and recorded in the Madison County Clerk's Office May 14th at 9 o'clock a.m. in Liber 163 page 155 described and bounded as follows, viz: On the north by lands owned by the Baptist Church & Society; east by lands formerly owned by Mary M. Ellis; on the south by land formerly owned by Russell Whitmore; on the west by the center of the highway; being a part of Lot No. 91 of said town, CONTAINING ¾ of an acre more or less.

ALSO ALL THAT TRACT OR PARCEL OF LAND DEEDED BY THE Trustees of the First Baptist Society of said town to Timothy Brown on the 15th day of August, 1882, and recorded in the Clerk's Office of the County of Madison on the 5th day of August, 1884 at 11 o'clock a.m. in Liber 161, page 20.

Plate 9-Instr#:2011-6312. 11/04/2011 P. 2

ALSO ALL THAT OTHER PIECE OR PARCEL OF LAND deeded by Zinah J. Mosely, Milton D. Allen and Mary his wife, Isaac Fletcher and Mercy, his wife to said Sarah H. Brown on the 22nd day of March 1871 and recorded in the Clerk's Office of the County of Madison on the 30th day of March 1871 at 11 o'clock a.m. in Book No. 123 of Deeds, page 347.

ALSO THE RIGHTS AND PRIVELEGES in and to a certain spring of water which was conveyed to the said Sarah H. Brown by a deed from Hiram N. Atwood and wife and George Curtis and wife and recorded in the Clerk's Office of the County of Madison on the 14th day of May, 1885 at 9 o'clock a.m. in Liber 162 of Deeds at page 140, to which said deed reference is hereby made for a more particular description of said water rights.

PARCEL II

ALL THAT TRACT, PIECE OR PARCEL OF LAND, situate in the Town of Georgetown, County of Madison, and State of New York, described as follows: BEING a part of Lot 91 of said town and bounded as follows: BEGINNING at a stake on the northwest corner of the lot now or formerly owned by Mrs. Fred Currier (formerly Ross) south line; running thence eaterly along said Currier south line about 199 ½ feet to a stake; thence in a southerly direction about 276feet to the corner of lands formerly owned by H. H. Whitmore; thence in a westerly direction about 323 feet to a stake; thence in a northerly direction 309 feet on the eat line of the old Cemetery to the northeast corner of said Cemetery; thence west about 9 feet; thence northerly about 97 feet to the place of beginning, CONTAINING about two acres of land, be the same more or less.

RESERVING THEREFROM a strip of land on the northerly end 65 feet wide on west line and tapering to 58 feet wide on east line.

PARCELL III

All that tract or parcel of land LYING AND BEING IN THE Town of Georgetown, County of Madison, State of New York and described as follows: Intending to convey that portion of the lands owned by the party of the first part (formerly) purchased from Gordon F. and Theresa B. Burgess on March 30, 1947 and known as the Whitmore Farm, described as follows: Said plot begins at the southeast corner of the Baptist Parsonage lot and continues easterly on the same course 241 feet to an iron post; thence in a northerly direction parallel with highway No. 26 for 267 feet to the line between the said Whitmore Farm and properties owned by Leemon R. Cossitt. The northerly boundary of this plot is the line of property now or formerly owned by Leemon R. Cossitt and the westerly line is the Baptist Parsonage lot.

Plate 10-Instr#:2011-6312. 11/04/2011 P. 3

Resurreccion Dimaculangan

Subject to covenants, easements and restrictions of record, if any.

The above described property consists of three separate tax parcels:
194.19-1-46
194.19-1-47
194.19-1-49
The property is on the east side of N.Y.S. Route 26S. Its postal address is 916 Route 26S, Georgetown, New York 13072.
The building on this property is registered on the U.S. National Register of Historic Places as the "Spirit House." [2006-06000160]

Being the same premises conveyed to Valentine T. and Helen B. Kartorie by Quit Claim Deed dated October 2, 1989 and recorded in the Madison County Clerk's Office on October 2, 1989 in Liber 895 of Deeds at Page 316.

TOGETHER with the appurtenances and all the estate and rights which the said Decedent had at the time of death, in said premises and also the estate therein, which the party of the first part has or has power to convey or dispose of, whether individually, or by virtue of said Estate or statute or otherwise.

TO HAVE AND TO HOLD the premises herein granted unto the Grantee, the heirs or successors and assigns of the Grantee forever.

AND the Grantor covenants as follows:

FIRST, the Grantee shall quietly enjoy the said premises;
SECOND, that the said premises are free from encumbrances;
THIRD, that the Grantor will execute or procure any further necessary assurance of the title to said premises.

This deed is subject to the trust provisions of Section 13 of the Lien Law.

IN WITNESS WHEREOF, the Grantor has executed this deed the day and year first above written.

In presence of:

Valerie K. Wilson

Intentionally left blank

Plate II-Instr#:2011-6312. 11/04/2011 P. 4

INSTR#: 2011-6312 11/04/2011 DEED Image: 5 of 5

STATE OF NEW YORK)
COUNTY OF ONONDAGA) ss.:

On the 3rd day of November, 2011, before me, the undersigned, personally appeared Valerie K. Wilson, personally known to me or proved to me on the basis of satisfactory evidence to be the individual whose name is subscribed to the within instrument, and she acknowledged to me that she executed the same in her capacity, and that by her signature on the instrument, the individual, or the person upon behalf of which the individual acted, executed the instrument.

Notary Public

GREGORY A. SCICCHITANO
Notary Public, State of New York
No. 02SC5081204
Qualified in Onondaga County
Commission Expires June 30, 2015

Plate 12-Instr#:2011-6312. 11/04/2011 P. 5

Town & County Tax Bill

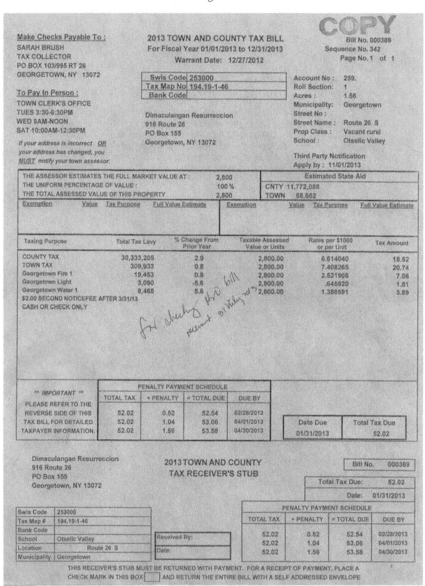

Make Checks Payable To :	2013 TOWN AND COUNTY TAX BILL		**COPY**
SARAH BRUSH	For Fiscal Year 01/01/2013 to 12/31/2013		Bill No. 000389
TAX COLLECTOR	Warrant Date: 12/27/2012		Sequence No. 342
PO BOX 103/995 RT 26			Page No. 1 of 1

GEORGETOWN, NY 13072

Swis Code	253000
Tax Map No	194.19-1-46
Bank Code	

To Pay In Person :
TOWN CLERK'S OFFICE
TUES 3:30-6:30PM
WED 9AM-NOON
SAT 10:00AM-12:30PM

If your address is incorrect OR your address has changed, you MUST notify your town assessor.

Dimaculangan Resurreccion
916 Route 26
PO Box 155
Georgetown, NY 13072

Account No :	259.
Roll Section:	1
Acres :	1.56
Municipality:	Georgetown
Street No :	
Street Name :	Route 26 S
Prop Class :	Vacant rural
School :	Otselic Valley

Third Party Notification
Apply by : 11/01/2013

		Estimated State Aid
THE ASSESSOR ESTIMATES THE FULL MARKET VALUE AT :	2,800	
THE UNIFORM PERCENTAGE OF VALUE :	100%	CNTY 11,772,088
THE TOTAL ASSESSED VALUE OF THIS PROPERTY	2,800	TOWN 68,662

Exemption	Value	Tax Purpose	Full Value Estimate	Exemption	Value	Tax Purpose	Full Value Estimate

Taxing Purpose	Total Tax Levy	% Change From Prior Year	Taxable Assessed Value or Units	Rates per $1000 or per Unit	Tax Amount
COUNTY TAX	30,333,205	2.9	2,800.00	6.614040	18.52
TOWN TAX	309,933	0.8	2,800.00	7.408265	20.74
Georgetown Fire 1	19,453	0.8	2,800.00	2.521908	7.06
Georgetown Light	3,090	-5.6	2,800.00	.645920	1.81
Georgetown Water 1	8,465	5.6	2,800.00	1.388591	3.89

$2.00 SECOND NOTICEFEE AFTER 3/31/13
CASH OR CHECK ONLY

for checks X 0 bill
paid or tally 2013

** IMPORTANT **	PENALTY PAYMENT SCHEDULE					
	TOTAL TAX	+ PENALTY	= TOTAL DUE	DUE BY		
PLEASE REFER TO THE	52.02	0.52	52.54	02/28/2013		
REVERSE SIDE OF THIS	52.02	1.04	53.06	04/01/2013	Date Due	Total Tax Due
TAX BILL FOR DETAILED	52.02	1.56	53.58	04/30/2013	01/31/2013	52.02
TAXPAYER INFORMATION.						

Dimaculangan Resurreccion
916 Route 26
PO Box 155
Georgetown, NY 13072

2013 TOWN AND COUNTY TAX RECEIVER'S STUB

Bill No.	000389
Total Tax Due:	52.02
Date:	01/31/2013

Swis Code	253000
Tax Map #	194.19-1-46
Bank Code	
School	Otselic Valley
Location	Route 26 S
Municipality	Georgetown

Received By:
Date:

PENALTY PAYMENT SCHEDULE			
TOTAL TAX	+ PENALTY	= TOTAL DUE	DUE BY
52.02	0.52	52.54	02/28/2013
52.02	1.04	53.06	04/01/2013
52.02	1.56	53.58	04/30/2013

THIS RECEIVER'S STUB MUST BE RETURNED WITH PAYMENT. FOR A RECEIPT OF PAYMENT, PLACE A
CHECK MARK IN THIS BOX [ ] AND RETURN THE ENTIRE BILL WITH A SELF ADDRESSED ENVELOPE.

Plate 13-Tax Account # 194.19-1-46

Notice the Deviation of this Document from the Deeded Acreage?

Otselic District School Tax Bill

Make Checks Payable To :		2013-2014 SCHOOL TAX BILL				Bill No. 000577

```
Make Checks Payable To :                2013-2014 SCHOOL TAX BILL                     Bill No. 000577
OTSELIC VALLEY CSD                  For Fiscal Year 07/01/2013 to 6/30/2014           Sequence No. 532
C/O NBT BANK                             Warrant Date: 09/01/2013                     Page No. 1  of  1
P.O. BOX 167
SOUTH OTSELIC NY 13155                                                    Account No :   259.
                                   Swis Code 253000                       Roll Section:  1
                                   Tax Map No 194.19-1-46                  Acres :        1.56
To Pay In Person :                 Bank Code                              Municipality:  Georgetown
NBT BANK                                                                   Street No :
1572 STATE HIGHWAY 26              Dimaculangan Resurreccion               Street Name :  Route 26  S
SOUTH OTSELIC, NY 13155           916 State Route 26 S                     Prop Class :   Vacant rural
                                  Georgetown, NY 13072                     School :       Otselic Valley    084401
If your address is incorrect  OR                                          NYS Sch Code : 606
your address has changed, you
MUST notify your town assessor.                                           Third Party Notification
                                                                          Apply by : 7/01/2014
```

THE ASSESSOR ESTIMATES THE FULL MARKET VALUE AT :		2,800	Estimated State Aid		
THE UNIFORM PERCENTAGE OF VALUE :		100 %	SCHL 5,522,532		
THE TOTAL ASSESSED VALUE OF THIS PROPERTY		2,800			
Exemption	Value Tax Purpose Full Value Estimate		Exemption	Value Tax Purpose	Full Value Estimate

Taxing Purpose	Total Tax Levy	% Change From Prior Year	Taxable Assessed Value or Units	Rates per $1000 or per Unit	Tax Amount
TOWN OF Georgetown					
SCHOOL TAX MONDAY - THURSDAY 9:00 AM - 3:00 PM FRIDAY 9:00 AM - 5:30 PM	3,068,703	2.1	2,800.00	18.366850	51.43

PAID - 4

OCT 01 2013

NBT BANK, N.A.
So OTSELIC NY

Your tax savings this year resulting from the New York State School Tax Relief (STAR) Program is: 0.00
Note: This year's STAR tax savings generally may not exceed last year's by more than 2%.

** IMPORTANT **	PENALTY PAYMENT SCHEDULE			
PLEASE REFER TO THE	TOTAL TAX	+ PENALTY	= TOTAL DUE	DUE BY
REVERSE SIDE OF THIS TAX BILL FOR DETAILED TAXPAYER INFORMATION.	51.43	1.03	52.46	11/01/2013

Date Due	Total Tax Due
10/01/2013	51.43

Dimaculangan Resurreccion
916 State Route 26 S
Georgetown, NY 13072

2013-2014 SCHOOL TAX
RECEIVER'S STUB **PAID - 4**

Bill No.	000577

OCT 01 2013

	Total Tax Due:	51.43
	Date:	10/01/2013

Swis Code	253000
Tax Map #	194.19-1-46
Bank Code	
School	Otselic Valley 084401
Location	Route 26 S
Municipality	Georgetown

	PENALTY PAYMENT SCHEDULE			
	TOTAL TAX	+ PENALTY	= TOTAL DUE	DUE BY
	51.43	1.03	52.46	11/01/2013

THIS RECEIVER'S STUB MUST BE RETURNED WITH PAYMENT. FOR A RECEIPT OF PAYMENT, PLACE A
CHECK MARK IN THIS BOX [ ] AND RETURN THE ENTIRE BILL WITH A SELF ADDRESSED ENVELOPE

Plate 14-Tax Account # 194.19-1-46

Notice the Deviation of this Document from the Deeded Acreage?

Notice the Deviation of this Document from the Deeded Acreage? There were four separate properties described on Parcel One of the Deed? Why are the other three parcels not taxed nor accounted for? Which one is this? From among these: 3/4 acre; 2 & 1/4 acres; 9' x 60 ' & 1/3 Rights to the Spring? No noted accounts of the Exemption /s.

Town & County Tax Bill

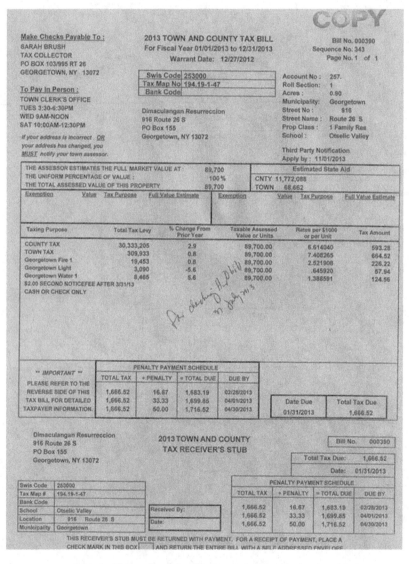

Plate 15–Tax Account #194.19-1-47

Notice the Deviation of this Document from the Deeded Acreage?

Otselic District School Tax Bill

Make Checks Payable To :
OTSELIC VALLEY CSD
C/O NBT BANK
P.O. BOX 167
SOUTH OTSELIC NY 13155

To Pay In Person :
NBT BANK
1572 STATE HIGHWAY 26
SOUTH OTSELIC, NY 13155

If your address is incorrect OR your address has changed, you MUST notify your town assessor.

2013-2014 SCHOOL TAX BILL
For Fiscal Year 07/01/2013 to 6/30/2014
Warrant Date: 09/01/2013

Swis Code 253000
Tax Map No 194.19-1-47
Bank Code

Dimaculangan Resurreccion
916 State Route 26 S
Georgetown, NY 13072

Bill No. 000578
Sequence No. 533
Page No.1 of 1

Account No : 257.
Roll Section: 1
Acres : 0.90
Municipality: Georgetown
Street No : 916
Street Name : Route 26 S
Prop Class : 1 Family Res
School : Otselic Valley 084401
NYS Sch Code: 606

Third Party Notification
Apply by : 7/01/2014

THE ASSESSOR ESTIMATES THE FULL MARKET VALUE AT :	89,700	Estimated State Aid		
THE UNIFORM PERCENTAGE OF VALUE :	100%	SCHL 5,522,532		
THE TOTAL ASSESSED VALUE OF THIS PROPERTY	89,700			

Exemption	Value	Tax Purpose	Full Value Estimate	Exemption	Value	Tax Purpose	Full Value Estimate
STAR B	30,000	SCHOOL	30,000				

Taxing Purpose	Total Tax Levy	% Change From Prior Year	Taxable Assessed Value or Units	Rates per $1000 or per Unit	Tax Amount
TOWN OF Georgetown					
SCHOOL TAX MONDAY - THURSDAY 9:00 AM - 3:00 PM FRIDAY 9:00 AM - 5:30 PM	3,068,703	2.1	89,700.00	18.366850	1,647.51

PAID - 4
OCT 01 2013
NBT BANK, N.A.
S. OTSELIC, N.Y.

Your tax savings this year resulting from the New York State School Tax Relief (STAR) Program is: 541.00
Note: This year's STAR tax savings generally may not exceed last year's by more than 2%.

** IMPORTANT ** PLEASE REFER TO THE REVERSE SIDE OF THIS TAX BILL FOR DETAILED TAXPAYER INFORMATION.	PENALTY PAYMENT SCHEDULE			
	TOTAL TAX	+ PENALTY	= TOTAL DUE	DUE BY
	1,106.51	22.13	1,128.64	11/01/2013

Date Due	Total Tax Due
10/01/2013	1,106.51

Dimaculangan Resurreccion
916 State Route 26 S
Georgetown, NY 13072

2013-2014 SCHOOL TAX RECEIVER'S STUB PAID - 4
OCT 01 2013
NBT BANK N.A.
S. OTSELIC NY

Bill No. 000578

Total Tax Due: 1,106.51
Date: 10/01/2013

Swis Code	253000
Tax Map #	194.19-1-47
Bank Code	
School	Otselic Valley 084401
Location	916 Route 26 S
Municipality	Georgetown

Received By
Date 10-1-13

PENALTY PAYMENT SCHEDULE			
TOTAL TAX	+ PENALTY	= TOTAL DUE	DUE BY
1,106.51	22.13	1,128.64	11/01/2013

THIS RECEIVER'S STUB MUST BE RETURNED WITH PAYMENT. FOR A RECEIPT OF PAYMENT, PLACE A
CHECK MARK IN THIS BOX [ ] AND RETURN THE ENTIRE BILL WITH A SELF ADDRESSED ENVELOPE.

Plate 16-Tax Account #194.19-1-47

Resurreccion Dimaculangan

Notice the Deviation of this Document from the Deeded Acreage?

Town & County Tax Bill

Make Checks Payable To :
SARAH BRUSH
TAX COLLECTOR
PO BOX 103/995 RT 26
GEORGETOWN, NY 13072

To Pay In Person :
TOWN CLERK'S OFFICE
TUES 3:30-6:30PM
WED 9AM-NOON
SAT 10:00AM-12:30PM
If your address is incorrect OR your address has changed, you MUST notify your town assessor.

2013 TOWN AND COUNTY TAX BILL
For Fiscal Year 01/01/2013 to 12/31/2013
Warrant Date: 12/27/2012

Bill No. 000392
Sequence No. 345
Page No. 1 of 1

Swis Code	253000
Tax Map No	194.19-1-49
Bank Code	

Dimaculangan Resurreccion
916 Route 26
PO Box 155
Georgetown, NY 13072

Account No :   258.
Roll Section: 1
Acres :   1.11
Municipality: Georgetown
Street No :
Street Name :   Route 26 S
Prop Class :   Rural vac<10
School :   Otselic Valley

Third Party Notification
Apply by : 11/01/2013

THE ASSESSOR ESTIMATES THE FULL MARKET VALUE AT :	2,200	Estimated State Aid	
THE UNIFORM PERCENTAGE OF VALUE :	100%	CNTY 11,772,088	
THE TOTAL ASSESSED VALUE OF THIS PROPERTY	2,200	TOWN 68,662	

Exemption	Value	Tax Purpose	Full Value Estimate	Exemption	Value	Tax Purpose	Full Value Estimate

Taxing Purpose	Total Tax Levy	% Change From Prior Year	Taxable Assessed Value or Units	Rates per $1000 or per Unit	Tax Amount
COUNTY TAX	30,333,205	2.9	2,200.00	6.614040	14.55
TOWN TAX	309,933	0.3	2,200.00	7.408265	16.30
Georgetown Fire 1	19,453	0.6	2,200.00	2.521908	5.55
Georgetown Light	3,090	-5.6	2,200.00	.645920	1.42
Georgetown Water 1	8,465	5.6	2,200.00	1.388591	3.05

$2.00 SECOND NOTICEFEE AFTER 3/31/13
CASH OR CHECK ONLY

** IMPORTANT **	PENALTY PAYMENT SCHEDULE					
PLEASE REFER TO THE	TOTAL TAX	+ PENALTY	= TOTAL DUE	DUE BY		
REVERSE SIDE OF THIS	40.87	0.41	41.28	02/28/2013		
TAX BILL FOR DETAILED	40.87	0.82	41.69	04/01/2013	Date Due	Total Tax Due
TAXPAYER INFORMATION.	40.87	1.23	42.10	04/30/2013	01/31/2013	40.87

Dimaculangan Resurreccion
916 Route 26
PO Box 155
Georgetown, NY 13072

2013 TOWN AND COUNTY
TAX RECEIVER'S STUB

Bill No.   000392

Total Tax Due: 40.87

Date: 01/31/2013

Swis Code	253000
Tax Map #	194.19-1-49
Bank Code	
School	Otselic Valley
Location	Route 26 S
Municipality	Georgetown

Received By:

Date:

PENALTY PAYMENT SCHEDULE			
TOTAL TAX	+ PENALTY	= TOTAL DUE	DUE BY
40.87	0.41	41.28	02/28/2013
40.87	0.82	41.69	04/01/2013
40.87	1.23	42.10	04/30/2013

THIS RECEIVER'S STUB MUST BE RETURNED WITH PAYMENT. FOR A RECEIPT OF PAYMENT, PLACE A CHECK MARK IN THIS BOX [ ] AND RETURN THE ENTIRE BILL WITH A SELF ADDRESSED ENVELOPE

Plate 17-Tax Account #194.19-1-49

Otselic District School Tax Bill

Make Checks Payable To :
OTSELIC VALLEY CSD
C/O NBT BANK
P.O. BOX 167
SOUTH OTSELIC NY 13155

To Pay In Person :
NBT BANK
1572 STATE HIGHWAY 26
SOUTH OTSELIC, NY 13155

If your address is incorrect OR your address has changed, you MUST notify your town assessor.

2013-2014 SCHOOL TAX BILL
For Fiscal Year 07/01/2013 to 6/30/2014
Warrant Date: 09/01/2013

Swis Code 253000
Tax Map No 194.19-1-49
Bank Code

Dimaculangan Resurreccion
916 State Route 26 S
Georgetown, NY 13072

Bill No. 000580
Sequence No. 535
Page No.1 of 1

Account No : 258.
Roll Section: 1
Acres : 1.11
Municipality: Georgetown
Street No :
Street Name : Route 26 S
Prop Class : Rural vac<10
School : Otselic Valley 084401
NYS Sch Code: 606

Third Party Notification
Apply by : 7/01/2014

THE ASSESSOR ESTIMATES THE FULL MARKET VALUE AT : 2,200
THE UNIFORM PERCENTAGE OF VALUE : 100 %
THE TOTAL ASSESSED VALUE OF THIS PROPERTY 2,200

Estimated State Aid
SCHL 5,522,532

Exemption	Value	Tax Purpose	Full Value Estimate	Exemption	Value	Tax Purpose	Full Value Estimate

Taxing Purpose	Total Tax Levy	% Change From Prior Year	Taxable Assessed Value or Units	Rates per $1000 or per Unit	Tax Amount
TOWN OF Georgetown					
SCHOOL TAX	3,068,703	2.1	2,200.00	18.366850	40.41

MONDAY - THURSDAY 9:00 AM - 3:00 PM
FRIDAY 9:00 AM - 5:30 PM

PAID - 4
OCT 01 2013
NBT BANK, N.A.
S. OTSELIC NY

Your tax savings this year resulting from the New York State School Tax Relief (STAR) Program is: 0.00
Note: This year's STAR tax savings generally may not exceed last year's by more than 2%

** IMPORTANT **	PENALTY PAYMENT SCHEDULE			
PLEASE REFER TO THE REVERSE SIDE OF THIS TAX BILL FOR DETAILED TAXPAYER INFORMATION.	TOTAL TAX	+ PENALTY	= TOTAL DUE	DUE BY
	40.41	0.81	41.22	11/01/2013

Date Due 10/01/2013
Total Tax Due 40.41

Dimaculangan Resurreccion
916 State Route 26 S
Georgetown, NY 13072

2013-2014 SCHOOL TAX
RECEIVER'S STUB
PAID - 4
OCT 01 2013
NBT BANK N.A.
S. OTSELIC

Bill No. 000580
Total Tax Due: 40.41
Date: 10/01/2013

		PENALTY PAYMENT SCHEDULE		
TOTAL TAX	+ PENALTY	= TOTAL DUE	DUE BY
40.41	0.81	41.22	11/01/2013

Swis Code	253000
Tax Map #	194.19-1-49
Bank Code	
School	Otselic Valley 084401
Location	Route 26 S
Municipality	Georgetown

Date 10.1.13

THIS RECEIVER'S STUB MUST BE RETURNED WITH PAYMENT. FOR A RECEIPT OF PAYMENT, PLACE A CHECK MARK IN THIS BOX [ ] AND RETURN THE ENTIRE BILL WITH A SELF ADDRESSED ENVELOPE

Plate 18-Tax Account #194.19-1-49

What is the acceptable margin of error for land measurement discrepancies?

Resurreccion Dimaculangan

? If tax exemptions render the parcel unaccounted in the tax map, why is the 501 (c) (3) designated religious organization next door in the map?

? Should efficient accounting of taxable property be accurately documented to avoid confusion, maintain clarity of records, transparency, and prevent the high cost of litigation and misunderstanding that resulted from dubious and incompetence of a few that should do their responsibilities but for whatever reason fall short as so often the cases?

? What safeguards and measurable steps can be taken and be put in place to protect the taxpayers and the coffers of the community /governance in ensuring that these types of mediocre practices come up to the standards of stellar excellence?

? Is there any one out there that care about these issues? Someone that can make a real positive difference in ensuring that property not be taken under every body's very nose?

Does this Commissioned Document Reinforces the DEEDED DESCRIPTIONS?

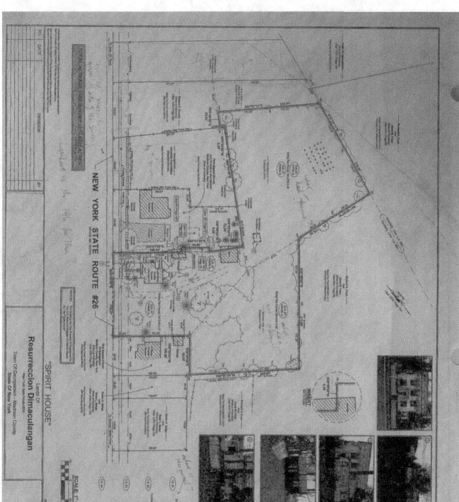

Plate 21

The Erroneous Mathematical Visual Translation of the DEED

Is this the face of 21st Century Math, Science & Technology in the World of GPS and pinpoint

Accuracy, Precision and Land Surveying Engineering: A Licensed Profession?

Plate 19-The Tax Map A

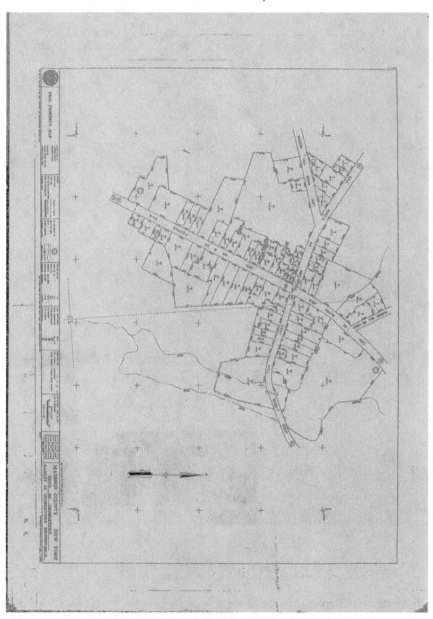

LOT 91 Map Version A [Take a real look for any difference]

Plate 20-The Tax Map

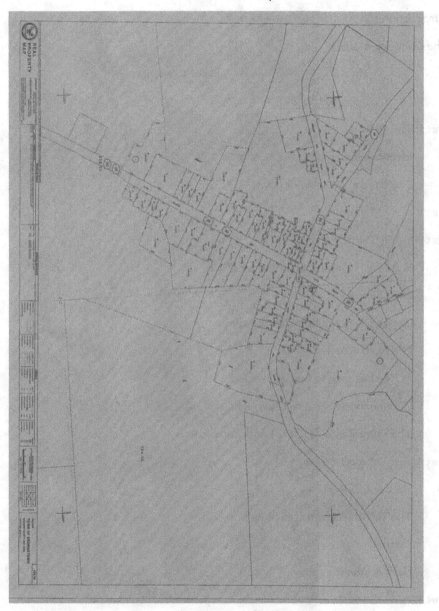

LOT 91 Map Version B [for comparative observation]

Table of Contents

1864 to 1895

"Towering genius disdain the beaten path. It seeks regions hitherto unexplored."

A.Lincoln

Introduction

It is no secret that moving Historic Sites into relevancy of purpose, and timeliness of function are directly tied with insightful planning, balanced foresight, selfless visionary approach, with conservative appropriations of fund availabilities: if there are even resources that can be dispensed with, at all. Most of the time, these elemental qualities do not come in a pot of gold, all stirred and ready to go. Particularly, talents wrapped with cash in abundance, are few in between.

These important building blocks are among the many challenges hard enough to contend with on their own; but to couple the lack thereof with antagonistic stance of people whose agenda totally go opposite directions from Conservation & Preservation Contexts that target Self - Sustainability in long Term Planning, quadruple the already heavy albatross into the gargantuan goal of a lifetime. These are true even with the use of applied research, testings, evolving design, welcomed efforts on innovative material experimentations, free exchanges of ideas, and free - flowing two way communications. Difficulties are aggravated more so, if these processes, and tools, are touted as wrong means, because of ignorance. Taking on the stance of refusal to understand the practice of environmental awareness by going Green as the overarching conviction of "waste not, want not"⁵ type of foresight make the climb to Mt. Everest, easy like eating Peanuts.

The Economics of Historic sites, and Museums as Viable Business Ventures, and not as an Entitlement Entities for Forever Grants Recipiency seemed to be the Hardest Sell. Views not new, but when being endorsed by someone like me, heard firsthand from

---

⁵ Proverb, self explanatory

my kind, intended to be acted upon, hands on by me - was tantamount to heresy. Sheer contradiction to the popular notion about Museums / Historic Sites. The ones, and the types of set up, that people around here are used to. At least, from how I understand it.

In this particular case, this economic fluidity was the first to have been ignored even from the nomination Stage for Land Marking Application. How so? The Streamlined use of a Singular Historical Context using one person's narrative, not only undermined the greater chance of Self - Sustainability for this Site, but also foreshadowed the deliberate reduction[6] of the titled land acreage that came with the House by knowingly, totally ignoring the Number One Resource of Informational facts - Deeds! The recorded, legal, legitimate accepted documentary proof of Ownership. Even at first glance, how can a less than 7 acre site not be self - sustaining? WHY? HOW?

I, then ventured on the quest to find some answers, if not the answer.

Fact checking, double checking, and ensuring authenticity of Facts. The very fundamental premise of Historical documentation. Also true in all other academic or non scholarly settings, both Theoretical and Applied. These should be common knowledge! Putting the Focus on architecture and a myth; ignoring the literal people that lived, and died with their stories, their contributions to the economics, social, cultural, growth and development of this community are so closely interwoven; the identification of the landscape that was then, as the acreages were deeded; and in this case were even worded with great clarity, are the very essence, the core of this Historical Story, but were never included. A misplaced understanding? Intentional or Schemed? Which? WHY?

The responsible accounting of what acreages were handed onto the House by the succeeding owners thereafter unto today is what authentic, efficient Registration

---

[6] NPS form 10-900 p.11 No.10. Wikipedia entries, and other web articles with reduced acreage entries.

should be. This falls into Provenance check. Was this omitted by deliberate neglect? Or to provide the platform for groups with vested interests to stitch the fabricated story, be stamped historical, and pass for legitimate because the efforts were backed and promoted by well connected, solidly networked Last names?. Have we as human beings lost our mind? Have we gone so low as ignore the truth for some concocted story?

This work attempts to adhere within the guidelines set forth by the U.S. Department of the Interior, National Parks Service in the "recommended standards for historic surveys, identification, evaluation, documentation and registration" of Sites, structures, landscapes of value. This Personal Historical account in book form aim to target the following inquiries:

* What contexts do this site fall into, to be considered important?

* Are these contexts based on factual evidentiary documents that, any Scientific and Scholarly approach can retrace back onto, with great accuracy and truth?

* Are the facts authentic, as compared to every evidentiary resource available, made available, and that which are out there?

* Was the filter for mistranslation, speculation, bias and other forms of omissions that favor an imbalance of factual presentation been rendered totally impermeable to such temptations?

The topics were arranged in a type of genealogical format useful as outright fact checking and cross referencing manual. At the same time, serve as a documentary explorative researched evidence, as well as a personal account of the journey to the quest for the Truth in the documentation of this historical site. All for the goal of healing the community with whatever ails the people all these years. First, the suppuration filled inflammation bump need be drained of pus. That is the stage of this circumstance. Either we all wait for the boil to pop on it's own like an implosion or use the guided, controlled incision to irrigate the wound. This is an attempt for a unification effort to make a positive difference one person at a time, as a lifestyle: a true badge of honor for the Old School American Spirit. A reminder: this is a living book. The search in ongoing.

The Conversion Guide

1	feet	inches	rod	rood	perches	poles	links
acre	43560		160	4	160	160	
chain	66		4		4	4	100
link	0.66	7.92					
rod	16.5		1	40 square rods	1	1	
perch	16.5		1	40 square perches	1	1	25
pole	16.5		1		1	1	
rood				1	40		

Plate 22

1 Township = 36 sections

1 Township = 6 miles long x by 1 mile wide　　　　1 Section = 1 mile x 1 mile wide

1 Township = 36 square miles　　　　1 Section = 640 acres

Note: While your Geometry, Trigonometry, Physics, Algebra Classes may seem to be of no consequence to you - young readers, you may be surprised that they really are. For the adults that have not practiced this stocked knowledge for a while, may somehow been neglected, yet embedded in the deep recesses of the subconscious, the subsequent pages contain numerical values, and situations that with some patience can be turned into productive teaching moments, and learning exercises for all ages. Life inevitably have to be explained mathematically. Especially so, in this particular case.

BROWN ~ Stevens ~

♡   ♡   ♡

[(1 & 1/2 acres)+(2 acres)]

1939 & 1947

Leemon Ray Cossitt

bought ~ out her family to render the legacy of the Brown's undivided

1920

Alice Stevens

[(3/4 acre) + (9' x 60')] + [(2 & 1/4 acres)+ (1/3 rights to a Spring)]

1864, 1872 & 1871, 1884

Timothy & Sarah H. Brown

This page aims to summarize at a glance

No. #06000160 ~ 2006

5

Cossitt Legacy

♡   ♡   ♡

[(1 & 1/2 acres) +(2 acres)] + [(3/4 acre) +(9' x 60') + (2 & 1/4 acres) + (1/3 rights to a Spring)]

1955, 1920

Alice S. Cossitt

[(1 & 1/2 acres) +(2 acres)]+ [(3/4 acre) +(9' x 60') + (2& 1/4 acres) +(1/3 rights to a Spring)]

1986

James & Valerie Wilson

[(1 & 1/2 acres) +(2 acres)]+ [(3/4 acre) +(9' x 60') + (2& 1/4 acres) + (1/3 rights to a Spring)]

1989

Helen & Valentine Kartorie

the Provenance of inheritance for Historic Site

USNational Register.

TimothySarahCoraSarahJohnFloydChaunceyJuliaElwinAliceBerthaAliceFrancesAlice.

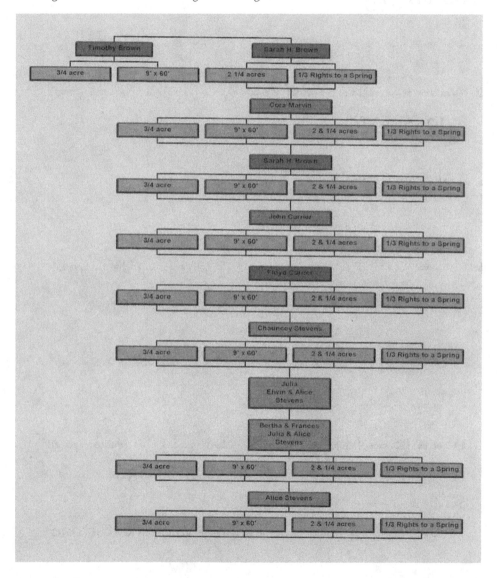

Plate 23-Chain of Ownership: 1864 to 1920

From 4 different Property Parcels to 6 Different Property Parcels

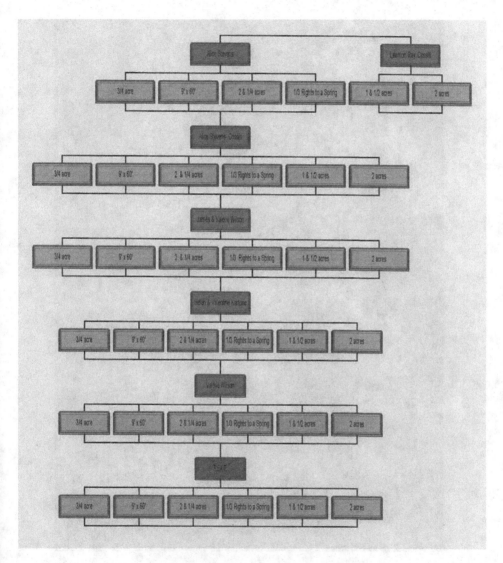

Plate 24~Chain of Ownership: 1920 to 2011

A. The Browns

Notice the Tax Mapper's Visual Translation of the DEED?

Plate 25-0734 Timothy & Sarah H.

Time Lines: extracted from the Documents the 2006 Historic Landmarking was Framed.

1965, January. Mr. Milton Chapin, then a student at Cornell; embarked on a Historic American
    Buildings Survey of Timothy Brown House (Brown's Temple or the Spirit House) HABS
    No. 5602. The House sits on a 3/4 acre land. Mrs. Cossitt was alive; did not sign on this
    effort to make the House be Landmarked Historical, then. WHY?

1991, The Georgetown Historical Society Compiled a ten paged Story of the House entitled "The
    Spirit House Georgetown, New York (Also referred to as Brown's Free Hall)" there was a
    small insert of a black & white picture of the House with the picket fence. A copy of this
    compiled document was autographed for me by Mrs. Estelle Evans. On this narrative, the
    House sits on a 3 & 1/2 acres with a barn and a garage. WHY?

2006, The Land Marking Application submitted & was approved, had taken only the Historical
    Contexts the 1965 Building Survey had. That Building survey never looked into the
    Deeds as the primary source of references except as to trace the named owners. In
    depth story used was filtered from narratives of people in the 1950's. WHY WAS THIS
    NOT UPDATED? Historical framework allows for 50 years and over.

2011, Setting the Records Straight, Comprehensive & Complete; A Work in Progress. This book
aims to factually present what the Deeds really say; show what authentic updated Historical
Contextual Survey is, even in its' ongoing process; and from there, move forward positively.

1.   Identity Clarifications & Questions

Finding the Identity of the right Timothy Brown and Sarah H. Brown first, and foremost would clear the Who, What, How, of the Issue at Hand. Even then, we found out first hand, people tend to have similar names. The chance of living in the same area is also quite possible. Thus, we tackled the issue of false identity head - on. Even the notion of possible switches, duplicities. Yes, even in the 1800's.

Cross referencing the facts, minding the words used, spelling, prolix, typographic markings & tendencies. Sourcing out other types of documents collected and recorded in the archives helped pin down the veracity of the names that go with the actual location of the sought property confidently. That is, in a scientifically proven standard of precision and accuracy. This includes the correct Lot number, in the exact Township, subdivision, and which side of that particular Lot number is the specific acreage positioned.

All data details are important in cross checking all the information, to eliminate the errors in filtering the facts that go together, & do not go together to formulate the Truthful Story. That - is this History's Story, Narrated by facts. It seemed that the names Timothy for males, Sarah for females, even the last name Brown were of common usage in that era. Going over the deeds on records produced names that are similar, descriptions that were seemingly identical, or alike. Whether names meant familial connectivity would be another topic, though. The strict adherence to the specific area in question on Lot 91 Subdivision Township 06; that parcel on the East side of the highway called Route 26 was concentrated on. Everything else were taken into contextual consideration to understand the overall picture without losing focus on the specific site mentioned. Data gathered revealed at least Three Timothy Brown listed in the NY Madison County archived directory of Records.

1). This first Timothy Brown seemed to had the most familial information on records.

    1795, Settled in Sullivan.

    1807 – 1816 Juror

    1807, Lieutenant in the Militia

    Died at the age of 72.

    Had a wife named Olive Clark.

    Four sons named: Herman

                William

                John

                Solomon

    Daughter married Anson Pearson. Land holdings stretched from Sullivan to Canaseraga and more. Without question, deed listings ruled out owning anything that was, and in Lot 91, Georgetown, Madison County, New York.

———————

2). There was a Capt. Timothy Brown, that served in the Militia. Not much was written about him.

———————

The above two Timothy Brown nomenclatural entrees did not have any property on record that connect to the one we are interested in. These two did not live, nor were associated with Georgetown, NY, Lot 91. The above data were further matched from the listing on p.36 by William H. Tuttle as Edited by Isabel Tracy (1984), on Names and Sketches of the Pioneer Settlers of Madison County, NY. Here's the third one.

Similar <u>Timothy Brown</u> Name from the Same Township:

3). 1853, December 28, from Timothy **G.** Brown & wife Malvina

                            Georgetown, Madison County, NY

                            Lot 55 Township No.06 , 11 acres of land

                            Lot 55 SE corner 43 & 3/4 acres

                            to Philinda A. Nichols of Georgetown

Liber BX pp. 181 - 18   Notarized: 28 Dec. 1853   Recorded: 22 Feb. 1854, 12 Noon

Is this our Timothy Brown?

Similar to the <u>Sarah H. Brown</u> Name; Same Township:

1884, May 06 Sarah **E.** Brown is the widow of Alfred A. Brown.

quitclaimed on the property in Lot 101, for $1.00

forty - three and three - fourth acres (43 3/4 acres)

mortgaged by Alfred A. Brown to Laura A. Reed

Liber 215 p. 389   Recorded: 05 May 1905, 8AM

The mortgage was held by the First National Bank of Morrisville. Having that Alfred A. Brown had passed, the surviving spouse Sarah E. Brown dealt with the situation. HOW?

While the work you are looking right into this moment, may still not answer all your questions; we can all go out of our way, and revisit this story any time, to retrace the steps left behind by these people through the pages of archived records, and other legally accepted proofs of ownership documentations available. An integral part of learning is an infinite quest to find answers to unanswered questions, that may have been left out to be discovered, or not. If we keep turning those pages, we'll have the higher chance of coming at answers. When we do, information is shared as a basic human trait. Different mindsets, see things through different lenses, all the time. True. Yet, facts are facts. Let us all stick to them. Let us do disseminate them as such. That was the over all goal attempted here. The collected information were then subjected to deductive reasoning and applied analytics used first to Establish the Identity of " Our Timothy Brown" as well as all the data, topics, views found in each of the pages so compiled here.

2. The Merger, A Union of Love?

1847, A person named Timothy Brown from Vermont, procured a piece of land on Lot 103 & 104 from Isaac V. Purdy, and wife Rebecca, of Georgetown. The acreages are respectively shown in an equation format here.

$$70 \text{ acre} + 30 \text{ acres} = 100 \text{ acres for } \$1,600.00[7]$$

It is brought up here again with great emphasis, that Timothy Brown's address on this particular land procurement transaction was the State of Vermont. This made him an emigrant, or the more popularly used spelling of immigrant. At this point, only his name on the deed of final sale was used. Yes, without the mention of a wife, nor the literal name of Sarah H. Brown.

Now, interestingly enough, a year after:

1848, This particular piece of land was then parceled out: Thirty - five acres were sold to Mr. Obadiah Caniff of Georgetown for $800.00. Again, it is noted here the change in the named signatories, and why that is important cannot be overly discussed here. The names of the Sellers at this point appeared as "Timothy Brown & wife Sarah, of Georgetown, NY."[8]

Lot 103 = 70 acres - 35 acres sold = 35 acres left

Lot 104 = 30 acres - 88 rods x 55 rod x 88 rods x 55 rods = 29.90 acres left

These parcels were cut from the North half of Lot 103 and Lot 104, respectively. There were now at this point roughly 64.90 acres of land still owned, this time by Timothy and Sarah H. Brown, instead of just Timothy Brown as the name appeared the year prior.

---

[7] Liber BH pp.471-472. dated 29 April 1847.Recorded 01 May 1847 at 5 o'clock PM

[8] Liber BO pp.305-306. dated 22 March 1848.Recorded 21 August 1850 at 3 o'clock PM.

Let me repeat, Timothy Brown included Sarah H.'s name in a deed of sale in 1848, a year after he bought the property in 1847, which was then on his name only.

While the information discussed in the previous pages may be useful to rule out Our Timothy & Sarah H. Brown, It is with assured confidence that strict measures were applied to filter out those that were just similar namesakes. Unfortunately, we have not narrowed down on the Properties this research was really intended for: the two parcels under Timothy Brown & the other two titles of Sarah H. Brown, geo - positioned on Lot 91, Township 06. Here are the Sarah H. Brown's contribution:

1871,   Taking a microscopic look at the document found on Liber 123 p.347 deed for the 2 & 1/4 acres, and the

1884   deed found on Liber 162 p.140-141 on the 1/3 share on the Spring of Water procured by Sarah H. Brown while she was already married. Notice that on both these transactions she only had her name on the deeds. These situations make me wonder what was going on here, then? Was this some Activism Statement?

Now, you have both instances of Timothy & Sarah H. Brown buying properties without " the name of either spouse on the legal documents." Should the query be "What was going on between the two?" or "What was going on in the World at large then? Especially in the context of Equal Rights, Civil Rights and Women's Rights in Particular? Property Law?" How do these events affected the relationship between them? That is, if they did? One thing stands out from all these though: that It does seem that each can dispense of funds and procure property individually, provided they sell them together as co - signors. If this was the rule then, I find it conveniently useful in today's modern family, and / or for any relationship as well. Finally, we are now at the right subdivision 6, Lot 91, town of Georgetown. Let us look at the details of these transactions. One more thing:

The usual reliance on the use of Dates for Birth, Death, Marriage as references were opted out. The primal reason for this is the fact that there were no tangible records found before the printing of this work. The narratives - widely popular, and there were many of those written, were just narratives. The numbers do not match with every other story, and every other story teller. The more in depth look for birth / death / marriage dates, is beyond the scope of the Accessioned land acreages' topic in front of us now. The widely used assertions of death for instance do not match the transactions recorded, for one cannot be transferring deeds after a person has died. If this angle is pursued, the issue of fabrication is raised. That one date of death undermines all the recording and documenting, and the entire archived records in the County. Suffice it to say for now that even the NY State Archives' Notice on the website stated that:

"... the Archives does not hold birth, marriage, and death certificates, only indexes them. The State Department of Health and local registrars of vital statistics are authorized to furnish uncertified copies of vital records for genealogical purposes." Also, that " NY began statewide registration of births, marriages, and deaths (vital records) in 1880-81, under supervision of the State and local boards of health. Compliance with the law was incomplete until 1913 or even later; therefore certificates are lacking for many events." An 1847 Law required the school districts in each town to collect vital statistics. They ceased doing so after a few years. The State Archives and the State Department of Health hold no records created under the 1847 law." Prior to 1784, couples intending to marry were required to obtain licenses from and file bonds with the provincial secretary, if the impending marriage was not announced in a church. The Marriage Bonds (A1893) were mostly destroyed in the 1911 State Capitol fire".

The real question here is not whether they were born or not, nor whether they died or even got married. The issue is about finding the Truth of the facts about the business transactions contracted. We are taking account of the landholding that the House own and is entitled to. That includes Painting the story of the lives lived, their contributions and legacies, to the best detailed information that these legally accepted documents have in them. This compiled data of the story is intended to bring the factual History to light. The account is to set the paper trail reference for what can be termed as the accessioned landholdings of this site. This is the core focus of this book.

Plate 26-0758 NorthWest Bay

We do not doubt that this was built by a Human being that walked this earth alive. What we want to account for, to accurately record History are the parcels that came with the House. Surely, the Structure needed land to stand on. There were six different land titles on the Abstract. Past, Previous, and Current Deeds, and Records hold the same. Those parcels of land holdings are construed as the Collections that came with the Structure. The quest to find a resolution to the stagnation of this Site had been embarked on, as a commitment in pursuit for a higher calling. The questions of: How much is the acreage, and what happened to them? Why are the efforts to bring them to account strongly rebuffed? It is long overdue - therefore, let us take an in depth look.

The Union of

$$a + b = c$$

Timothy & Sarah H. Brown

(5,461.00) **+** *($425.00 + $66.00)* **=** *$5,952.00*

∴

$5,952.00 − $5,179.73 = $772.27

*Capital − Expenses = Net Worth**

916 State Route 26 South, Georgetown, New York

All the other land holdings in the different Subdivision lots were considered, and taken into account, to paint a fuller picture of their finances, and to corroborate the facts shown here. So, let us continue:

1864, November 21, Timothy Brown then, procured 3/4 acre of land on Lot 91 from Samuel Clark & wife Maria, of Eaton, for $350.00 recorded in Liber 102, p.434.

1872, April 15 Timothy Brown bought 12 acres of land for the price of $3,500.00 from Elnathan Ellis and wife Diana[9] as recorded in Liber 126, p. 70-71. Both these procurement transactions were made with only Timothy Brown's name on the deed:.

1871, Taking a microscopic look at the document found on deed Liber 123 p.347 for the 2 & 1/4 acres for the sum of $425.00, this one on Sarah H. Brown; and the

1884 deed found on Liber 162 p. 140-141 for the 1/3 undivided share on the Spring of Water for $66.00 procured by Sarah H. Brown on her own: while married.The total capital land investment amounted to $5,952.00 in dollars. Deduct the total dollar amount of sold off pieced - out parcels to the tune of $5,179.23. This brought $772.27 Net worth of capital invested in what would be the Timothy & Sarah H. Brown acreage legacy that would be further discussed in the next pages. Put in mathematical sentence: $A + B = C$

I   (Timothy Brown) + (Sarah H. Brown) = total investment in real estate

$$[(\$1,600.00) + (\$350.00) + (\$3,500.00)+(\$10.00) +\$1.00)] + [(\$425.00) + (\$66.00)] =$$

$$[(\$5,461.00)] + [(491.00)] = \$5,952.00$$

Thus:(C - total land sales transactions) = dollar assigned valuation for their Legacy

II $(\$5,952.00)-(\$5,179.73) = \$772.27$

---

[9] 1843 Elnathan Ellis' wife is Mary M. Ellis refer to Liber AZ p.475.

Yes, $ 772.27 Seven hundred seventy - two dollars, and twenty - seven cents start - up valuation for the house, and the 3/4 acre, the 9' x 60', the 2 & 1/4 acres, and 1/3 undivided rights to a Spring. I call it the Net worth. This is in the mid to late 1800.

1847, April 09	to Timothy Brown	fr. Isaac V. Purdy	Procurement	$ 1,600.00
1864, Nov. 21	to Timothy Brown	fr. Samuel Clark	Procurement	$ 350.00
1871, Jan. 28	to Sarah H. Brown	fr. Zinah J. Moseley	Procurement	$ 425.00
1872, April 15	to Timothy Brown	fr. E.Ellis/ Diana	Procurement	$ 3,500.00
1872, Nov.01	to Timothy/Sarah	fr. O.Dutton/ Martha	Procurement	$ 10.00
1882, Aug. 15	to Timothy Brown	fr. Baptist Church	Procurement	$ 1.00
1884, Dec. 16	to Sarah H. Brown	fr. Atwood & Curtis	Procurement	$ 66.00

Total procurement Investment $ 5,952.00

1848, March 22	to Obadiah Caniff	Sold	$ 800.00
1850, December 09	to Jonathan Robie	Sold	$ 102.00
1851, Oct. 21	to Wheeler Dryer	Sold	$ 1,200.00
1855, October 03	to Harry Robie	Sold	$ 30.00
1872, September 23	to Nathan Pritchard	Sold	$ 500.00
1872, Nov. 01	to Orlando Dutton	Sold	$ 10.00
1873, November	to J. Henry Stanbro	Sold	$ 500.00
1874, March 19	to Horace Hawks	Sold	$ 500.00
1874, July 10	to Milton D. Allen	Sold	$ 150.00
1874, August 01	to Mary J. Johnson	Sold	$ 45.00
1874, November 14	to Edwin Joaquin	Sold	$ 150.00
1877, February 08	to Jane Saunders	Sold	$ 232.73
1877, October 23	to OrvilleMack et al.	Sold	$ 850.00
1882, August 15	to FBaptist Church	Sold	$ 100.00
1884, January 28	to Reuben Mawson	Sold	$ 10.00

Total Generated Income from land Sales $ 5,179.73

From the list of their landholdings, solid assets, and invested liquid resources, we can deduce the following: From 1847 to 1884.

1847, April 09	to Timothy Brown	fr. Isaac V. Purdy	Procurement	$ 1,600.00
1848, March 22	to Obadiah Caniff		Sold	$ 800.00
1850, December 09	to Jonathan Robie		Sold	$ 102.00
1851, October 21	to Wheeler Dryer		Sold	$ 1,200.00
1855, October 03	to Harry Robie		Sold	$ 30.00
1864, Nov. 21	to Timothy Brown	fr. Samuel Clark	Procurement	$ 350.00
1871, January 28	to Sarah H. Brown	fr. Z. J. Moseley	Procurement	$ 425.00
1872, April 15	to Timothy Brown	fr. E. Ellis/ Diana	Procurement	$ 3,500.00
1872, September 23	to Nathan Pritchard		Sold	$ 500.00
1872, Nov. 01	to Orlando Dutton		Sold	$ 10.00
1872, Nov.01	toTimothy/Sarah B.	fr. O/MDutton	Procurement	$10.00
1873, Nov.	to J. Henry Stanbro		Sold	$ 500.00
1874, March 19	to Horace Hawks		Sold	$ 500.00
1874, July 10	to Milton D. Allen		Sold	$ 150.00
1874, August 01	to Mary J. Johnson		Sold	$ 45.00
1874, November 14	to Edwin Joaquin		Sold	$ 150.00
1877, February 08	to Jane Saunders		Sold	$ 232.73
1877, October 23	to OrvilleMack et al.		Sold	$ 850.00
1882, August 15	to FBaptist Church		Sold	$ 100.00
1882, August 15	toTimothy Brown	fr. FBaptistC.	Procurement	$ 1.00
1884, January 28	to Reuben Mawson		Sold	$ 10.00
1884, December 16	to Sarah H. Brown		Procurement	$ 66.00

Back to those numerics that were taken as data, to represent this husband and wife team living life using monetary values. From the amount of $5,952.00 the Browns built a life together. What the records showed, was that this dollar values supported Sarah H. Brown over her walk towards the Sunset on her own; afterTimothy Brown had given up the ghost. From the same seed investments, came what we now have as the site

#06000160. Now, let me do the chronological ordering of these documents gathered, to illustrate this viewpoint of Budgets, Funds at Disposal, or Investment Capital.

The above list of transactions were the documents pertinent to the establishment of the identity of the Timothy Brown & Sarah H. Brown, that owned the House. There must be a lot more to add to the Historical facts here. For now, suffice it to say that the transactions collected were a fair representation of the land holdings of the Browns specifically on Lot 91, from 1847 to 1895 to the year Sarah H. Brown finally transferred the responsibility of taking care of this Masterpiece.

The rest, $ 5,179.73 from the proceeds of apportioned land parcels sold off were spent for living allowance, improvements etc. That is factoring the narrative accounts, and other hear says that Timothy Brown may not have been a good provider, as he was busy building the House. Though that is not what I believe the records show, and addressing this part of the story into the perspective of numerics on neutral grounds; I had placed the income on record that were generated out of land sales into an equation format to present a visual, of cash invested then. Life moved on cash flow, it still does.

This is to demonstrate that actual dollars were used in these investments. I am sure there were more to all of these in the reality of their life then, than what were left on the records. Since the documents for the specific Lot 91 are all I have for referencing, those are the values I used for the investment numerics, not ZERO dollars as many of the people feel. This is for illustrative purpose. Adamantly not to weave a lie or a new story but to point out that monetary investments need returns to continue the cycle. Even regular couples like Timothy & Sarah H. Brown knew that, all the way to circa 1840. Regular people helped build the economics of Main Street: Is that story so bad?

This is but one of the many angles featured here to reinforce the request to either review, correct, or scrap that landmarking designation. The quest to Answer why this multi - faceted contextual story of History is not the story proliferated, nor what was presented in the application form? In it's place was the incomplete information based on legends written in print form that became the rubber stamped historic story of this site.

Today, in this generation; I was subjected to this "free for all - any time" notion observed, expressed by the behavior of habit from people, exercised as " we can just come in as we please" attitude; use, take or leave refuse, into, or from the site without responsibilities, nor accountabilities, are samplings of the many overt acts of kindness received. These are in a manner of saying, that as a new comer I was expected to see them as? I wrack my brains to find a rationale that may render them easier to explain here. I cannot. Maybe the sort of new form of civilized democracy? You tell me, you readers may be able to interpret these acts better, so as not lose any in translation.

Anyhow, taxes have to be paid, does any one know that? "The HELP: the Farm Labor", so the label goes, have to be paid. Day to day indoor, and outdoor maintenances cost money. What more of Improvements? Besides, it is a private abode, and not quite ready, nor set up to receive the public yet.

Do people have no shame, or self respect in a country that fly the flag of Freedom, Democracy, Liberty, and Constitutional Bill of Rights for Property Ownership? Particularly this one, that is under Habilitation: a Work in Progress? Not ready to receive Visitors, Paying or Not. Have living in the rural area bode cause for all human values to leave all the senses? How would any one that profess love, and appreciation to this Magnificent House express those feelings in measurable, visible, tangible ways? What kind of people would bully their way to entitlement use of a Privately owned landmarked site not ready to receive any form of visitation? For free?

"Let the girl slave herself so we can all take the credit and benefits off it" attitude. Enterprising con men hold paid tours, rites, ceremonies, and social gatherings without benefit of commerce to the House or the Rightful owner. Total Disrespect.

These acts reek Prejudice. Have Society gone so low so fast, it became second skin? Surely, the least that can be done is to have the 501(c)(3) Organization [a school, a church, a historical society, a hospital, the local government or any benevolent group whose mission is to improve the quality of life] apply for grants that would shoulder the fees for the people that cannot afford the admission fees to respectfully enter, and enjoy the premises of a landmarked site that is open and operational.

Since this one is not yet ready to serve the public, and as no public funds have been received in the Project of Preservation & Conservation from the grounds up for Sustainability, why then do people keep coming as if it is their right to be welcomed? It is a Private Residential Dwelling. It had been past, present and will be in the future. That is factually documented. The right to happiness, and privacy in one's own property is a Constitutional Right. I am bringing this issue here as this site may not just be the one caught in the same situation as this: Having a Historical marker does not signify open season to trespass. That should be basic knowledge. Respect is missing here.

If not one person care, then let the Project move forward without distraction, or disturbance, or even harm. There are public lands for hunting and living off the land, not somebody else's land, please! Correct, permits have to be paid for that use of public land for hunting, and yes following the open or closed season schedule. I strongly believe that people are principled enough not to resort to barbaric actions. Trapping game in someone else's land: Is money really that hard to come by, that even the Food Bank cannot be visited? Surely with appropriate conversations, and dialogues, these challenges can be taken civilly, as dignified, and privately as can be, in a Nation called America, a State as NY, even in the suburbs? Getting the True History Right. Prepare for safety. Get ready; be organized before hosting paid or unpaid guests. Thus is the fervor for this Project. The affection for my newfound Community. Is this hard to comprehend?

This is one facet from the many lenses that I see this Site with. The monetary valuation is first. The declaration of love and care, respect and honor, including the enjoyment of freedom, entail quantification; measurable. For this one, I opted to express the equation using assigned values in dollars, found in the procurements / sales transactions data Timothy & Sarah H. engaged in, as baseline standards.

All in the hopes that people would understand: History, Historic Sites, Museums, among other noble causes operate in dollars. This particular Project need not be dependent on taxpayers dollars for it's lifetime, but is geared to long term self - sustainability. That, at least can be applauded, not discouraged nor smeared campaigned for, even if there is nothing else one sees positive going on, at the moment.

Let me be clear in expressing that utmost diligence was applied in casting a wide net research processes, even if the documents included here focused on the owned properties located on Lot 91, Township 6, which were passed on legally for $65,000.00. Since I had the gall to put that up, surely the Respect to one's Property as Delineated in the Bill of Rights in our Constitution is understood by every person that is a Citizen of this County. Do we not have the International Cognizance for respecting the rights of Humankind? Of Private domicile? Still, the Disdain of many Continue.

I hang on to prayers, and positive thoughts. We are hoping: Civility will Prevail. The hope for unification using History based on facts seemed to have been buried in sub storied levels underground. The consensus to believe the twisted convolutions of myths readily accepted to be facts, repeated in automation without question, nor factual proofs, and authentic evidences are widespread. These are keys to regress back in the dark ages again. These constituted the audience demographics I found myself in.

America, the Country that allow the use of the brain for critical analyses, for independent thinking, for inquiries, and for the Truth: What happened? There is Science, there is Technology. We are about to go in space on a regular basis like flying coast to coast. Math is at its best. GPS can pin point to the needle in the haystack from space. Hard facts we believe in. Let us remain so. Yet here I am taunted to dare prove that Recorded Deeds are even the Provenance for this site. From RPAPL Article 3 section 301: it is stated that" conveyance is the record and evidence"; Section 311 talks about: "presumption of possession from legal title". The work to account for what acreages left as the true legacy of the House continues, and is ongoing. In the name of Provenance, let us find the veritable facts here. That History not be trampled to mediocrity and obscurity. Let not the authentic story of this site be totally expunged.

Stop the underpinnings of distrust, prejudice, one track mindedness that undermine the values of the Country professing High Standards of Civility, Equal Rights, and Respect for Women but tottering on the fine line of not practicing what is being preached? This is a Wake up Call. Please, stop letting the years roll by! This is insanely crazy waste of time and resources. From 1986, it's 29 years and going. Are these issues predicated on biased preconceived notions of, but a few? Have this community evolved into full blown bigots? Take heed, this is not the kind nor side of History you want to be a part of? Is it? I sure hope so: You want the free flow of innovation, creative mind set, new ideas based on factual historic facts, inclusion, and unity that bridge cultural understanding; then let me be free to exercise that: then all of us will be set free of the trappings of this mega nightmare plaguing this site and had been ongoing all these years!

Please do consider. I sincerely thank you, in advance.

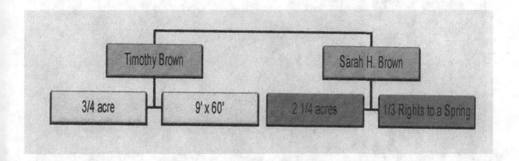

Plate 27   Tim & Sarah H. inventory

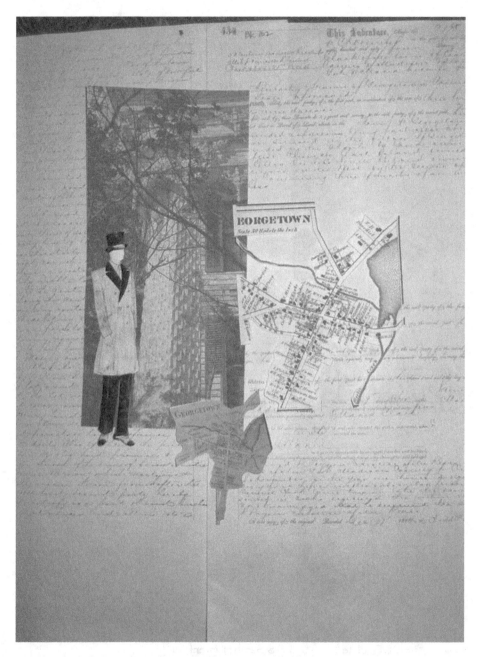

Plate 28-0485   The Face of an 1847 Immigrant, Stateside

II. Timothy

This name needs no introduction. His name is synonymous to the House. Still, there's more we can all learn about the owner of this masterpiece. Yes, even I would not, as I cannot, nor would not even come close if I wanted to describe this enigma of a man. The individual persona behind the name can be anybody, that is for sure. Case in point, is that I do not want to cover the entirety of who he is.

This page is but an effort at best to just want to dare add a touch of an interesting glimpse to what had been factual. The traits that stood out of the informational data gleaned from the deeds and titles he had signed, co - signed, and signed off on, were used freely in lavish adherence to the facts. These data were crossed referenced with other information, collective hear - says, printed and oral narratives. A combination of stoic, skeptical and neutral viewing lenses were used for wider perspective.

The soundness of the choices, and the sustainability of this Brown couple's decisions together, presented the examples of enduring contributions that shaped lives, brought communities together in a cohesive progressive culture. Records showed that these actions promoted diversity of mindsets; such that the strength of positivity continued for generations.

The proof is right before our eyes. This structure still stands even after being subjected to the most adverse of conditions. The overall Main Street laid out the way it is mostly seen now was because of the use, function, designs and the people of the past. One main decision maker was Timothy Brown, as he continued the subdivision of the land that became Main Street. These are the types of stories that abound behind the pages of archived records worthy of bringing forth to light, here.

For instance, he believed in mobility. The use of technology and planning. The Importance of ROW cannot be excessively emphasized here, as the people then subscribed to the idea of ease of transport, conveyance, access to land for the growth in commerce. Why should we not think the same today? It is important to mention that Timothy Brown in all his dealings had always taken into account the huge role of Ingress & Egress. The room for movement, expansion, growth. This is particularly of note in today's mode of living. NYS Property law cover this in Section 335 - a Easements of Necessity:

" The owner of any lot, plot, block, site of other parcel of real estate being a subdivision or apart of a subdivision of any larger parcel or parcels of real property shown upon a map of said parcel or parcels of real property and its subdivision or subdivisions, filed in the county or of the register of deed of the county where the property is situated, prior to the sale or conveyance of such lot, plot, block or site or other parcel, or subdivision thereof by the seller thereof, upon which map any road or street is indicated or shown as giving access to or egress from any public road or street to such lot, plot, block, site or other parcel of real estate thereon indicated or to any part thereof, sold or granted after such filing, and the owner of any lot, plot, block, site or other parcel of real estate, the conveyance whereof shall specifically give the right of access to or egress from the same by any private road or street over lands belonging to the maker of such conveyance and which road or street is described in such conveyance, may, when necessary to the enjoyment of the lot, plot, block or site or other parcel of real estate so sold or conveyed and when the same is not bounded by a public road, lay, beneath the roads or streets indicated and shown upon such map or described in such conveyance as giving access to or egress from any public road to such property so sold or conveyed as aforesaid, wires, and conduits for the purpose of supplying the said property with electric light and telephone service...."

The actions of Timothy Brown as a what we may not call a Developer is apparent in all his transactions. The collaborative reach outs and the cooperative outreach of the people left what we have now as MainStreet. Unfortunately, that most of what was laid out for the best of the inhabitants are being threatened. It is the purpose to show here that the foresight for the planning of the groundwork in the literal, that were already implemented, recorded, can be of better value now, as it had been then. That the Singular enjoyment of the benefits of this pre - planning is against the very grain of the Spirit and the State of being a human entity. It would stifle progress economically, undermine cultural heritage, and couple that with the shortchanged Historical documentation of the Legacy that narrate the Story of this Town is unconscionable.

The data were subjected, to rigorous analysis with open minded curiosity for what, and where the facts will lead to. Even then, what were compiled here would only be pertinent to his land ownership of the land parcels in Lot 91. The six titles, the acreages that would be in contextual relevance to the site of what is now landmarked as of Historic Importance.

Although mentions of his owning different parcels in different lot numbers within the Township may coincide with some references used, the area of concentration being introduced, and clarified here would be centered and focused on Lot 91. WHEW! That was one of the many issues. The saga of challenges continue here.

Adjoining land documents were looked into as detailed, and conscientiously studied to find the rationale as to the Departmental Deviations from their own Standards:

1   WHY are the following departments contain recorded acreages that do not match deeded acreages? Not one of each entree dovetail one another. How come?

1.a	Real Property	1.b	Records Dept.	1.g	Historical
1.c	Commissioned Survey	1.d	Mapping		Context &
1.e	Taxation & Assessment	1.f	Treasury		Survey

2   WHAT brought the above discrepancies?

3   WHY are the agencies in charge have not done anything even after this issue of discrepancy was brought to their attention respectfully, for three years and running?.

4.   Why did the application process ignore the prescribed document resources for sites, structures, happenings, or landscapes, to fully grasp the contextual totality from which Historic designations or recognition be based upon?

It is unfortunate that efforts to establish communication in a civil manner were brushed off, in all fronts. This compiled data, and the story are intended to bring the factual story to light. Keep turning the pages, we are quite ready indeed to unravel the mystery, yet. Please, I beseech the people to try to understand, this is a fact finding mission to find the answers on why the Truth is being buried under a pile of inconsistencies. For now, let us try to address it from the taxation exemption point:

RPTL Article 16   Consolidated Assessing Units

    Section 1610. Assessor

This section details what the "powers and duties generally applicable to the title of Assessor". One such, under "(b) Determines the exempt status of real property"

It is under this Law that the inquiries about the taxable acreage discrepancies were brought upon to document accordingly the inventoried acreages that came with the House. What is being sought, is the affirmation of whether what exemptions the law had provided for, had been applied to the properties whose acreages are not taxed. These were not indicated on the forms. This inquiry is to set the assumption to rest, and turn that discrepancy into an accounted official documentation.

Let me share you the sections of PRTL Article 4 Exemptions, Title 2 Private Property:

Section 446.	Cemeteries
Section 456.	Municipal railroads
Section 489 - dd.	Exemption of railroad real property from taxation

RPTL § 446. Cemeteries

1. Real property actually and exclusively used for cemetery purposes shall be exempt from taxation and exempt from special ad valorem levies and special assessments.
2. In addition to the exemption provided in subdivision one of this section, unimproved land, which is not presently used for cemetery purposes, but in which interments are reasonably and in good faith anticipated, shall be exempt from taxation, special ad valorem levies and special assessments. An exemption pursuant to this subdivision shall be granted only upon application by the owner of the property on a form prescribed by the commissioner. The application shall be filed with the assessor of the appropriate county, city, town or village on or before the taxable status date of such county, city, town or village.
3. The term "cemetery purposes" as used in this section shall mean land and buildings, whether privately or publicly owned or operated, used for the disposal or burial of deceased human beings, by cremation or in a grave, mausoleum, vault, columbarium or other receptacle. Such term shall also include land and buildings actually used and essential to the providing of cemetery purposes including, but not limited to, and the on site residence of a full- time caretaker and storage facility for necessary tools and equipment.
4. No real property shall be entitled to receive an exemption pursuant to this section if the owner or operator of such real property or any officer, member or employee thereof, shall receive or may be lawfully entitled to receive any pecuniary profit from the operations thereof, other than reasonable compensation for services performed, or if the ownership or operation is a guise for directly or indirectly making any other pecuniary profit for such owner or operator or for its officers, members or employees.

Add, L 1958, ch 959, §1, eff Oct 1, 1959; amd, L 1981, ch 920, § 3, eff Jan 1, 1982, L 1984, ch 473, §§ 5,6, eff July 20, 1984, L 2010, ch 56, § 1(Part W), eff June 22, 2010.

RPTL § 456. Municipal Railroads

Real property held and used for railroad purposes by any corporation, all of the capital stock of which is owned by a municipal corporation of this state, shall be exempt from taxation and exempt from special ad valorem levies and special assessments to the extent provided in section four hundred ninety of this chapter.

Add, L 1958, ch 959, §1, eff Oct 1, 1959, with substance derived from Tax Law §4.

RPTL §489- c Assessment of real property of railroads

1. Railroad real property shall be assessed according to its condition and **ownership** as of the first day of July of the year preceding the year in which the assessment roll on which such assessment will be entered is filed in the office of the city or town clerk, except that it shall be assessed according to its condition and **ownership** as of the first day of July of the second year preceding the date required by law for the filing of the final assessment roll for purposes of all village assessment rolls.

RPTL §489- d. Exemption of railroad property from taxation

2. Subsidized railroad real property shall be exempt from taxation. The **exemptions shall be granted each year only** upon
   (a) Application of the owner of said property on a form prescribed by the commissioner and
   (b) Submission of such proof as may be required by the commissioner that the property is subsidized railroad real property.

The application and proof shall be filed with the appropriate assessing authority on or before the appropriate taxable status date, with copies thereof simultaneously filed with the commissioner and the department of transportation.

RPTL § 410 Special Districts

Real property owned by a special district, or the property owners therein, within its boundaries used exclusively for the purpose for which such district was established shall be exempt from taxation and exempt from special ad valorem levies and special assessments to the extent provided in section four hundred ninety of this chapter, except as otherwise provided in section two hundred seventy- two of the county law.

Add, L 1958, §1with substance derived from Tax Law §4; amd, L 1974, ch 71, §1, eff March 19, 1974.

III. The Three - Fourth Acre

Many pages of registered records pored over, and... Here it is: Timothy Brown, Lot 91.

1864, November 21 to Timothy Brown from Samuel Clark of Eaton,

3/4 of an acre for $350.00

Liber 102, p.434 Recorded: 17 Dec. 1864 at 3 PM.

"... being part of Lot 91 bounded on the North by lands owned by the Baptist Church & Society; East by lands formerly owned by Mary M. Ellis; on the South by land formerly owned by Russell Whitmore; on the West by the center of the highway; being a part of Lot No. 91 of said town, Containing 3/4 of an acre, more or less."

This particular piece of land was the only one of all his land investments that happened to be included in the application for nomination of the House, as a structure of architectural importance and as part of some sort of religious movement. This is sad, very sad indeed. WHY? On what categorical context did this parcel excluded the rest of the landholdings left in his possession, their possessions?

It is my strong belief that there was stark bias in the gathering of facts. Information that are authentic. Data that withstand scientific, legal, and mathematical scrutiny, if at all any Real Historian would be interested in. The Accuracy.Truth. The Veracity of Facts. Even the Government Agencies that handle all Historical Landmarking, posted the guidelines on how to appropriately take the most contextual scope that can represent the Truthful Story, worthy of Historic deference. Why were the guidelines deviated from? www.parks. Was that context taken, and chosen, designed to be singular? To ensure the greater odds of entitlement [receipt thereof; as in grants be given year in year out], instead of self - sustainability? How can context and acreage be remarkably unaccounted and diminished? The information used in assessment and taxation documents are glaringly incongruent from the recorded and archived data in the County Records. Not one person in the approving agency ever questioned those inconsistencies even after bringing them to their attention. Double check, Cross check, Fact Check? What happened to quality control? Accuracy? Surely, there is not one human that would be beyond fact checking? Are we infallible?

This 3/4 acre did not come with proof that the House was in the literal placement there either. At least my research have not unearthed any. I beseech any one of the readers, if the factual document or record that is in a legally accepted proof beyond reasonable doubt ever existed? Building permits, architectural design, taxation, for instance? The same is true with Mr. Timothy Brown literally building the structure. There is no tangible proof on record, except the hearsay that had been narrated over and over, written and re - written, then became the accepted truth without question. How is this History? Thus, I am questioning this belief to be just that. A tale. A myth. A legend. A make - believe. Why do we not say so? Stop passing unproven facts as so.

Even in that era, there were such things as records. Provenance, foolproof, and genuine. Accurate. Thus, I feel that the deeds of the dead are being shortchanged by not taking into context the factual basis of the lives of these people according to the number one source of information. The Deeds. Allow me then to present the very much ignored facts. Facts that may render sore feelings to come to life, illicit smirks, and curses, nevertheless they are the Truths found archived. It is my unique position as an owner, privileged to be University trained, even if touted to be inexperienced, to tell the facts as they are, as they were written to be sources of recorded information, testaments to what deeds the previous owners did with real properties, glimpses of lives lived, in this case beautifully, before they died.

At a glance, can you find where and what from the cartographic illustration?

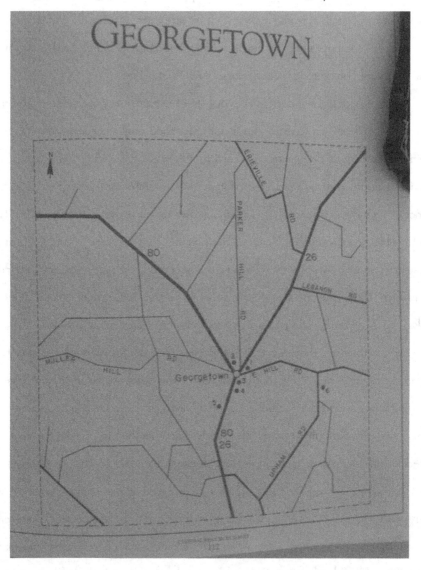

Plate 29 Cultural Resources Survey

A compilation of Madison Historical Society, accessed through Hamilton Library History Collection through the kindness, and open mined practice of information sharing and cross referencing. TYjoan.

3.   Most Referred Roads & Highways circa 1800

Let me hold you off a minute here. Defining the whereabouts of what, and which highways we are reading about, and were used as reference points in these documents are important. That way, we lessen the odds of losing data in translation, perception, and misunderstanding.

Highway that cuts through the center of Lot 91:

Route 26 runs North & South

Highway that run from the Village of Georgetown to Otselic

Route 26 runs North & South

Highway that run from the Georgetown Mills to DeRuyter

Route 80 connects to Route 13

Highway that run from Georgetown to Nelson

Route 26 connects to Nelson via Erieville Road

Highway that run from Georgetown over the Hill to DeRuyter

Muller Hill Road

Highway that run through Timothy Brown's land:

On Lot 91: Route 26 passes the front of the house, placing the property on the East side of the highway.

Route 26 [North and South]   Route 80 [East and West] crosses Route 13

Railroad to Georgetown Station

Mill Street [East and West] now called East Hill Road

1839, Highway leading from Otselic to Nelson Liber AU p.418-419

1839, Highway leading from DeClerq's Mills to New Woodstock Liber AU p.418-419

1872, West Road Liber 126, p. 70-71

1872, Creek Road Liber 126, p.70-71

1873, Old Plank Road Liber 133, p. 430

1874, Highway from the Village of Georgetown to DeRuyter Liber 138 p.516

.... Highway that run through Timothy Brown's land…

———

1874, November 14 This Liber 138 p.516 deed came from the 12 acre that Timothy Brown bought from Elnathan Ellis. This particular piece to Edwin Joaquin then, is situated in Lot 91 thus at least 2 major Highways both intersect close, and within this grid Lot 91: Route 26 & Route 80. Then a couple of streets namely: Mill St, Brown Street, West Street, and Muller Road. Important things to consider here, and baffling, as there should be no reason why the changes in Street names would not be documented, and records be open to the public for information, for study, for knowing, for accurate referencing. Today, 2014, where this original Mill Street was, is now called East Hill Road.

What was then West Street, would be now straight Route 80.

Brown Street is now called Playground Street.

Muller Road seemed to be still the same.

The local Town Clerk, and the County DOT had not revealed any data for me to peruse, unfortunately. Of course, if you happen to be more familiar than me about these roads, please do add on the information, to update. Corrections would be welcome too. A new media format is in the works as of this writing.

Let us take an up close look here:

The CREEK ROAD also known as the Georgetown & Otselic PLANK ROAD:

1893, December 27 Liber 182 p. 388 Recorded: 02 January 1894 H. Hamlin Whitmore to Albert E. LaSalle (same premises as described in both Liber 363 pp.56-61 & Liber 375 pp 131-136) as had been transferred:

1946, March 31 Liber 363 pp.56-61; first paragraph page 58 "... Also excepting and reserving therefrom all that piece or parcel of land being part of Lot No. 103 and bounded and described as follows viz: On the northerly and westerly by the center of the highway running from the creek road through part of said lot and other land now or formerly owned by Albert E. LaSalle, on the south by land now or formerly owned by Wm. F. Drake and on the easterly by the center of the creek road formerly known as the Georgetown and Otselic plank road,..."

1946, Sept. 19 Liber 375 pp.131-136; first paragraph page 133" Also excepting and reserving therefrom all that piece or parcel of land being part of Lot No. 103 and bounded and described as follows viz: On the northerly and westerly by the center of the highway running from the creek road through part of said lot and other land now or formerly owned by Albert E. LaSalle, on the south by land now or formerly owned by Wm. F. Drake and on the easterly by the center of the creek road formerly known as the Georgetown and Otselic plank road,..."

The above are representative samples of little details buried in a document that mentioned facts that should have been recorded chronologically. Information that can be made open for public understanding of changes that were made or that happened then. A distinctive attribute that can enhance the value of property.

Note:

Creek road as the same as Plank Road: Is this true only for this part of the Road or the entire length regardless of Township?

Check out J. Devenport; Wm.P. Hare; the Cemetery; the Church; & the Parsonage on the West.

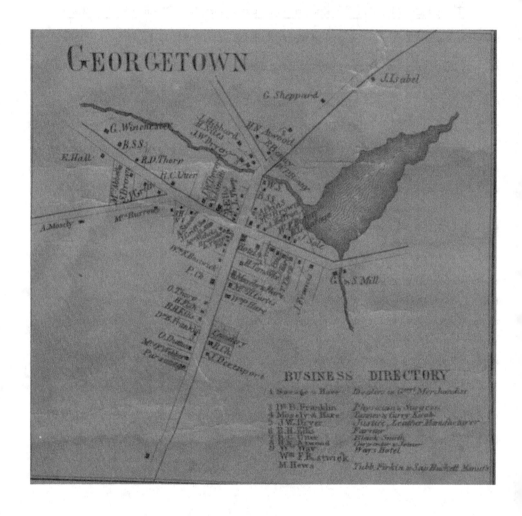

Plate 30-0742 Main Street, 1859

Accessed from the Madison County, NY, Records.

Check out J. Devenport - now O.H. Whitmore; Wm.P. Hare - still there, still longer than adjoined measured parcels; H.N. Atwood now added; the Cemetery - now enlarged; the Church - remained smaller than the cemetery as was in 1859; Brown Hall now there; & the Parsonage on the West unaccounted here.

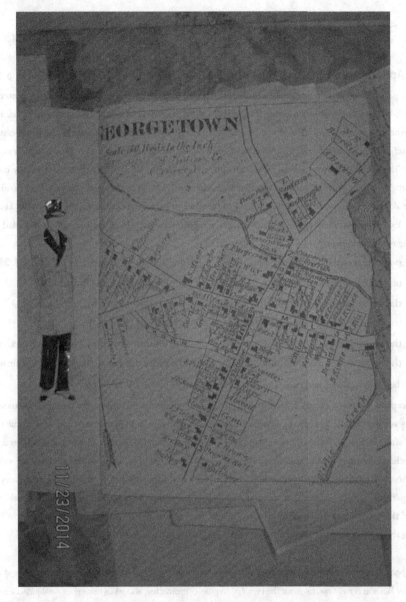

Plate 31-0256 Georgetown, 1875

Courtesy of: Madison County DOT Engineers Office. Such cartographic document was made available by other Historical Societies conferred with, and private collections of history enthusiasts.

4. Here's where Most of **Main Street** came from:

1872, April 15 from Elnathan Ellis and Diana[10], his wife for $3,500.00 Liber 126, p. 70-71

"... being part of Lot 91 beginning at the center of the Creek Road at a point of junction with the center of the West Road leading to DeRuyter running thence south 33 degrees West along the center of said Creek Road to the Northeast corner of lands now owned by Isaac Fletcher thence W 33 degrees N along the Northeast line of said Fletcher's land 12 rods to the Easterly line of lands owned by said Fletcher thence Northeasterly along said Easterly line to the Southwest corner of the lot formerly deeded to Ira P. Wood thence a Westerly course to the Southeast corner of the Dibble lot so called thence a North course to the center of said West Road thence Easterly along the center of the said West Road to the place of beginning containing twelve acres of land more or less. Excepting & reserving therefrom the several pieces or parcels or land heretofore deeded to the following named persons to wit

one half acre deeded to Seth Smith	one acre & 59 rods deeded to Zinah J. Moseley
one half acre deeded to Calvin B. Stowel	the Congregational Church lot
the lot owned by William F. Bostwick	the lot now owned by John Griffith
the lot now owned by Joseph Thorpe	the School House lot
the lot now owned by Sila Wadsworth	the lot now owned by Henry W. Saunders
the lot owned by Henry Sunders and	the piece deeded to Mrs. Wm. H. Johnson

for a further description of said parcels of land reference is [sic] had to the respective deeds."

"Also excepting the piece of land sold to Alvin Moseley, said premises sold subject to a mortgage thereon of the sum of seven hundred dollars held by Warren Brown which mortgage & the interest which shall accrue thereon from & after the 23rd day of November 1871. Said second party hereby assumes to pay and satisfy as a part of said purchases money with the appurtenances and all the estate title and interests therein after the said party of the first part and the said Elnathan Ellis doth thereby covenant & agree to & with the said party of the second part his heirs & assigns that the premises thus conveyed in the quiet and peaceable possession of the party of the second part his heirs & assigns he will forever warrant & defend against any person lawfully claiming the same or any part thereof except under said mortgage....".. recorded May 21, 1872, 10 AM.

This is where Scientific Analysis & Mathematical Acumen come in handy - In the systematic accounting of land division wannabes' like you & me. Now, take out the Pencil, Compass & Protractor, and let us remember Analytical Geometry

---

[10] 1836, Liber AO p.422-423; Elnathan & wife Mary M.;

1843, Liber AZ p.475 Elnathan Ellis' wife is Mary M. Ellis: Is Diana the second wife then?.

Let us back track a few archived pages more, and find out where this particular piece was cut off from which particular parcel. Then, clarify the adjoining names cited as monuments for referential purposes.

****1839, January 12 from Epaphroditus Whitmore, John Brown & Emily,
      Samuel W. Barnett & Eleanor **to Elnathan Ellis**
      for $350.00 Liber AU p. 418-419 Recorded: 17 Oct. 1839
      Georgetown Lot 91, Township Subdivision No. 06, County of Madison.

"... bounded as follows viz beginning at the center of the highway leading from Otselic to Nelson thence south 33 degrees West along the center of the said highway to the building lot now owned and occupied by the said Ellis thence West 33 degrees North 12 rods to the Southwest corner of the building lot deeded to Ira P. Wood containing a Westerly course to the Southeast corner of lot owned and occupied by Doct Whitmore known by the name of the Dibble lot thence a North course to the center of the new road leading from Niles Settlement to De Ruyter thence Easterly along the center of the highway to the place of beginning in the center of the highway leading from Declerq's Mills to New Woodstock."

"Reserving therefrom:

        one half acre deeded to Seth Smith

        one acre & fifty nine rods deeded to Zinah J. Mosely[11] being the Northeast
            corner of said piece

        one half acre deeded to Calvin B. Stowel

        one half acre deeded to Ira P. Wood, be the same more or less..."

Note: This transaction already had it's Reservations, four (4) in all. It is also interesting that all the other men had their wives' names added, Elnathan Ellis' wife not mentioned here.

subdivision process, that seem to baffle even the most Professed Elite Engineers & Surveyors, that include all combined with what you remembered in the HS Trigonometry Classes. It better be brilliant stock knowledge.

---

11 1836 Zinah J. Moseley's wife, Mary Liber AN p. 474-475.

1839, January 12 Reservations from Epaphroditus Whitmore, John Brown & Emily, his wife, Samuel W. Barnett & Eleanor his wife, to Elnathan Ellis. Four lot parcels.

Seth Smith	one half acre
Zinah J. Mosely[12] Northeast corner	one acre & fifty - nine rods
Calvin B. Stowel	one half acre
Ira P. Wood	one half acre

1872, April 15 to Timothy Brown from Elnathan Ellis & Diana[13], his wife. This was the 12 acres bought for the price tag of $3,500.00 recorded in Liber 126, p. 70-71. There were thirteen reservations by the time Elnathan Ellis transferred ownership to Timothy Brown.

Seth Smith	1/2 acre	Congregational Church lot[14]	1 acre
Zinah J. Moseley	1 acre & 59 rods	William F. Bostwick[15]	1 rood & 4 rods
Calvin B. Stowel	1/2 acre	John Griffith	
Joseph Thorpe		the School House lot	
Sila Wadsworth		Henry W. Saunders	
Mrs. Wm. H. Johnson[16]	40 sq.ft.	Henry Sunders	

*Alvin Moseley, said premises sold subject to a mortgage $700.00 held by Warren Brown mortgage & the interest due 23rd day of November 1871.

---

[12] 1836 Zinah J. Moseley's wife, Mary Liber AN p. 474- 475

[13] 1836, Liber AO p.422; Elnathan & Mary M.;1843 Elnathan Ellis & Mary M. Liber AZ p. 475

[14] 1883, May 05 Liber 156 pp. 329 - 331 one acre Congregational Church

[15] 1966, August 05 Liber 626 p. 306 presently the Georgetown Fire Dept., One rood 4 rods

[16] 1871,Oct. 28 Liber 125 p.283 ; 1966, August 05 Liber 626 p. 306: 40 feet square

5. The Itemized Accounting of the Twelve Acres:

How Timothy Brown & Sarah H. Brown Subdivided the twelve acres further, helped shaped Main Street bustled with Economics:

From the land titles that originated from Elnathan Ellis and from E. Whitmore, John Brown, & Samuel W. Barnett [on the previous pages that are comparatively facing each other] to Timothy & Sarah H. Brown. The subdivision of this land to the following titles and their respective new owners; some included details of their specific purposes, others of forthcoming community improvements planned.

1872, September	23	to Nathan Pritchard	$500.00	half acre
1872, November	01	to Orlando Dutton	$ 10.00	5 &4/10 rods
1872, November	01	to Timothy Brown	$ 10.00	9 & 4/10 rods
*** Timothy Brown & Sarah from Orlando Dutton & Martha				
1873, November	01	to J. Henry Stanbro	$500.00	2 roods, 4 & 1/2 rods
1874, March	19	to Horace Hawks	$500.00	3 roods
1874, July	10	to Milton D. Allen	$150.00	16 & 1/4 rods
1874, August	01	to Mary J. Johnson	$ 45.00	40' x 51' & 6"
1874, November	14	to Edwin Joaquin	$150.00	?
1877, February	08	to Jane Saunders	$232.73	64 rods
1877, October	23	to Orville Mack et al.	$ 8.50	6 & 130/1089 rods
1882, August	15	to FBaptist Church	$100.00	3 rods
*** Timothy Brown from the Baptist Church 9' x 60'				
1884, January	28	to Reuben Mawson	$ 10.00	144 square ft.

1872, September 23 to Nathan Pritchard $500.00 half acre Liber 516, p. 127

"…part of lot 91…bounded as follows: beginning at a point on the Westerly line of the Congregational Church lot a distance of seventy five links South Westerly from the Northwest corner of said Church lot running thence S. 84° 20' W. three chains to a point on the Westerly line of C.S.C. [sic] said lot thence N 64° W. one chain sixty seven links thence 34° 20" E. three chains thence S 64° E. one chain sixty seven links to the place of beginning containing one half acre of land."

Here's the interesting twist on this particular business of buying - selling / selling - buying transactions on that very same date, between Timothy Brown & wife Sarah, and Mr. Orlando Dutton & wife Martha. It is noted here, as this seemed to be a way of doing things with Mr. Brown and the local people: as such transpired with The Baptist Church & Timothy Brown with the 9' x 60' parcel.

There were three transactions dated 15 August 1882, all at the same day, yet recorded in different times and years.

This manner of business procedures show inclination to do things with ease. They adapted schedules synchronization to manage time and resources. Please consider that they did not operate in cyber time then, plus the speed of travel is not on today's transportation efficiency as well. While this process achieved their goals; to us now, in our generation - comprehension of their intentions may not come straightforward if we are not careful to take the aforementioned elements as facts. They can create a disconnect that can be quite confusing, especially, if the documents are not studied together and taken at the whole context of occurrence.

1872, November 01 to Orlando Dutton $ 10.00 5 &4/10 rods Liber 127 p. 520

"... part of lot 91... bounded as follows: beginning in the center of the highway on the Northwest corner of a piece of land deeded by Russell Whitmore and wife to the said Orlando Dutton running thence N.35° E. along the center of the said highway sixty two and one half links thence S. 56° E. one chain eight links to the North line of said Dutton line of land thence N. 85° W on said North line one chain twenty five links to the place of beginning containing five and four tents rods of land."

The deed from Timothy Brown to Orlando Dutton was recorded on Dec. 28, 1872 at 12 o'clock; and the one below from Orlando Dutton to Timothy Brown was recorded at 2PM. Whereas with the logged time sequence the page number assignment on the actual book rendered the reverse. Timothy Brown to O. Dutton on page 520 and Dutton to Brown on page 519.

1872, November 01	to Orlando Dutton	$ 10.00	5 &4/10 rods	Liber 127 p. 520 at 12 Noon
1872, November 01	to Timothy Brown	$ 10.00	9 & 4/10 rods	Liber 127 p. 519 at 2 PM

1872, November 01 to Timothy Brown $ 10.00 9 & 4/10 rods Liber 127 p. 519

"... being part of lot 91... bounded as follows: beginning on the South line of lands owned by the said Timothy Brown, at the East corner of a piece of land this day deeded by the said Timothy Brown and wife to the said Orlando Dutton running thence S. 85° E on said South line one chain sixty five thence S. 35° West eighty three links to a stake thence North 55° W. one chain forty links to the place o beginning containing four tenths rods of land."

Was this transaction between Mr. Dutton and Timothy Brown a sort of swap? This one is an interesting point to look further into. Here is the description of another parceled piece, out of that twelve acres. What is interesting on this one, is that this one mentioned the Old Plank Road. This transaction was 1873. There were other Deeds around this vicinity that had mentioned the Plank Road, and the highway in different sentences, on the same paragraph. This would have to be addressed, and expounded on a different platform. For now, suffice to point this fact here.

1873, November 01 to J. Henry Stanbro $500.00 2 roods, 4 & 1/2 rods Liber 133, p.430.

"... part of Lot 91... bounded as follows: beginning in the center of the Old Plank Road at the Northeasterly corner of Isaac Fletcher's village lot running thence Northwesterly on the Northerly line of said village lot three chains twenty five links thence Northeasterly on the Easter line of lands owned by said Isaac Fletcher one chain fifty links to the Southerly line of lands owned by said Timothy Brown thence Southeasterly in said line & on the Southerly line of the village lot deeded by said Timothy Brown to Levi Dutton three chains twenty five links to the centre of said road thence Southwesterly along the centre of said road one chain 75 links to the place of beginning containing two roods four & one half rods of land more or less."   ... recorded May 25, 1874, 4 PM.

This Old Plank Road seemed to be the most elusive of all. I wonder WHY? So I am bringing here a digested form of MS. M.E.Cochrane - Folsom Raft to Railroad p. 58 on Plank Roads in the Village of Green in the late mid 1800.

M.E. Cochrane wrote a piece about the Plank Road North of Greene in the old days:

"... this plank road was put down by private concern or corporation. Just outside of the village a toll gate was built and the toll house still stands and is in use as a dwelling. The teamsters who used this road felt for a long time that they were on top of the world. No mud, nor ruts, nor stone. Even old Doobin was delighted. But after many years it seems that the road company was interested only in the collecting of tolls. Planks got broken and teamsters had to pry them loose and throw them aside, and none were replaced. So it gradually ceased to be a plank road any longer. Still the users had to pay toll.".. February 11, 1869: " The Farmers' Plank Road Company has taken steps to abandon the road from Greene to Smithville Flats. It has been one of the best roads in this section and we hope the inhabitants along the line, to whom it will revert, will do their duty and keep the road in good condition" The toll gate was sold in auction. In 1872 Alonzo Marvin was living in it."

6. Old Plank Road

> *"The probability that we may fail in the struggle ought not to deter us*
>
> *from the support of a cause we believe to be just."*
>
> *A.Lincoln*

6.   Old Plank Road

The old plank road. I have read and seen this mentioned in numerous documents, but not one person wanted to acknowledge this. The following are the representative sampling of the Deeds using the Old Plank Road as a site reference monument to denote where a piece of land started, ended. This Old Plank Road was the geopositional marker.

1873, November 01 to J. Henry Stanbro $500.00 2 roods, 4 & 1/2 rods Liber 133, p.430.19

" ... in the <u>center of the plank road at the Northeasterly corner of Isaac Fletcher's Village lot</u>.."
1878 December 04 Recorded: 27 March 1882 Liber 153 p. 67 as it changed hands in:

1944, July 30 Noel Jackson & ano. To Ella M. Trass Liber 252 p. 190 to:

1946, March 31 Liber 363 p.56-61 Maud J. Upham to Gorgon F. Burgess: 4th parag. P. 57

"Excepting and reserving therefrom all that tract or parcel of land situate in the Town of Georgetown aforesaid, being a part of Lot No. 103 and bounded as follows: Beginning in the center of the Gulf about 37 rods south of the northwest corner of Lot 103; thence easterly along the center of the said Gulf to the highway leading from <u>plank road over the hill</u> of Wm. Dutton's; thence southeasterly along the center of the said highway to the west line of said lot; thence north along the west line of said lot to the place of beginning, containing by estimation 10 acres of land be the same, more or less. Being the same premises conveyed to Otis H. Whitmore by Russell Whitmore and wife.

1878 December 04 Recorded: 27 March 1882 Liber 153 p. 67
1878 December 04 Recorded: 27 March 1882 Liber 153 p. 67." as it changed hands in:

1946,Sept. 19 Liber 375 p. 131-136 Gordon F. Burgess to Gordon F. Burgess & wife Theresa B. Burgess; 4th paragraph page 132

"... Excepting and reserving therefrom all that tract or parcel of land situate in the Town of Georgetown aforesaid, being a part of Lot No. 103 and bounded as follows: Beginning in the center of the Gulf about 37 rods south of the northwest corner of Lot 103; thence easterly along the center of the said Gulf to the highway leading from <u>plank road over the hill</u> of Wm. Dutton's; thence southeasterly along the center of the said highway to the west line of said lot; thence north along the west line of said lot to the place of beginning, containing by estimation 10 acres of land be the same, more or less. Being the same premises conveyed to Otis H. Whitmore by Russell Whitmore and wife, 1878 December 04 Recorded: 27 March 1882 Liber 153 p. 67." On this part of the same deeds, this information was gleaned:

1893, December 27 Liber 182 p. 388 Recorded: 02 January 1894 H. Hamlin Whitmore to Albert E. LaSalle as it changed ownership in 1946.

The CREEK ROAD also known as the Georgetown & Otselic PLANK ROAD:

1946, March 31 Liber 363 pp.56-61; first paragraph page 58 "…Also excepting and reserving therefrom all that piece or parcel of land being part of Lot No. 103 and bounded and described as follows viz: On the northerly and westerly by the center of the highway running from the creek road through part of said lot and other land now or formerly owned by Albert E. LaSalle, on the south by land now or formerly owned by Wm. F. Drake and on the easterly by the center of the creek road formerly known as the Georgetown and Otselic plank road,…" As well as the same document here below, the same year:

1946, Sept. 19 Liber 375 pp.131-136; first paragraph page 133 "… Also excepting and reserving therefrom all that piece or parcel of land being part of Lot No. 103 and bounded and described as follows viz: On the northerly and westerly by the center of the highway running from the creek road through part of said lot and other land now or formerly owned by Albert E. LaSalle, on the south by land now or formerly owned by Wm. F. Drake and on the easterly by the center of the creek road formerly known as the Georgetown and Otselic plank road,…"

Here is another set of those deed descriptions that pertain to the actual location of the old plank road:

1917, Jan. 19 Noel E. Jackson to Mrs. Ella M. Trass for $10.00

"… Being part of Lot ninety - one (91) of said Town and bounded as follows: On the northeast by lands formerly owned by Wm. P. Hare (deceased); On the southeast by lands owned by Sarah H. Brown; on the southwest by the cemetery; On the northwest by the center of the old plank road; containing two roods and twenty three perches of land, more or less, excepting and reserving the right and privilege of conveying water across said premises in a pipe as is, unless said pipe shall be in the way of digging a cellar on said premises...."

1967, April 26 Floyd Trass, Executor for Ella Trass to Millie Moore a.k.a. Camilla M.

Brown Liber 631 p. 29-30 (William Trass died 1947: equal share with Millie Moore)

"... Being a part of Lot 91 in said Town, and bounded on the Northeast by lands formerly owned by Wm. P. Hare, on the southeast by lands owned by Sarah H. Brown, on the southwest by the Cemetery, and on the northwest by the center of the old plank road; containing twenty - three perches of land more or less; subject to the water pipe right as set forth in the deed recorded in Madison County Clerk's Office in Liber 252 of Deeds at Page 190. The said premises were owned by Ella M. Trass at her death on July 30, 1944..."

Excerpt of Liber 252 p. 190 "...

1977, June 23 Camila Brown to Audra Slocum Liber 699 p. 457 $1:00

"... Being part of lot 91 in said Town, and bounded on the northeast by lands formerly owned by Wm. P. Hare, on the southeast by lands owned by Sarah H. Brown, on the southwest by the Cemetery, and on the northwest by the center of the old plank road; containing two roods and twenty three perches more or less; subject to the water pipe right set forth in the deed recorded in Madison County Clerk's Office in Liber 252 of Deeds at page 190."

The following paragraph had been added to this document on the following two deeds and absent on the previous two deeds excerpted from the document drawn 1917 & 1967. I have seen versions of this deed that was not on the record. I wonder why?

... " Subject to all easements, grants, rights of way, liens, exceptions, restrictions and covenants of record and to any state of facts that an accurate survey may show. Title to the above described premises has not been examined." Here the ROW and the matter of ingress and ingress had been given importance to be annotated.

2005, October 01 Liber 1350 p. 222 Recorded: 03 Oct. 2005 Here below is the excerpt showing the same descriptions as the one in 1977; delineating the chain of changes.

"... Being part of lot 91 in said Town, and bounded on the northeast by lands formerly owned by Wm. P. Hare, on the southeast by lands owned by Sarah H. Brown, on the southwest by the Cemetery, and on the northwest by the center of the old plank road; containing two roods and twenty three perches more or less; subject to the water pipe right set forth in the deed recorded in Madison County Clerk's Office in Liber 252 of Deeds at page 190." ... " <u>Subject to all easements, grants, rights of way, liens, exceptions, restrictions and covenants of record and to any state of facts that an accurate survey may show.</u> Title to the above described premises has not been examined." There should be no reason why the Plank Road can be mistaken as some old fool's rant.

Among all other challenges, one is clarified and here is the transcribed copy of the actual record of incorporation dissolution for the Plank Road dated 05 July 1865. There really was one, and the remnants are stark sharp.

Book 2 Register of Incorporations p.144

The Directors of the <u>Georgetown & Otselic Plank Road Company</u> feel desirous of Abandoning their road it lying situate in the Counties of Madison & Chenango. Now therefrom we the undersigned directors of said Company do hereby Abandon said road & thenceforth became the public highway the subject to all provisions of the Laws of its State in relation to highways agreeable to an act of the Legislature of the State of New York passed February 11, 1785 In Witness whereof we set our hands & seals this fifth day of July 1865. WM W Hare Alfred A. Brown EM. Brown ZJ. Moseley HW Way Directors of the Georgetown Otselic Plank Road Company Witness ES Savage Madison County WMHare being duly sworn deposes & says that he is President of the Georgetown & Otselic Plank Road Co. That A.A Brown, EM Brown ZJ Moseley & HMWay are directors of said Company who have subscribed to the above statement The statements made above in relation to the abandonment of said road to are true & correct in all respects WM. Hare President of Georgetown and Otselic P.R.Co Sworn before me this 19 July 1865 JMDryer

5cd_stamp attached cancelled _ July 19, 1865.Recorded July 21, 1865 Whitford, Clerk.

What happened with the Plank Road in Georgetown? And to the one that traversed two Counties? Did it suffered the same fate as the one in Greene? Was this the same plank road, or road route that got converted or portions thereof into the Otselic Valley Rail Road circa 1906? Was there a House built in it? In the center of it? If it happened in Greene then, there might be chances that this was so, in Georgetown? Why keep that Fact under wraps? That House would be in a unique geo - position. That fact would be a featured novelty.

SYRACUSE DAILY JOURNAL LAST EDITION VOL.LIII.-NO.184 WEDNESDAY AUG. 4, 1897

BINGHAMTON INTERESTED: BUSINESS MEN LOOK WITH FAVOR ON THE PROPOSED OTSELIC VALLEY RAILROAD.

Binghamton, Aug.4 1897 - The Binghamton Board of Trade is becoming interested in the proposed Otselic Valley Railroad, which would extend from this city to Madison County. It is probable that a special meeting of the board will be called on some evening the last of this week for the purpose of discussing this project and trying to determine what steps can be taken to go by way of Castle Creek instead of running parallel to the Delaware, Lackawanna & Western as far as Whitney's Point.

Several business men of this city are interested and it is thought that the project will soon surmise definite shape. It is understood that capitalists living at the upper end of the proposed route are ready to help build the road; and the farmers along the way are said to be enthusiastic over the subject, many of them having offered to donate the right of way, and some of them being ready to assist in the grading of the line.

General Edward F. Jones and the other members of the board of trade believe it will be possible to interest Binghamton business men so their northern neighbors can be met halfway in the effort to build the line, which would practically open up a new country and could not help but be of great benefit to this city. They are anxious that everyone who is interested in the subject will attend the meeting which will be called later.

What happened to abandoned Roads in NY State?

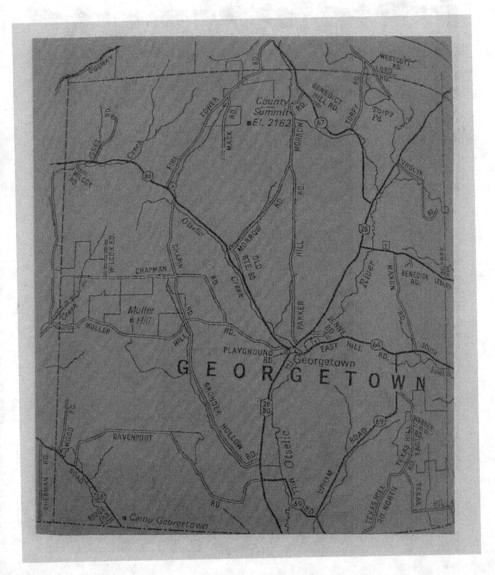

Plate 32-0742 Modern Main Map 1859 from the Cultural Resources Survey

A compilation of Madison Historical Society, accessed through Hamilton Library History Collection

through the kindness, and open mined practice of information sharing and cross referencing. TYjoan

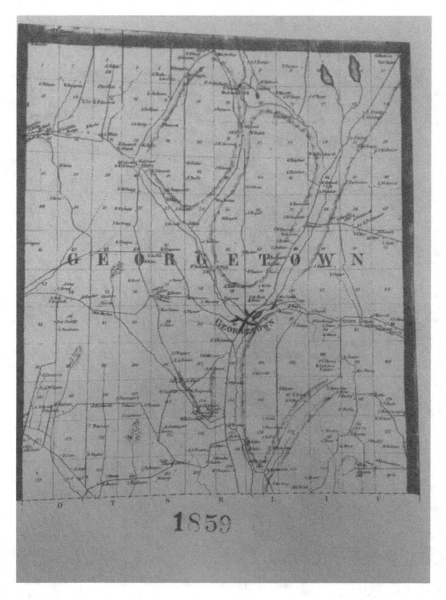

Plate 33- 0081 Georgetown, 1859

Both Maps were found common in different locations as the County Records, Brookfield Historical Society, Kellogg

Library, Mr. Vredenburgh's Collection, on line, and many anonymous contributors.

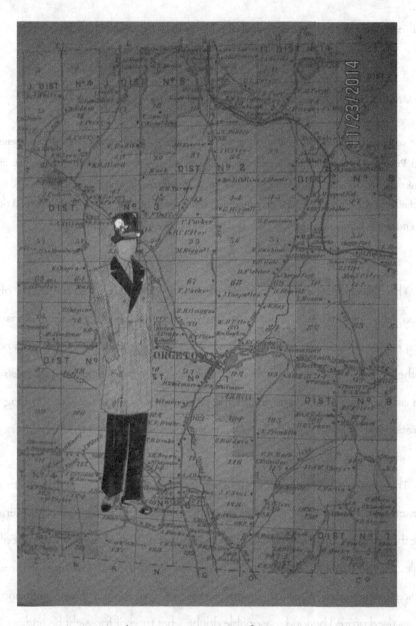

Plate 34-0255 East Line of Lot 91?

What can be observed from the evolution of the maps?

Both these parceled pieces mentioned of a highway to be established, thus made

1874, March 19 to Horace Hawks $500.00   3 roods   Liber 133 p. 365.

"... part of Lot 91...bounded as follows: beginning at the Northwest corner of land now owned by Nathan Pritchard running thence South 34° 20' West on said Pritchard's Westerly line two chains fifty links thence N.64° W. three chains thence N.34° 20' E. two chains fifty links thence S. 64° E. three chains to the place of beginning, containing three roods of land. Said premises extend on the North end to the center of a highway after said highway shall established & opened."

... recorded April 28, 1874, 2 PM.

This called for an extension on the North end of the parcel to the center of the highway, even before the highway was marked and laid out. There were plans that already swirled around about this roadway. Whether this road was for the train or for any other, remains one of the focus of further research, but if you already guessed it based on the maps attached in one of the pages here, Congratulations. Do blog that information back please. One thing for sure, this plan was not for a tow path or another road made of planks.

This property's expansion would then increase the frontage to the North end. This exemplified the trait of MR. Brown, and his fellow entrepreneurs of the era, of having the foresight, and the exercise thereof in business transactions. It was part of the lifestyle. For the credit to Mr. Brown, his house still stand today. That type of foresight in choices of materials, type of design, manner of execution of the design and the materials used proved beyond reasonable doubt, what type of foresight he had.

provisions for the extension of the lot sold. Were the Highway & extensions realized?

1874, July 10 to Milton D. Allen $150.00   16 & 1/4 rods   Liber 133 p. 535

"...part of Lot 91...bounded as follows: beginning at the Southwesterly corner of lands owned & occupied by Wm. F. Bostwick running thence N. 65 1/2° W. ninety links to a stake thence N. 34° 20' E. one chain twenty - five links to a stake set at the Southwesterly corner of lands of Wm. H. Johnson thence S. 65 1/2° E. on Southerly line of said Johnson's land ninety links to the Westerly line of said Wm. F. Bostwick land thence S.34° 20' W. on said line one chain fifteen links to the place of beginning containing sixteen and one - fourth rods. Said piece if intended to extend Southerly to the center of a highway after said highway shall be laid out and marked."

...recorded July 13, 1874, at 10AM.

The opposite page talked about extension on the North. This one for Mr. Allen was on the South part of the parcel to the center of the highway once the highway project get realized. Again, this plan was to increase the frontage of the property Southerly.

7. "...The Highway to be established..."

The Allen and the Hawks parcels mentioned in the last two pages have the highway to be laid out. This road was yet to be. Which one was this?

Consider the following data:

1874, March and July: the documents were drafted.

> Route 80 that intersects Route 13 going to DeRuyter was not yet laid as we now know it today: Route 80 and Route 26 changes names along a point in it's line.

1897, August 04 There was a press release about the interests of the Binghamton Trade in the proposed Otselic Valley Railroad. This was 23 years after that deed was drawn. What happened to the floating land, meaning the land that was intended to be expanded to if the road had not been realized?

> Was this one reason why there were issues on that corner parcels of Main Street a few years ago, as had been rumored?

Also, found lacking in documentation available for public perusal:

1   The changing of street names, the when? Why?

> eg. Mill Road to East Hill Road

> Brown Road to Playground Road

2   Should there have been an ordinance to record this, and a public hearing of some kind? Or just plain record of a name change?

This page is a work in progress more than the other pages. We'll appreciate any contribution that can be made to complete the facts therein.

8. Continuation of 12 acre Accounting:

Now, we resume looking at the subdivided chronicle of this twelve acres. This transaction seemed to be just an add – on to what was already owned and occupied by MS. Mary Johnson. This was a little more than a half acre or 2,115 square feet.

1874, August 01   to Mary J. Johnson $ 45. 00   Liber 135 p. 26

"...part of Lot 91...bounded as follows: beginning at the Northwesterly corner of lands owned by the said Mary J. Johnson N.34° 20' E. fifty one feet and six inches to the Southerly line of lands owned by George Griffith thence Easterly on said Southerly line forty feet to the Westerly line of lands occupied by Benjamin Franklin thence Southerly on said line and on the Westerly line of lands owned by the said Mary J. Johnson fifty one feet and six inches thence Westerly on the Northernly line of said lands forty feet to the place of beginning." ...recorded August 17, 1874, at 2PM.

On the transaction with Mr. Edwin Joaquin, the remarkable reference point was the Highway that run from the village of Georgetown to DeRuyter. Also, mentioned another highway that run into Timothy Brown's land. There is a Brown Street that connects Rt. 26 to Muller Road that intersects West Mill St.

1874, November 14   to Edwin Joaquin $150.00   Liber 138 p. 516

"...part of Lot 91...bounded as follows: beginning at the Northwesterly corner of lands owned by Isaac Fletcher and George Curtiss in the highway running from the village of Georgetown to DeRuyter and thence running Southerly along said Fletcher and Curtis' West line to the Southwest corner of said Fletcher & Curtis' South line to the center of the highway running Southerly from the above described highway through said Timothy Brown's land. Thence Northerly along the center of the last described highway to the center of the first described highway, thence Easterly along the center of the first described highway to the place of beginning be the same more, or less.

...recorded August 11, 1876, at 4PM.

This one also was to just expand on a land area that was already owned by MS. Jane Saunders. Yes, this is one of those things I am talking to you about, the conversion guide was placed in the front of the book. Take a scrap paper and compute for the accounting and conversion of these measurements from Imperial to the metric or any unit you are interested in.

1877, February 08   to Jane Saunders $232.73   64 rods   Liber 139 p. 263

"...part of Lot 91...bounded as follows: beginning at the Southeast corner of the village lot now owned by Jane Saunders house Southerly on a Straight line with the East line of the said line 6 rods 9 feet and ten inches thence Westerly at right angles 12 rods 7 feet six inches to the East line of Alvin Moseley's land thence Northerly six rods nine feet and ten inches to the Southwest corner of the aforesaid Jane Saunders lot thence Easterly along the South line of the said Jane Saunders lot ten rods eight feet and three inches to the place of beginning containing by estimation Sixty four rods of land be the same, more or less."   ...recorded February 9, 1877, at 12 Noon.

Why are these transactions important to be detailed here?

For Responsible Stewardship.

This is a fraction of the undertakings to account for the acreage inheritance of the House. This include the seemingly minute, negligible, details. Yes, that few square feet.

That, of the 9' x 60' titled land parcel.

If this is not important, why is it that this started to be missing in 2011? This is land one cannot carry in one's purse. This is literally on the ground. It cannot walk by itself, nor be taken without knowing. In this case: Is it is a matter of encroaching? Or being subjected to adverse possession? This issue was not clarified enough so we can all move forward.

If this is not about the problem of covetousness, perhaps non-accountability in parking space use compensation, or just plain getting away without coverage for insurance liability burdens, even for the safety of public / parishioners use, what is it? Why can we not account for it then deaccession this piece accordingly as prescribed by lawful ownership? This is a housekeeping effort to narrow down what is the truth, in this story of History.

The mere fact that the previous owners took the time to document this piece, record, and continued to be conveyed for over 167 years then, suddenly become unaccounted for in my time, is really very fishy. On my end: It stinks of prejudice, and discriminatory intolerance that was even calculated. That is what is excruciatingly painful. Not a very good story to be historically recorded. Surely, this is not what a good practicing Christian would want to be known for? If this is not so, why can we not put the documents in order?

First, acknowledge the documents of conveyance on record, instead of a thick wall of silence and behind the scenes. Then, we deaccession from the truthful Legacy of this Site, as it was adversely possessed. That's history too. This is the antagonistic, hostile adversaries to the unified continuance of the legacy Alice Stevens - Cossitt so bravely acted upon single handedly, as a person, as the intelligent woman that she was.

To a responsible Registrar in any field of discipline, it is crucial to account for accessioned holdings. It is standard procedure to be able to, either, or, or both: mathematically explain; scientifically prove to the iota; numerically chronicle; especially with financial denominations, why the process of Deaccession was undertaken, needed to be taken, and HOW, to legally undertake the process.

9. The Three, 15 August 1882 Land Transactions

1882, August 15 There were three land sales transactions contracted that concerned the Browns. For in depth study, and in the pursuit of clarifications, the details were included here for documentation, and ease of referencing.

These three business deals consummated at the same time are crucial in understanding one of the contexts being brought to light for the historicity of the site. The intertwined relevance and complex relationship to the adjoining landscape cannot be understood best unless we delve into these three. The origin of the church the way we see it now started as a meetinghouse.

This is the excerpted description of that meetinghouse parcel:

1840, March 24 Recorded: 19 September 1854 at 10 AM.
"...Beginning at the southwest corner of the burying ground thence running easterly along the south line of the burying ground eight rods thence southerly by a line parallel with the highway eight rods thence westerly by a line parallel with the south line of the burying ground eight rods to the highway thence northerly along said highway eight rods to the place of beginning containing one rood and twenty for rods of land be the same more or less..."

The meetinghouse, to be further appreciated need be viewed from it's spatial relationship with the cemetery. The burying ground as we see it now is not the way it was before.

It is crucial therefore to establish these points to be able to precisely account for the retracing of the three parcels being discussed here in the following pages devoted for them. You will find the record of how the Church rearrange what we now view as the cemetery lot. The specific dimensions I was not privy with, and thus I present what data I was able to have the privilege of gathering as the circumstances presented themselves.

Here is the first of the three transactions in relation with the Meetinghouse:

1   From Orville Mack et al. to the Board of Trustees of the first Baptist Church & Society Liber 157 p.56 $1.00. This was same exact description of land bought 23 Oct. 1877 from Sarah H. Brown & Timothy Brown. Notice how Timothy's name appeared as a secondary signor.

"...Beginning at the south East corner of what is known as the Meeting House lot of the Baptist Church and Society in said town of Georgetown and running east in a direct line with the South line of said Meeting House lot 43 feet; thence North from this point 28 feet in a line parallel with the east line of said Meeting House lot; thence West 22 feet in a line parallel with the south line of said Meeting House lot; thence North 22 feet in a line parallel with the east line of said Meeting House lot, thence West 21 feet in a line parallel with the South line of said meeting House lot; thence South along the east line of the Meeting House lot to the place of beginning, containing six and 130/1089 rods of land more or less..."   Recorded: 07 May 1883, 11 AM

The cemetery had been made reference monuments for land parcels close to it. Whether the size had been as what we view it now or not, the fact that there were references to it meant that there was some semblance of it even before the other transactions were made. I came upon the records from the 501 (c) (3) organization next door that can shed more light to the question of integrity as to the dimensions of the cemetery the way we view the lay out of the grounds today.

The 1966 Report alluded to the alterations made under the directives of the Trusted Officers called Trustees. By 1968, the act of repositioning the fencing to expand the grave site had been completed. Further down this book, under Burial Ground, these reports would be discussed more in deep relevance to the surrounding parcels.

Before we continue to the other two transactions made on this day 15 August 1882, let me just show what the deeded descriptions of the Meeting House is again in this page, as drawn by the Trustees of the First Baptist Church and Society with Elnathan Ellis & wife Mary. This is for ease of comparison to the second transaction. Here is the excerpt below:

1840, March 24"... Beginning at the south west corner of the burying ground thence running easterly along the south line of the burying ground eight rods thence southerly by a line parallel with the highway eight rods thence westerly by a line parallel with the south line of the burying grounds eight rods to the highway thence northerly along said highway eight rods to the place of beginning containing one rood & twenty four rods be the same more or less..."

Recorded: 19 September 1854 at 10 AM.

Quick Conversion: 1 Rood = 1/4 of an acre

24 rods = 4 × 16.5' = 66'

2   From Timothy Brown & Sarah H. Brown to the Trustees of the First Baptist Society, their successors in Office. $100.00 Liber 157 p.57

"... Beginning at the South west corner of what is known as the new part of the Cemetery lot in the village of Georgetown, thence running easterly along the southerly line of the Cemetery lot six rods and three links to the corner of the said Cemetery thence south 37° west five rods and three 1/2 links to a stake thence west 37° north two rods and twenty one links to land owned by to the first Baptist Society of Georgetown thence northerly on easterly line of said Society's lot to the place of beginning Containing about twenty three rods of land be the same more or less. Hereby allowing the party of the second part the privileges of erecting sheds upon the line the eaves to run upon the lands owned by parties of the first part...recorded: May 07, 1883 at 11 AM."

Note: This begins at the new part of the cemetery. If you consult the maps & compare 1859 with 1875. Focus on the lay out of the cemetery and the church, it had evolved.

IV.   The 9' x 60' Parcel:

1882, August 15 This is the third transaction of this date, and year.

3   From The Trustees of the First Baptist Church Society of Georgetown,

Madison County, NY. to Timothy Brown. $1.00 Liber 161 p.20

"... his heirs and assigns, ... Being a strip of land nine feet wide by sixty feet long. Commencing at a stake on the eastern boundary of land deeded by said Timothy Brown to Orville Mack et al the 23rd day of October 1877 and running westerly along the south line of said lot 60 feet parallel with said lot to a stake on Society's lot fifteen feet west of said Timothy Brown's barn and nine feet north of said Society's south line...recorded: August 05, 1884 at 11 AM."

Interesting Facts about the Deed for 9' x 60'.

3.1   This particular deed is markedly important to be placed in a legal documentation of a transaction. This was even recorded.

3.2   This was in good faith, as this only cost Timothy Brown $1.00.

3.3   This transaction is self - evident of human relationship that was amicable, peaceful, reasonable, understanding, open minded, Christ - like practice in everyday. I wonder what happened?

3.4   This 9' feet x 60' at present seem to be missing on the ground. Efforts to account for the piece on the literal grounds for the commemorative landmarking were met with hostility. WHY?

3.4   There is the notion of the Garage and the Barn of the House as encroaching entities on the acreage of the Church, instead.

3.5   This is also not accounted for in taxation, tax map, botched survey, etc.

3.6   If this be an issue of a mistake, there must be some mathematical, and scientific explanation that are acceptably sound to allow for the legitimate deaccessioning of this land from the current title or 2011 deed on record. It had been conveyed for over 167 years without any change.

3.7   Would it not be more Christian to have this accounted, or legally transferred, versus owning by adverse possession? Taking something not one's own is stealing, no matter how petty. Is this what the IRS designation of 501(c)(3) is all about?   For the improvement of the quality of life? By taking someone else's property?

3.8   Repatriation.

We always feel celebratory when we hear stories of something lost but found. More so when unexpectedly returned after a long journey. A Welcomed closure. We can then move forward in harmony, co - sharing, co - habitation, synergistically, not parasitically.

3.9   Responsible use.

Public Parking spaces are either free, which meant that the cost of maintenance and operations are shouldered by taxpayers dollars; or paid using quarters, prepaid card and charged for by the minutes. This space belong to the House. The House costs upkeep, taxes, maintenance, improvements, the whole enchilada. What is Christlike to do? Take the land, or give what is due based on ownership, accountability, and in consonance to the 501 (c) (3) Mission of Improving the Quality of life?

3.9   Provenance.

Even animal breeds are prized for an unquestionable pedigree. The distinctive unquestionable quality of the background history. Be it in man, animals, objects d' artes. We all still have that chance to correct what are not quite kosher here. Let us please all come together in an effort, a Christ - like effort to right what is wrong, even when no one is looking. Especially when no one is looking.

RPL Article 9 § 381. **Survey, map or plan to be filed**

There shall be filed with the registrar a survey, map or plan of the land the title to which is sought to be registered, which shall be made by a competent surveyor and shall be subject to the approval of the court, and which shall clearly show the exact boundaries of the land and its connection with adjacent lands and any adjoining or neighboring streets and avenues, and the distances from such adjoining or neighboring streets or avenues, and all encroachments, if any, and all other facts which are usually shown by accurate surveys. If any adjacent land is already registered, the **survey must properly connect and harmonize** with the survey of such previously registered land. There shall be attach to such survey, map or plan and filed with it, an affidavit of the surveyor by whom it was made, that it was made by him personally or under his immediate supervisor and direction; that it is a survey, map or plan of the property described in the petition or the official examiner's report of title, and that according to the best of his knowledge and belief said property is included in the boundaries shown on such survey, map or plan, without any encroachments or improper erections, except as follows: (stating and describing any encroachments or improper locations of buildings, fences or other structures). After the original registration of any parcel of land, a new survey, map or plan of the same showing a subdivision thereof into lots may be filed with the registrar after compliance with the provisions of section 334 and 335 of RPL, as amended, and chapter 620 of the laws of 1926. The filing of such a new survey, map or plan shall outline the registered portion of the property, shall be noted as a memorial on the certificate of title to which it relates, and thereafter the land or any interest therein shall be transferred or encumbered by reference to it; in the event that the old description is used, reference must also be made to the new map.   Add, L 1909, ch 52, amd, L 1929, ch 575, eff July 1, 1929. Ams, L 1991, ch 640, § 3, eff Jan 1, 1992.

Note: Different law opinions were surfed out and had been gathered here:

One says that "this section requires the filing of a map of any parcel sought to be registered (the process of verifying ownership without constructing an abstract of title)".

In the Site's case, there is the required abstract and the documents therein contained were compared with the documents personally re - opened and re - cross checked again from the County Records Department. Also another angle of WHY the Survey not only did not connected and harmonized, [there is only one survey of the adjoined land: what was the Wm P. Hare, of today] but totally held this 9' x 60' ; 1/3 Rights to a Spring and 2 & 1/4 acre parcels of deeded and described properties unaccounted for was because of this explanation?

"Where a conveyance of a property has already been recorded, the submission of a survey along with another copy of a conveyance would be a reformed deed. The filing of such reformed deed would include the original deed, the survey, and a cover (grantee to grantee) indicating that the deed was being reformed by virtue of addition of the survey."

Why would a deed description of less than 7 acres be surveyed for a little more than three acres? There is no lien on the deed, written or oral, on record; and in consonance with the requirements of these sections RPL § 333 - a; RPL §333 -b; RPL § 334.

Tax Exemption do not render the land out of commission, nor disappear without trace?!?

10. His Contribution

Continued & Finished the Subdivision of Land to become Main Street

Lived the lifestyle of positive spontaneity.

Equality in the fair treatment of Women.

Diversified Mind in the Era where this was a volatile Issue

Continuation of the Burial Ground

Rights of Way for ease of access when roads & travel were most difficult

Owner of a Magnificent House, we still marvel at, today

Promoted Technology and the use thereof that rendered life easy and beautifully adapted to the mores of the period

While the actual factual document or record that came with the notion that Timothy Brown built the House with his bare hands cannot be found nor established with acceptable records like permits or blue prints, what is found to be factually true is the fact that even in the 1800's there were what were and are called engineers, artisans, architects, designers, the craftsman guild, and builders. Take for example how Mr. Solomon R. Guggenheim commissioned the famed Mr. Frank Lloyd Wright to design the Guggenheim Structure in Manhattan. Also the White House (1792) having been designed for the American People in mind by the well - known Architect Mr. James Hoban, an Irish Immigrant. These are historical facts. Since we are in the factual knowledge that Timothy Brown had the financial means, he could have engaged any of those methods to have a magnificent home. The census stated that he was a carpenter, farmer. DIY can be true as well. What is undiluted information, is that Mr. Timothy Brown owned the House, and made multiple functions out of it, apart from the prime purpose of being a home.

11.   The Timothy Brown in all of Us.

Whether the House was literally built or not, when or how by Timothy Brown are not the queries within the scope of this analytical study at this point. Suffice it to note here in it's final affirmation, that the Structure and the property we are dissecting the origin of, belonged to him. It was his American Dream. He was able to provide for the family and afford the lifestyle that in all common sense were the expectations of humanity. The standard for any person in which to measure up with. Fact is, what was gleaned was that he was a man of:

1   Good taste - we still are mesmerized with the House he nurtured his Home in, a testamentary Taj Mahal[17], or if one would question my use of the word Shrine for the love he had, for the "love of his life", "his wife" - Sarah H. Brown. You raise your eyebrows. Why? Now, you seek for the rationale and question the "how can I write about the house this way"? The angle that I am using are the facts herein given with the documents I was lucky to have the visuals of, during the research:

A man marries a woman, they have to have a home. If it would have been the birds, they would have built a nest, for some four footed animals, a lair. It is reasonable to deduce that Timothy built the home for him and his wife - Sarah H.. Whether he contracted an architect or not, the structure was built. The parallel with the Love story from India, was the Romantic attestation of love were made tangible in both structures, so beautiful, people come far and wide, all around the world just to behold.

2   Economic foresight - as exemplified in the final expanded form of Main Street through his procurement of the 12 acres that he further subdivided.

––––––––––––––––––––
[17] Testament of love

72

3   Developer - the expanded form of Main Street, the continuation of the burial grounds, easily accessed to in an era where transport ergonomics was a challenge

4   Social Consciousness - the Home was also a gathering place

5   Cultural Awareness - his use of technology and the Arts, as well as applied patron of artisan pursuits

6   Respect in Equality - he allowed his wife the ability to make her own financial investments. He harbored a nurturing Spirit for Sarah's intellectual growth and development. A true biblical interpretation of "why God in creating Eve - was taken from the ribs of Adam," that is to be partners - productive partners. This was modern. To practice such at the time where issues of Equality, Human Rights, Suffrage were at the crux of turmoil, is ballsy.

7   Superb Intelligence - the transactions he had made fulfilled what were the dictates of legal procedures of the time, that we are still able to reference them today.

8.   Timelessness - of his actions that still appeal to us today 167 years to date.

9   Business Acumen - like every person that delved in the lifelong adventure to generate revenue, the ups and downs always come, such that they were always likened to a wheel of fortune. Timothy had his, a couple of them, those were facts, too. An example chosen here would be the mortgage his wife concurred with Job Mack. A quitclaim documentation from Job Mack and the receipt by Sarah H. Brown & Timothy Brown of the discharged mortgage, were all written at the same document. A &A book 7 of records pp.374- 375 was dated 23 October 1877, recorded two years after, dated 21 January 1879 at 2PM. Five years after, on this very same note, the date 23 October 1877, was the same date Orville Mack et al, received this very same parcel descriptions from Timothy and Sarah H. Brown. The same parcel & descriptions were deeded by Orville

Mack et. al. to the Trustees of the First Baptist Church on the 15th August 1882. To continue, there were a total of three deed sale transactions that happened on this 15th day August 1882 that included Timothy Brown and Sarah H. Brown. Efficiency, time conservation, and getting the job done decisively. These are the traits that show their Spirit of entrepreneurship.

10   Environmental awareness & Innovative Spirit - the harnessing of the water from Otselic River to run the Mill. Sharing this technology, by selling the rights to others. Also, the strict adherence to the responsible use of design, manner of construction of the dam as a structure, it's maintenance, to protect the area from water and current surges and fluctuations, showed advanced planning with a great amount of foresight.

11   Leadership Qualities - he was able to continue from where MR. Ellis, E. Whitmore, J.Brown & S.W. Barnett left off, in developing Main Street to a bustling viable economic enclave of varied businesses through land subdivision of the 12 acres.

12   Progressive, Diverse Mindset, a Doer - he took on different areas of industry himself. A land developer, a farmer, an engineer, architect, laborer, modernist spouse. He can easily be a cross of a Mr. Hughes, Brad Pitt, and Joel Osteen [that is, if he had ever preached?] in one.

As a community today, this type of man is no shabby icon for a town like Georgetown. Besides, it is better than just any other designation or town moniker. To have the structure that was his Home still standing is really a remarkable achievement that attest to these natural traits ands qualities 167 years after. Would you not be proud? Yes, a resident of Georgetown, NY. A migrant from Vermont. It is not new therefore, to have a newcomer do great deeds in Georgetown, for Georgetown. We should embrace this notion. It is productive. It is positive. A true Symbol of Human Spirit. An American Spirit.

12.   Death 1

I cannot imagine how Mrs. Timothy Brown would have felt when she realized that life had to go on without her husband. I would not delve into speculation of emotions as that is not what this Project is about. So, dear readers, we will continue in the path of basing analysis on recorded documents. Amidst the day to day handling of end of time issues, facts showed us that Timothy Brown was able to get his affairs in order. He transferred the 3/4 acre to Sarah H. Brown 05 May 1885. Now this brings us to the topic that seemed to be leaving a sore spot whenever I make the efforts to inquire accountability as to the whereabouts of this 9'x 60' parcel of land that was deeded back by the First Baptist Church to Timothy Brown.

Even if this parcel was not turned over in the manner that Timothy Brown did with the 3/4 acre, this 9' x 60' deed of sale was part of the three deed transactions that occurred the 15th of August 1882. Sarah H. Brown had to sign off literally on the documents of sale - being the spouse of Timothy Brown. Even if her name was not on the procurement documents, these transactions occurred while they were married. Communal Property. On his death, she was the primary heir apparent. On the principles of moral values, and the merits of right and wrong [especially Christ - likeness], it was hers, unquestionably. The fact that she was able to sell this 9' x 60' as traced in the ownership chain, meant that this was honored from then onwards.

Why is it that by the time 2011 came, this cannot be accounted on the literal physical, ground, anymore? Yes, this 9' x 60' is still in the deeds.

13. Heirs & Inheritance

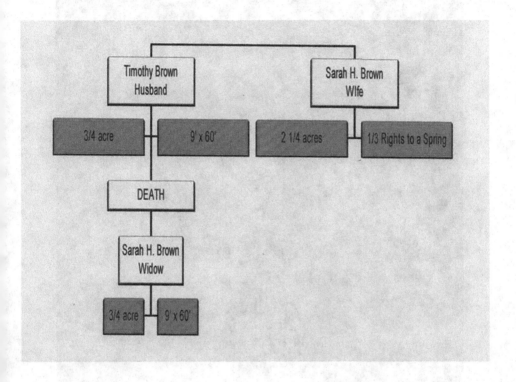

Plate 35 Tim to Sarah H. Transfer

The Charted Origin of the 4 properties. An Inventory.

Plate 36-0550 Sarah H. Brown: Mourning

V. Sarah H.

Sarah H. Brown was hardwired to sustainability. Attesting to this trait were the investments she indulged into on her own, while basking in the sacrilegious circle of marriage. Remember, this was right smack mid 1800's. Victorian era. The following land procurement transactions exemplified her head for business. Her errors and hard falls. She kept trying, feistier, more energized fortunate to be with a supportive spouse beside her. Her entrepreneurial spirit showed both personal and collective purposes for the greater good of society. Her actions directly benefitted the local community. Here below is the digest of those two procurement transactions she engaged in. The business deals were broken down to be sampled and better understood.

A. First Procurement Conducted:

| 1 | 1871, January 28 | 2 and 1/4 acres of land |

Business Deals Engaged Into with the First Procured Parcel:

1876, July 28	I.A mortgage
1877, October 23	I.B mortgage discharged
1877, October 23	I.C mortgage released
1877, October 23	I.D mortgaged parcel sold
1884, January 28	I.E another parcel sold, for burial purposes

B. Second Procurement:

| 2 | 1884, December 16 | October 1/3 Rights to a Spring |

There is the question of: Did this second Procured Investment generated Revenue? It would be best for all, if Decency be accounted for, so that the facts of what transpired be known, and let not be obliterated to oblivion or be twisted to mediocrity.

VI. The TWO & ONE – FOURTH ACRES of LAND

A Business Investment Strategy acted upon solely by SARAH H.

How can this not be viewed as a Social Statement for Women's Rights for Equality?

Circa 1871

The excerpt was made available below:

1871, January 28   to Sarah H. Brown $ 425.00   2 1/4 acres   Liber 123 p. 347

from Zinah J. Moseley, Milton D. Allen & Mary; Isaac Fletcher & Mercy

"...part of Lot 91...bounded as follows: On the North by land owned by the late William P. Hare deceased on the East by the East line of said Lot 91 on the South by Russell Whitmore's land on the West by land owned formerly by Job Davenport the Baptist Church the burying - ground and thence on a line parallel with the Easterly line of the burying ground to the South line of Wm. P. Hare's lot excepting & reserving therefrom a piece of ground bounded as follows commencing at the S.E. corner of the Burying Ground hence East nine feet, thence North thirty two feet, thence West nine feet thence South thirty-two feet to the place of beginning: the premises hereby conveyed are supposed to contain about two and one fourth acres of land more or less."

...recorded: 30 March 1871, 11 A.M.

Essential Notes from this deed that need Clarification:

A   Established Location of the EAST LINE of LOT 91.

B   N : Wm. P. Hare

C   S : Russell Whitmore

D   W : Job Davenport; Baptist Church; Burying Ground

E   One exception & reservation: 9' x 32'; SE cor. Of Burying Ground

*This is different from the 9' x 16' = 144 sq.ft. sold to Reuben Mawson for burial use. Compare.

The Grid of the Land mass of the Township, up close.

The earth as the substance of land surface is a <u>stable</u>, dense, nonvolatile inorganic substance found in the ground; exact words from the dictionary; an unquestioned truth, scientific fact, common sensibly, obvious? Or is it?

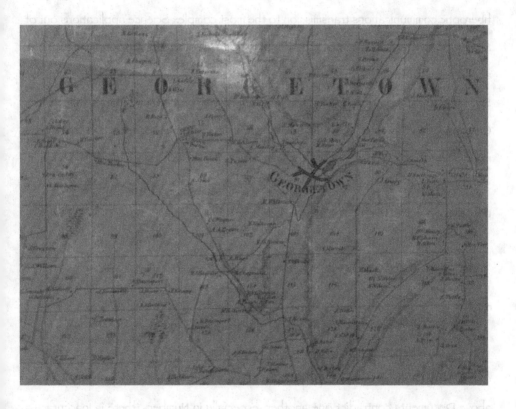

Plate 37-0683 NESW on GRID

Can you spot the location of the East line of Lot 91?

14. The EAST LINE of LOT 91

If any one of you dear Readers remember the GRID in your Math classes, or if you have seen or even used these grid lined paper for Number lines, graphs, Quadrants etc. Well, the philosophy ingrained in these series of little squares are real serious business. Money is made and lost, big time. From athletics like football, be it energy grid, fiberoptic communications transmission to the most complex Science applications out of Space. So that is how essential to find and identify the lines, their positioning as in the applied use of the GPS. The equatorial regions, those that fall in the quadrant of NESW. So is the application of the Grid lines in a Township. The Lot subdivisions fall into the Grid lines of a Township, for easy identification, for ease of location. Do these lines move? Should be permanent; but guess what? This Grid Line in Lot 91, found in Subdivision #6 called East Line of Lot 91 is not only having movement, it was unaccounted for in the following legally accepted Documents:

on the Survey

where Taxation Map & Township Map should Coincide

where Assessment is based upon

how the Taxed Amount is derived

then, Title / Deed Acreage = Tax Acreage = Survey Acreage = Mapped Out Acreage = the actual acreage one has in one's land, no more no less. When all the above Documents contradict one another, especially in Numbers, there is Inaccuracy = Problems. If there is an Issue = Investigate, Collect Evidence, Analyze + Compare = Solve. Unless we weave a web of deceit in the practice to deceive? Please do consider the fact that inattention to accuracy threaten the integrity of every agency dedicated for public service. This would be especially expected in the system of Archiving, of Records, that were designed to ensure the safety and well being of the tax paying citizens of a civilized nation that is based on the premise of Democracy!

Let me allow my thoughts to wander. This 2 & 1/4 acre parcel was procured with Sarah H. Brown as the sole purchaser. The year 1871 makes me wonder what else was going on in the world out there. The Civil Rights, Women Equality, Right to vote, and so forth were incendiary topics. It would be noteworthy to inject the issue of Property Ownership for Women[18] in that generation. Back then, I was told: women can only own property if passed on by the spouse and first born son if there were children, that is. The mother being the guardian, only if the child have not reached the age of majority.

Also, even if the woman inherited property from her own father or family before marriage, once she marries, the male spouse became the property owner. She then, can just hope and pray that this male person treats her kindly and fairly, instead of gambling the money away as was the more commonplace predicament of many a family from the bottom tier of society to the highest echelon.

Sarah H. had been really lucky as a Woman. She was able to engage in business transactions on her own. Especially at that era. This was the first procurement transaction made by Sarah H. Brown on her name only, as the records showed. Again, this cannot be emphasized enough. The timing indicated that this business deal was conducted during the time they would have been married. Look again at the 1848 sales transaction of a piece of the Purdy land then sold to Mr. Caniff, Sarah H. was listed as "wife".

---

[18] Ch.3.pp. 90-113 paragraph 2.a Business & Property Law. Robert Stone. The Foundation Press. Chicago. 1941.

15. Mortgaged, Discharged, Released, Sold

A Couple of things to pay detailed attention here:

1.   This parcel description was a subdivision

2.   Besides, this document showed that this encumbrance was paid off,

3.   The mortgage was discharged,

4.   The title used as collateral was released

5.   and on the same this piece of land was released, was sold off to the man that had the same last name.

So, let us not be confused here. The Mortgaged parcel to Job Mack, was discharged, released, on 23 Oct. 1877. This then was sold off by Sarah H. to Mr. Orville Mack and Associates, same date 23 Oct. 1877. Hold your horses off. Job Mack and Orville Mack are two different persons. Orville Mack was the one that then, sold this piece to the Baptist Church. This parcel had direct correlation with three other transactions on August 15, 1882.

1876, July 28	Original Mortgage	Liber 74 p. 324
1877, October 23	Assigns & Assignations	Book 7 pp. 374-376.

Now here is a comprehensive transcription of the Mortgage contracted by Sarah H. Brown, on the day the encumbrance was discharged, and the collateral released. Timothy Brown signed off on this transaction, as a secondary signor. Was this a signature of support to Sarah H.'s ventures? Not just as the man following after the woman who was the one wearing the pants in the family? It was apparent that she was the primary borrower here. Sarah H. acted as the Primary borrower was a statement by itself. To completely show the dynamics of Aug. 15 transactions, and get a fuller view of where the parcels came from, this document was presented here in a more comprehensive form of excerption. This is Really important for you, and everyone who would be interested to debunk the mystery, that was not so mysterious after all.

1877, October 23 From the book called Assigns & Assignations Book 7 pp. 374-376.

Mortgage of Sarah H. Brown & Timothy Brown to Job Mack

" ... Witnesseth that whereas Sarah H. Brown and Timothy Brown her husband by an Indenture of Mortgage bearing date the 28th day of July 1876 for the consideration therein mentioned, and to secure the payment of the money therein specified did convey certain lands and lien amounts of which the lands herein after described are part unto Job Mack of the Town County and State above mentioned. And whereas the said party of the first part at the request of the said party of the second part has agreed to give up and surrender the lands herein after described unto the said party of the second part and his heirs and assigns and to hold and retain the residue of the said Mortgaged lands as security for the money remaining unpaid on the said mortgage. And this Indenture Witnesseth that the said party of the first part in pursuance of the said agreement and in consideration of One dollar duly paid at the time of the unsealing and delivery of these presents being a part of the money secured to be paid by the said Mortgage the receipt whereof is hereby acknowledged has granted released quitclaimed and set over and by these presents does grant release quit claim and set over unto the said party of the second part and to her heirs and assigns all that part of the said mortgaged lands described as follows.

All that tract or parcel of land situate in the Town of Georgetown and being part of Lot 91 in said town and bounded and described as follows. Beginning at the south East corner of what is known as the Meeting House lot of the Baptist Church and Society in said town of Georgetown and running east in a direct line with the South line of said Meeting House lot 43 feet; thence North from this point 28 feet in a line parallel with the east line of said Meeting House lot; thence West 22 feet in a line parallel with the south line of said Meeting House lot; thence North 22 feet in a line parallel with the east line of said Meeting House lot, thence West 21 feet in a line parallel with the South line of said meeting House lot; thence South along the east line of the Meeting House lot to the place of beginning, containing six and 130/1089 rods of land more or less. Together with the hereditaments and appurtenances of the said party of the first part of in and to the same to the intent that the lands hereby conveyed may be discharged from the said mortgage and that the residue of the lands in the said Mortgage specified may remain to the said party of the first part as heretofore: To have and to hold the lands and premises hereby released and conveyed to the said party of the second part her heirs and assigns to her only proper use benefit and behalf forever free clear and discharged of and from all lien and claims under or by virtue of the Indenture of Mortgage aforesaid. In witness whereof the said party of the first part has hereunto set his hand and seal the day and year first above written Job Mack LS. Liber 74 page 324. Recorded January 21st 1879 at 2PM John N Woodbury, clerk"

The following are Points to consider regarding the above transaction. This will allow for an accurate re - trace to better pinpoint where exactly this parcel was cut off, at what position. Also for proper land marking on the ground; in the hopes of laying the acreage clarification questions to rest. This particular parcel of land used as collateral to a mortgage was subdivided from the bigger parcel of Sarah H. Brown. That important detail of Sarah H. being the Primary signor for these business deals tells a lot more than just being a signee. From the Procurement of the land, having six and 130/1089 rods sliced off it, to mortgaging, recovery and then literally selling that portion of the land.

An excerpt of the description was presented here for in depth accounting.

1877, October 23 $8.51 Liber 143 p. 529   recorded: July 21, 1879 at 2 PM.

"...Beginning at the south East corner of what is known as the Meeting House lot of the Baptist Church and Society in said town of Georgetown and running east in a direct line with the South line of said Meeting House lot 43 feet; thence North from this point 28 feet in a line parallel with the east line of said Meeting House lot; thence West 22 feet in a line parallel with the south line of said Meeting House lot; thence North 22 feet in a line parallel with the east line of said Meeting House lot, thence West 21 feet in a line parallel with the South line of said meeting House lot; thence South along the east line of the Meeting House lot to the place of beginning, containing six and 130/1089 rods of land more or less..."

What happened to this sliced off six and 130/1089 rods sold to Orville Mack and Associates? Mr. Orville Mack et al., sold it to the Trustees of the Baptist Church, on 15 August 1882. The three August 15 transactions were laid out in detailed account under

Timothy Brown Chapter, if the reader recalls. These transactions were interconnected as the parcel sliced off by the Browns to sell to the Church and the 9' x 60' piece that the Church sold back to Timothy Brown, including this piece that Sarah H. sold to Orville and Orville to the Church gave directions on the exact locations the pieces were sliced from and tied together, vice versa.

This 9' x 60' parcel had always been included in every sales transactions without question all these 167 years. Even the most recent 2011 title transfer that included all these six titled parcels, the deeds' descriptions remained unchanged. The 2011 efforts to try to individually account them on the ground, and correctly mark them as the accessioned inherited landholdings of the House for appropriate precise landmarking, were adamantly rebuffed by some very prominent local people.

The questions of WHY, WHY NOT rose it's ugly head. Then a whole Pandora's box opened, a hornets' nest seemed to have been disturbed?

Did I missed out on something here? What is being hidden? Why the secrecy? Where is Transparency?

Three long years of asking very respectfully. In person, via private letters, private postings, and open letters to the public. The circumstances are giving me no other choice. I have not placed myself and this venture in cyberspace for the reason that a little town surely can sort out this little misunderstanding. The patterns indicated strongly otherwise. It has become an error as well. Non - factual one sided views populate the internet. See for yourself. If this is the type of History that the Community desires, then it would be. On my part, in all due Respect to the Wonderful Legacies of the key People behind this Magnificent Structure, in the Spirit of Human kind, this story, this venture, should and must come to a Positive Union.

16. The Burying Ground

The burying ground as a monument of reference point to mark adjoining land parcels were first recorded in Timothy Brown's sales transactions on Lot 91. Retracing his transactions with Elnathan Ellis, year 1872 revealed that in 1839 E. Whitmore et. al sold this parcel to Mr. Ellis. Portions were cut off, and one such piece mentioned the burial ground, as a monumental point in marking the boundary of the parcel. Here it is:

1836, December 3rd   to William P. Hare   Liber AO p.422-423.

"...beginning at the center of the highway twelve rods North thirty two degrees East from the Burying Ground from thence North thirty two degrees east along the center of the said highway five rods thence thirty degrees South ten rods then South thirty two degrees West five rods thence West thirty two degrees North ten rods to the place of beginning containing one rood and ten rods of land be the same more or less. Together with all and singular the hereditaments and appurtenances."

The above document therefore attest to the fact that the burial ground had been there, at least 46 years from this 1836 deed used as a sample here. This is before there was even a Hillside Cemetery in 1882. By 1884 this burying grounds use continued. The question of: Was that because the embalmer, funerary implements, and the proximity to Main Street made it the easiest accessible place of rest, especially in Winter versus the newer, farther Hillside?

The Formation of Hillside Cemetery.

1882, February 16   Liber Miscellaneous B p.262

Notarized: 18 February 1882   Recorded: 23 February 1882 at 3PM

This meeting was held at the Brown Hall, Village of Georgetown, NY.

In 1884, Sarah H. Brown sold a parcel to MR. Reuben Mawson. Obviously there had been a need to have an interment plot be added on to this cemetery. A strip of land from the adjoined land area was allocated. This sampler of an actual Deed from Sarah H. & Timothy Brown documenting the sales transaction of a land parcel to be used only for such purposes. It was excerpted here:

1884, January 28   to Reuben Mawson $ 10.00   144 square ft. Liber 190 p. 262

"...part of Lot 91...bounded as follows: Commencing at the Northeast corner of the Georgetown Village Burying Ground and running from thence South along the East line of said Burying Ground sixteen (16) feet to the burying ground lot owned by Edgar G. Mack thence East nine (9) feet along the Northerly line of said Edgar G. Mack's burying lot; thence sixteen (16) feet in a line parallel with the East line of said burying ground thence West nine (9) feet to the place of beginning, containing by estimation one hundred and forty four square feet of land be the same, more or less. This land to be held forever for burial purposes."   ...recorded April 14, 1896, at 9:30AM.

Winter. This would be when the weathering conditions would be the harshest. The distance of the internment from the place of funerary processing would be of real import especially when the major form of transport was horse, carriage, or buggy. As I recall, it was not the general practice to have a pre - paid, pre - planned, and pre - arranged funeral preparations then. Sarah H. Brown did.

If my recollections serve me right, and of course you can all fact check this again; death, dying, and internment were not as welcomed a topic, or an expected occasion, nor something of a barber shop story even if everyone knew it's coming at some point. We have come a long way now; that in some areas, it is now regulated, or at least an option for the terminally ill - whether meeting the Creator can be at an appointed time and be as scheduled. The most advance liberal mindsets, part of the arrangements are plans for what to say in the Eulogy, to the words on the Headstone, style and type of stone; even how lavish the after party would be. On the other hand, the majority of the States still make assisted dying, a crime. Culture had evolved. The point is: We care about Death, the placement of the human remains: meaning procedures and documentation would have existed.

WHO OWN the BURIAL GROUNDS? What of the Care & Maintenance?

This was lifted off from the official communique of the First Baptist Church that were left in the House. When I moved in, I was not just the owner moving in a House to make a Home out of. I am the enthusiastic newcomer in the discipline of Museology. A Masters Degree on Hand, looking for a niche to carve out a Professional Expertise, I am looking at anything and everything on the prism of the story of the History. Nothing was thrown out without passing though a chromatograph. These information were gleaned from those pamphlets copied verbatim, including typographic error. Points to ponder:

1966 Trustees' Report submitted by Ronald Davies, Secretary: Page 3

3   Fencing purchased to go around the cemetery (money from the Witmer Estate)

#7   Mr. Dunham took down the fence and cleaned up around the cemetery.

1968 Trustees' Report submitted by Ronald Davies, Chairman: Page 6

Note: The booklet had been printed 1968; crossed out with a green marker, changed to 1967: A typographical error?.

#6   The cemetery fence has been built. By changing the fence a space has been left so that several new graves could be added.

#7   The men voted to donate their time on the fence building and cemetery repair toward a fund painting the church. At this time, this is not completed so we do not know what the cost will be.

#8   A new strong box was purchased for the church recrods. After it was discovered to be too small, the small one was traded for a larger safe.

Note: Is that Witmer a typo of the name Whitmore? How many more graves were added?

Questions: How much space was used? The area and space where they re - arranged the fence, was that the piece that they owned? If that was so, then the current accounting of the measurements in the deed description for the church should now include the cemetery portions that were added. This therefore would not extend to the acreage that belong to the House, anymore. They would have used up what belonged to them. That is of course, in all honesty. That is the question. They are not talking.

Also to be noted the domino effect this what seemingly simple act of accommodating new graves on the overall integrity of the adjoining land parcels. Here is another example to mull over:

"114 feet from the northeast corner of the cemetery", if there was no immovable marker there, that measurement of 114 feet was already undermined. Yes, it may seem trivial or oh but it was just a trifle; correct, if time had stopped, and the people that agreed to it ver grew old, died, sold the property, but you and I know that is not the case. Worst is when with all the legal documents, and court rulings in the world, are even in placed but once in a little while, Society produces a villainous character that would want to intentionally ruin everything, then the rest is exactly the reason you are reading this. It is because of that.

This is not the first time, nor would be the last: but if we take more caution and set all safety nets and support the education of the youth that would not know otherwise, then we would not have more of these types of issues. You see, passing on the correct facts, the authentic truth to the young impressionable youth help improve the betterment of Society: But, if we somehow screw the truth and devise fraud, forgery, theft and scheming dishonest deeds that are validated; then what are the chances of the truth ever coming up? The choices are within you, within all of us. Make yours today.

CHURCH CLERK REPORT

Members on roll 12/31/65   163
Lost by death in 1966   3
Lost by letter in 1966   4

Gained by baptism in 1966   2
Members on roll 12/31/66

                 161

Active members on roll   72

            Respectfully Submitted

            Alice Cossitt
            Church Clerk

FLORAL COMMITTEE

In remembrance of our members who have passed away we have given flowers or money to their families.

We also have tried to have flowers in the sanctuary for the sunday services.

            The Floral Committee
            Alice Cossitt

TRUSTEE'S REPORT 1966

The trustees held two meetings during the year with much discussion and not much action taken.

Some of the things action was taken on were--
1. A new Rex-Roto electric Mimeograph purchased
2. A new 40 gal water heater installed at the parsonage
3. Fencing purchased to go around the cemetary (money from the Witmer estate)
4. The chimes were worked on and played O.K. for about two weeks, repair parts have arrived at F. T. Chapin's and are waiting to be installed.
5. A load of gravel was spread on the parsonage drive.
6. The Willing Workers had a new wall put up and painted in the church dining room.
7. Mr. Durham took down the fence and cleaned up around the cemetary.

            Respectfully submitted

            Ronald Davis, Secretary

CRADLE ROLL DEPARTMENT

Cradle Roll--Mary Jane Brown, Peter Andrew Kalin, II, Vanessa S. Verger, Alan Edward Parkhurst.

Transferred to the Nursery Department--Blake Stewart Brown.

The Cradle Roll Packet published by the Scripture Press is being used.

            Respectfully submitted

            Rosemary R. Walrod

Plate 38-0664 Nineteen 66Report

Photo taken from an Original 1966 Trustees' Report, Part of the House Inherited Papers & Documents.

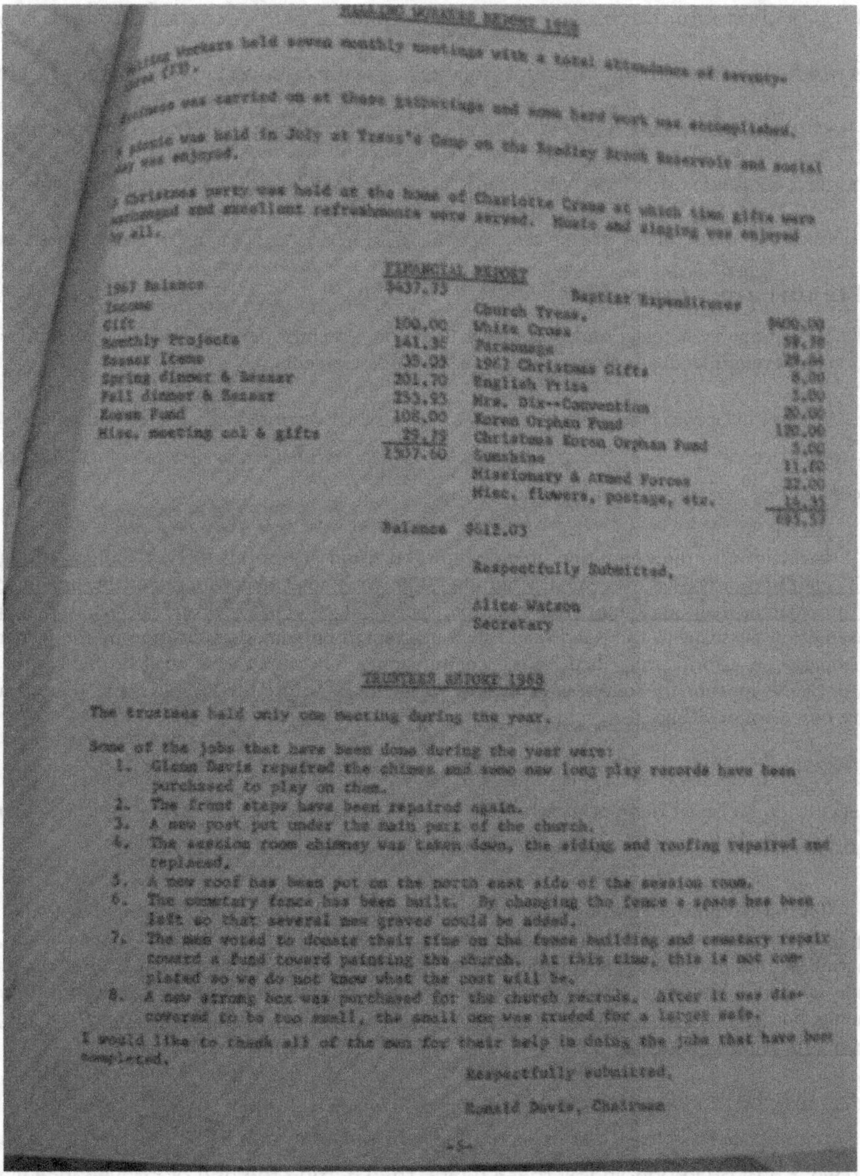

WILLING WORKERS REPORT 1968

Willing Workers held seven monthly meetings with a total attendance of seventy-three (73).

Business was carried on at these gatherings and some hard work was accomplished.

A picnic was held in July at Trass's Camp on the Bradley Brook Reservoir and social day was enjoyed.

A Christmas party was held at the home of Charlotte Crane at which time gifts were exchanged and excellent refreshments were served. Music and singing was enjoyed by all.

FINANCIAL REPORT

1967 Balance	$437.73		
Income		Baptist Expenditures	
		Church Treas.	
Gift	100.00	White Cross	$400.00
Monthly Projects	141.35	Parsonage	58.38
Bazaar Items	30.05	1967 Christmas Gifts	28.44
Spring dinner & Bazaar	201.70	English Prize	8.00
Fall dinner & Bazaar	253.93	Mrs. Dix--Convention	1.00
Korean Fund	108.00	Korean Orphan Fund	20.00
Misc. meeting col & gifts	29.75	Christmas Korean Orphan Fund	120.00
	1307.60	Sunshine	5.00
		Missionary & Armed Forces	11.60
		Misc. flowers, postage, etc.	22.00
			14.35
			695.57

Balance $612.03

Respectfully Submitted,

Alice Watson
Secretary

TRUSTEES REPORT 1968

The trustees held only one meeting during the year.

Some of the jobs that have been done during the year were:

1. Glenn Davis repaired the chimes and some new long play records have been purchased to play on them.
2. The front steps have been repaired again.
3. A new post put under the main part of the church.
4. The session room chimney was taken down, the siding and roofing repaired and replaced.
5. A new roof has been put on the north east side of the session room.
6. The cemetary fence has been built. By changing the fence a space has been left so that several new graves could be added.
7. The men voted to donate their time on the fence building and cemetary repair toward a fund toward painting the church. At this time, this is not completed so we do not know what the cost will be.
8. A new strong box was purchased for the church records. After it was discovered to be too small, the small one was traded for a larger safe.

I would like to thank all of the men for their help in doing the jobs that have been completed.

Respectfully submitted,

Ronald Davis, Chairman

-5-

Plate 39-0667 Nineteen 68Report

Photo taken from an Original 1968 Trustees' Report, The yellow cover page had a green marker crossed out the 7 of the 8; On this inside page the report clearly was typed with 1968 as the year.

Is RPTL Section 446, the reason as to the WHY the 2 & 1/4 acres of Sarah H. Brown does not have its own tax ID account Number, or not mentioned in one of the accounts that had the 3/4 acre taxed on? Why is an explanation to any such tax exemption not an accounted for fact, and one that is easily accessed via freedom of public information? Much more, if the question of this discrepancy had been inquired upon plenty of times?

RPTL- 161 § 446. *Cemeteries*

1   Real property actually and exclusively used for cemetery purposes shall be exempt from taxation and exempt from ad valorem levies and special assessments.

Note: Sarah H. Brown had sold a plot 9' x 16' or 144 square feet for burial purposes. This was part of her 2 & 1/4 acres, adjoined the already referred point of memorial marker as the "burying ground" since 1836.

2   In addition to the exemption provided in subdivision one of this section, <u>unimproved land, which is not presently used for cemetery purposes, but which interments are reasonably and in good faith anticipated, shall be exempt from taxation, special ad valorem levies and special assessments.</u> An exemption pursuant to this subdivision shall be granted only upon application by the owner of the property on a form prescribed by the commissioner. The application shall be filed with the assessor of the appropriate county, city, town or village on or before the taxable status date of such county, city, town or village.

Note: If this 2 & 1/4 parcel had been receiving exemptions; should it not be a practice of transparency to be of note somewhere in the tax records that it is so? Should this acres of land suddenly be out of commission and disappear without paperwork?

3   The term "cemetery purposes", as used in this section shall mean land and buildings, whether <u>privately</u> or publicly owned or operated, used for the disposal or burial of deceased human beings, by cremation or in a grave, mausoleum, vault, columbarium or other receptacle. Such term shall also include land and buildings actually used and essential to the providing of cemetery purposes including, but <u>not limited to, the on site residence of a full-time caretaker and a storage facility for necessary tools and equipment.</u>

Note: Is this the reason that people had insisted to be the one to mow the lawn; thinking that by doing so, then they can claim any benefit out of it, and if the carrying on is what really what had been ongoing all these years, then getting the title or conveyance made without the real owner knowing about it would be the reason of this muscling activities being given to me in sanctioned doses????

4   No real property shall be entitled to receive an exemption pursuant to this section if the owner or operator of such real property or any officer, member or employee thereof, shall receive or may be lawfully entitled to receive any pecuniary profit from the operations thereof, other than reasonable compensation for services performed, or if the ownership or operation is a guise or pretense for directly or indirectly making any pecuniary profit for such owner or operator or for any of its officers, members or employees.
Add, L 1958, ch 959, § 1, eff Oct 1, 1959; amd, L 1981, ch 920, § 3, eff Jan 1, 1982, L 1984, ch 473, § § 5, 6, eff July 20, 1984, L 2010, ch 56, § 1 (Part W), eff June 22, 2010.

Note: If this is the situation of this parcel at the moment, and then apply GOL title 3 Section 5 - 331. Is this why the Church was so keen on trying to slice this part away from the true deeded documents of this Site using the Survey? As they were not able to siphon this by deed transfer from Alice, Valerie & Helen? Are they willing to twist the truth, and ensure that this Magnificent structure of a House gets totally erased so as they can have the parking space, and benefit from the rest of the 2 & 1/4 acreage that was the legacy of Sarah H. Brown? Why not forge a more authentic, amiable relationship instead? Like a fair, square business with accountability! Not like "when JESUS toppled the tables in the temple type of business"?.

What is baffling to me no matter how I twist the documents to fit the mazes of convoluted justification of what really is going on with this Site being the way it had been and is threatened to continue as is - is because of GREED. Singular individual vested interests each wanting to be able to take a piece here and there of this property that:

1   does not belong to them.

2   they do not want to shell out money for; either because they cannot afford, does not want to, pretend not to want to or just plain grabbers.

3   But why? When human civilized collaborative efforts can build this estate into something far more than how it is now, had been all these years! Everyone can design each experience in a responsible, respectful manner without breaking the estate.

VII. ONE - THIRD RIGHTS TO A SPRING

Sarah H.'s Second INVESTMENT:

1884, December 16 to Sarah H. Brown $ 66.00 1/3 right to a Spring

Liber 162 p. 140-41 recorded 14th May, 1885 at 9 AM.

from Hiram N. Atwood & wife, Sarah Atwood,

and George Curtis & wife, Mary Curtis

"...to them duly paid have sold and by these presents do grant and convey to the said party of the second part her heirs and assigns forever one undivided one third interest in a certain spring or well situated in the side hill lot in the town of Georgetown aforesaid and near the large elm tree on the premises deeded to Jabez E. Tillotson on the fifth day of May 1883 by the executors of the estate of Isaac Fletcher deceased together with a lead pipe on said premises running from said spring or well to the house now owned by George S. Carver and to the house owned by Mrs. Eliza A. Smith and Mrs. Caroline L. Day. Said party of the second part shall have the privilege to enter on the premises on which said spring or well is located to repair any breaks that may happen to said pipe spring or well, and said party of the second part shall after such repairs place the earth back, the surface of the ground to be left smooth, stones removed, ground reseeded if so before and all done in a workmanlike manner with as little damage to the premises as possible and all done within a reasonable length of time. ..."   ...recorded 14th May, 1885 at 9 o'clock A.M

Inquiries:

1   What could have happened to this Spring of water?

2   Did it dry out?

3   Did it further the cause of making a positive difference, and brought in new investments to become a legitimate business of potable water, bottled, piped both or otherwise?

4   Even if the legitimate claim for revenues for the rightful owners be cast aside as nil; shouldn't transparency still be the rule of thumb in any business venture?

The answers and the questions are not only within the merits of legal accountability, but also morally upright and would free everyone from always looking behind the shoulders as to the what if?

These topics are left wide open to be analyzed more in depth on their own. That independent look into the make up of the facets of this multi - dimensional, interesting Story; so encompassing that it transcended generations, timelines, race, color, creed, that enticed even me, is just too beautiful a privilege to pass.

Baffled as to the rationale why these twists, turns and complexities of life changing decisions based on great choices made by real people of old had to be framed in the perspective that need be expunged? All in favor of make - believe mythical concoctions that were rubber stamped history, but are in reality, in actuality nothing but legends, from the narrow personal designs of a few? Why not call it as that, then?

To the people of this community, to the region, the state and all of America, let it be known, that I stepped up the plate and took on the duty to say something, and stand up for what is right for this site. This scam of not using recorded deeds describing the six titles of the Estate that belong to the House is not acceptable, and would not be quieted, nor " be reined in" so the naysayers say.

Though much damage from deep angst imperil the consistent forward direction of the Project, defer timely responsible preservation, conservation efforts that would render the task to suffer costly diversions and setbacks: It continue to be the hope with prayers, that a unification to make a positive experience out of something beautiful though threatened to be made dirty, can rise up above it all to share the testaments of love, of kindness, and human dignity.

17. The other 2/3 rights of Spring

Whose are they? What became of this Business Transaction?

1883, May 05 Between Palmer Hopkins & Hervy W. Mann, executors

last Will and Testament of Isaac Fletcher

to Jabez C. Tillotson of Cazenovia for $1300.00

Liber 156 p.329-331   Recorded May 7, 1883 at 11 AM

"... All that tract or parcel of land situate in the town of Georgetown County & State aforesaid and known as being part of lot No. 91, of said town & bounded as follows. Beginning on the west line of said lot at a stone set in the ground running thence north on said west line 8 ch 32 links to the center of the highway thence south 80 and 1/2 E along the center of said highway 3 ch 40 links thence south 69 3 ch 50 links Thence south 58 and 1/2 E along the centre of said highway 3 ch 37 links Thence south 3° E 7 ch 70 links to a stake &atones set in the north line of lands owned by said decd hereinafter described Thence north 73 and 1/4° W on said north line 11 ch 2 links to the place of beginning. Containing eight & a half acres more or less.

Also all that tract or parcel of land situate in the town of Georgetown in the County of Madison being a part of lot 91. and bounded as follows, viz: beginning at the Northwest corner of Elnathan Ellis village lot near & opposite to the village burying ground running thence westerly to the southwest corner of land formerly owned by Alvin Mosely Thence north on the west line of said Mosely land to the <u>centre of the highway leading from Georgetown Village over the hill to DeRuyter</u> thence westerly along the centre of said highway to the west line of said lot No.91. Thence south on the west line of said lot to the NWest corner of land owned by the Russell Whitmore thence east on the north line of said Whitmores land to the <u>centre of the plank road</u> Thence north westerly along the <u>centre of said plank road to the North east corner of Elnathan Ellis village lot thence westerly on the north line of said Village lot</u> & also one acre of land conveyed by E. Whitmore to the First Congregational Church of Georgetown.

Reserved:

A   eleven acres by Benjamin Franklin & wife to Alvin Mosely , 1856 Sept. 4, CD p. 443

B   one rood 2 and 24/100 rods described as - beginning in the centre of the highway at the south easterly corner of a village lot formerly conveyed to Orlando Dutton & running thence south 45° 45' W87 links on the centre of the highway 50°30'W 3 ch. Thence north 45° 45' East 89 links thence south 56° east three chains to the place of beginning.

C   15 acres 2 roods & 6 rods by Orlando M. Dutton by Benjamin Franklin & wife & afterwards by Isaac Fletcher & wife to WmThompson Liber III page 83

D   also <u>excepting & reserving the water rights conveyed in & by the last above described conveyance & subject to the conditions therein contained.</u>

E   Also reserving the right to WmPHare to take <u>waste water</u> from the dwelling house on said premises October 30, 1869

F   <u>Reserving the water rights by Elnathan Ellis to A. Stanton dated March 13, 1871.</u> The premises hereby conveyed are the dwelling house & premises owned & occupied by said Isaac Fletcher at the time of his death supposed to contain thirty - six acres of land be the same more or less."

In my never ending blockaded quest to uncover what really happened, and efforts to piece the story closest to the truth that can be factually gleaned, I chanced on this document from a eureka moment. This happened to be the page opened in front of me when I opened the book the first time. Normally, I would not have paid attention. Just carefully flipped the pages to the intended page. This time I took the time to read. This became the habituated standard thereafter.

Here is the page, and what it was about:

1888, April 19 from John H. Chapin & wife Betsy S. of Sloan, Woodbury County, Iowa
to Otis H. Whitmore, Georgetown, NY

Liber 171 p. 119

" ... part of Lot 91... bounded as follows: On the East by the center of the creek road leading from the village of Georgetown to Otselic, on the south and west by lands owned by A. H. Tillotson, and on the north by lands owned by Burdette Curtiss and containing one half acre of land more or less.

These being the same premises sold on a mortgage foreclosure:

18th May 1878 at L.B. Kerns Law Office, DeRuyter Madison County NY.

John H. Chapin and Betsy L. Chapin being the purchasers of said premises.... said Statute Foreclosure was recorded in the Clerk's Office of Madison County in:

Book 79 Mortgages p. 68

1st October A.D. 1878 at 5 o'clock P.M.

Also this Deed is intended to convey to the party of the second part his heirs and assigns forever One undivided fifth part of the lead pipe and one undivided fifth part of this water which now and thereafter shall run therein or in a pipe of the same size from a Spring located on land now owned by A. H. Tillotson of the town of Georgetown aforesaid which said pipe was laid by one Elnathan Ellis from above mentioned Spring on and cross lands now owned by A. W. Tillotson to or near the dwelling house of the parties of the first part subject to the agreements set forth in the deed conveying said pipe and water. Which deed was given by A. H. Tillotson and Eliza N., his wife,

21 October 1884 Recorded: 8th December 1884 at 10 o'clock AM

Book 161 p. 262 Deeds, Madison County, N.Y."

Questions Raised:

1   How was it, that after the titles changed hands, the fractional descriptions for the sharing of the water changed dramatically?

2   The same source of Spring water it seemed, yet the division of sharing had changed?

Remember, the original sharing was between three parties. If any one of the 1/3 share of a party was divvied up into five different shares, then that would be 1/5 of 1/3 share. This would not be a direct 1/5, as the deed on the Sarah H. remained 1/3 share. What happened to the other 2/3? Which 1/3 part did this 1/5 come from? Why was this information not part of the annotation or contract clause?

If the mathematical errors were mistakes due to misunderstanding, intentional, deliberate or not; the question now is: How can we move forward in rectifying these errors straight to their final resting place? Were they real mistakes?

If they were intentional and deliberately choreographed errors, designed to confuse and cause misunderstanding, WHY and to What Positive purpose? Is there: Was there a positive point to any of these hullabaloos?

THE Facts were vividly delineated as to the precise location of this Spring. Unfortunately, and Currently:

The 1/3 rights to a Spring was a sore spot to be accounted for when I try to find answers from the supposedly guardian of history, local leaders & long time residents;

The spring cannot be pointed as to the whereabouts by the commissioned survey nevertheless, even if as you can read here the placement description is quite clear;

There are a number of documents too bulky to all include here at the moment;

The generated revenue from the spring as a source of Water was never received by the House? When did it stop? If it did?

Surely, one that had brought so much in economic sustenance; sanitary & hygienic practices of piped running water to the many houses in Main Street, the very essence of life had to be deposed of recognition, respect and immortalization by historic marking? Why?

The original parties involved here were:

A. Sarah H.

B. Mr. Tillotson

C. Mr. Hiram Atwood

Note: More on this topic in the future. Inputs welcome.

Meanwhile, let us take a look at what the law says about why this 1/3 rights to the Spring is not appearing in the taxation account number with the taxed 3/4 acre or by itself. As to the Official Explanation of unaccountability had not been obtained. Was this lost with the incorporation of this Town's Water Cooperative System? How was this justified?

RPTL § 410. Special Districts

Real property owned by a special district, or the property owners therein, within its boundaries used exclusively for the purpose for which such district was established shall be exempt from taxation and exempt from special ad valorem levies and special assessments to the extent provided in section 490 of this chapter, except as otherwise provided in section 272 of the county law.

Add, L 1958, ch 959, § 1, with substance derived from Tax Law § 4; amd, L 1974, ch 71, § 1, eff March 19, 1974.

RPTL § 410-a. Special Districts

Real property owned by a special district, or the property owners therein, not within its district boundaries which is used as a sewage disposal plant or system, including necessary connections and appurtenances, or real property owned by a special district used as a water plant, pumping station, water treatment plant, or reservoir, including necessary connections and appurtenances, shall be wholly or partially exempt from taxation and exempt from special ad valorem levies and special assessments to the extent provided in section 490 of this chapter, by any municipal corporation in which located, providing the governing board thereof shall so agree in writing.

Add, L 1973, ch 933, § 1, eff Jan 1, 1974.

RPTL § 485- d. Water - works Corporations

Real property situated in a city with a population of one million or more owned by a water - works corporation subject to the provisions of the public service law and used exclusively for the sale, furnishing and distribution of water for domestic, commercial and public purposes, shall be wholly or partially exempt from taxation provided that the local legislative body of such city within such property is situated adopts a local law so providing.

Add, L 1985, ch 726, §1, eff Aug 1, 1985 and applicable to assessment rolls prepared in connection with fiscal years commencing on or after July 1, 1985.

Note:

If this is the stand of the law by 1958, 1985 to present, I am sure this is quite true in the early years of piped water system. It is for the betterment of life. Why would this exemption if applied then, not be an easily available information to account for?

Whichever of the above sections had been used to exempt this water system, source and the actual pipeline; surely should not be a concern of national security to be undisclosed?

More on this, soon.

Here is section 490, the ad valorems and special assessments exemptions in correlation with the special districts exemptions.

RPTL Title 3 Miscellaneous Provisions
§ 490. Exemption from special ad valorem and special assessments

Real property exempt from taxation pursuant to:

subdivision 2 of § 400, subdivision 1 of § 404, § 406, § 408, § 410, § 410-a, § 410-b, § 418, § 420-a, § 420-b, § 422, § 426, § 427, § 428, § 430, § 432, § 434, § 436, § 438, § 450, § 452, § 454, § 456, § 464, § 472, § 474, and of § 485

of this chapter shall also be exempt from special ad valorem levies and assessments against real property located outside cities and villages for a special improvement or service or a special district improvement or service and special ad valorem levies and special assessments imposed by a count improvement district or district corporation except

(1) those levied to pay for the costs, including interest and incidental and preliminary costs, of the acquisition, installation, construction, reconstruction and enlargement of or additions to the following improvements, including original equipment, furnishings, machinery or apparatus, and the replacements thereof: water supply and distribution systems; sewer systems (either sanitary or surface drainage or both, including purification, treatment or disposal plants or buildings); waterways and drainage improvements; street highway, road, and parkway improvements (including sidewalks, curbs, gutters, drainage, landscaping, grading, or improving the right of way) and

(2) special assessments payable in installments on an indebtedness including interest contracted prior to July 01, 1953, pursuant to of §242 of the town law or pursuant to any other comparable provision of law.

Does this Town have any law about this? This section 242, or something parallel to this? I do not recall seeing this with the copy of ordinances they shared with me, 2011. They had been mum about any questions I had asked. The other local agencies had been quiet about this, as well. What ever happened to governance with transparency, accountability, and public service? Also, freedom of Information? To think that I had been searching for answers all these years?

Again, to reiterate the importance of pursuing the solemn obligation of ensuring the facts of this Site not be lost in misinterpretation. This is what authentic guardians of History is about; this is reinforcing the essence of Humanity. The 1/3 Rights to a Spring.

Why would this be such a secret? Why is this property interests unaccounted?

Plate 40-0504   Contemplation

18. The 1893 Covenant

The Sarah H. Brown whom we met a few pages ago, now have been thinking of her golden years. Her actions and decisions show that she was a very efficient woman: a woman of substance. She laid out the plan on how the years ahead that would render her in a feeble state of one form or another, can be handled in a manner that would be financially funded, the caretakers be provided, and the type of provisions and care, she hoped to receive would be executed with love, with compassion.

A lot can be learned from Sarah H. Brown. Her agreement document opened windows and doors of understanding to the different facets of her life alone, circa 1893. Let me take you out of the realm of Georgetown. Then try to imagine the many beautiful, and not too beautiful things were happening around her, during this period. By these times, what I mean is to connect her life with what we can draw from a sampling of the available facts.   First, Women's Rights, Suffrage and Equality.

Technologies & Inventions: Thomas Edison was busy in his Menlo Park, Jersey. So was Tesla, and many other inventors, scientists.

The art of Counterfeiting currency, refrigeration in a grand scale, electrification, rubber vulcanization were already debuted.

Fashion: never ceases to amaze, always evolving, total statement of freedom, a symbol of a free spirit

Financial & Economic Growth: the big drought called the dust bowl, rail system at its peak; the Vanderbilt, Morgan, Roosevelt, Rockefeller, to name a few titans & magnates here.

The Terms of Agreement: Sarah H. Brown & Cora V.

This document was transcribed in its entirety, for ease of reading; and clarity.

1893, March 13   Sarah H. Brown to Cora V. Marvin $1.00   Liber 187 pp.166-168

"... Witnesseth that the said party of the first part in consideration of the sum of One Dollar and other considerations hereafter named to her duly paid has sold and by these presents does grant and convey to the said party of the second part her heirs and assigns, all the tract or parcel of land situate in the village of Georgetown County of Madison State of NY deeded to her by Timothy Brown May 5th 1885, Recorded in Madison Co. Clerk's Office May 14, 1885, 9AM. Liber 163 Page155 described and bounded as follows. viz. On the North by land owned by the Baptist Church. East by land formerly owned by Mary M. Ellis, on the South by land formerly owned by Russell Whitmore. On the West by the center of the highway containing three - fourths of an acre more or less. The above described land is part of Lot.91 of said Town of Georgetown, NY. Also all that tract or parcel of land deed by the Trustees of the First Baptist Society of Town Georgetown Madison County NY to Timothy Brown of said town, on the fifteenth day of August 1884 at 11 o'clock AM in Liber 161 page 20. Also all that tract or parcel of land deeded by Zinah J. Moseley, Milton D. Allen and Mary his wife Isaac Fletcher and Mary his wife of the Town of Georgetown County of Madison State of NY to Sarah H. Brown of the same place of residence on the 22nd day of March in the year one thousand eight hundred seventy one and recorded in the Clerks office of the County of Madison State of NY on the 30th day of March 1871 at 11 o' clock AM in Book No. 123 of Deed at page 347. And this conveyance is upon the express conditions hereafter named and upon the failure of either of said parties to fulfill the terms herein after named and upon their failing to satisfactorily settle the same themselves and after such disagreement they shall go before the Surrogate of Madison Co., NY and a failure on his part to satisfactorily adjust said disagreement then this transfer to be void and of no effect. Contract as follows between Sarah H. Brown of the Town of Georgetown County of Madison NY of the first part and Cora V. Marvin of the same place of residence party of second part. Witnesseth this deed to remain as security for the fulfillment of this agreement until said Sarah H. Brown dieth then to be of full force and virtue provided the terms of this agreement have been fulfilled, and said Cora V. Marvin shall have all the right title and interest in the personal property as well as all her estates to have and to hold for herself, her heirs and assigns forever, after the death of said Sarah H. Brown, said party of the 1st part shall have all moneys paid her for the use of the hall for town purposes to use and hold as her own during her natural life after which what is left if any to be given to Cora V. Marvin. The premises otherwise with all the avails thereof to be the property of said Cora V. Marvin upon which she shall make necessary repairs. Said parties of the first part Sarah H. Brown reserves to herself the South front room and a room in the rear and a small clothes room for her own exclusive use and benefit. The remainder of the buildings to be used by the said Cora V. Marvin as she may deem best. In consideration of this property the party of the second part agrees to take care in sickness or in health and furnish all the necessary medical care and aid to said party of the first part Sarah H. Brown. Also all provisions necessary for her maintenance all clothing when the income from the town hall fails. Also, all things necessary for her burial and funeral and all expenses attendant thereto shall be paid by said Cora V. Marvin. Said Cora V. Marvin shall furnish fuel and lights for said party of the first part. The parties of the first part shall have and hold according to a deed given said Sarah H. Brown all her right title and interest in a certain deed given to Hiram Atwood & George Curtiss of the water now owned and running on her said premises. And the parties hereto agree that all differences arising between them shall be settled by the Surrogate of Madison County, NY. Possession to said property and all the avails thereof is hereby given to the said Cora V. Marvin on the day & date above written in consideration of the agreements herein specified. With the appurtenances and all the estate title and interest therein of the said party of the first part. And the said Sarah H. Brown does hereby covenant and agree to and with the said party of the second part her heirs and assigns that the premises thus conveyed in the quiet and peaceable possession of the said party of the second part her heirs and assigns she will forever warrant and defend against any person whomsoever lawfully claiming the same or any part thereof. In witness whereof, the party of the first part has hereunto set her hand and seal the day and year first above written Sarah H. Brown..."

...recorded: March 26th, 1894, 2PM.

Plate 41-0554   Ponder

19. Cora V. Marvin: back to Sarah H. Brown

A comparative look at the Covenant upon return of the same, a year after.

1894, April 10   Cora V. Marvin to Sarah H. Brown   for $50.00   Liber 187, pp. 364-65

"...This Indenture made this tenth day of April in the year of our Lord one thousand eight hundred and ninety - four. Between Cora V. Marvin and C. Larverne Marvin her husband of the town of Georgetown County of Madison and State of NY of the first part and Sarah H. Brown of Georgetown aforesaid of the second part. Witnesseth that the said parties of the first part in consideration of the sum of Fifty Dollars and other goods and valuable consideration to them duly paid have sold and by these presents do grant and convey to the said party of the second part her heirs and assigns. All that tract or parcel of land situate in the village of Georgetown County of Madison and State of NY deeded to her by Timothy Brown May 5th 1885, recorded in Madison Co. Clerk's Office May 14th 1885 at 9 o'clock AM. Liber 163 page 155 and bounded as follows, viz. On the North by lands owned by the Baptist Church, east by lands formerly owned by Mary M. Ellis, on the South by lands formerly owned by Russell Whitmore, on the West by the center of the highway containing by estimation three - fourths of an acre more or less. The above described land is part of Lot 91 of said town. Also the tract or parcel of land deeded by the Trustees of the First Baptist Society of the town of Georgetown to Timothy Brown of said town on the fifteenth day of August 1882 and recorded in the Office of the Clerk of the County of Madison on the 5th day of August 1884 at 11 o'clock AM in Liber 161 page 20. Also all that tract or parcel of land deeded by Zinah J. Moseley, Milton D. Allen and wife, and Isaac Fletcher and Mercy his wife, of Georgetown aforesaid Sarah H. Brown of the same place on the 22nd day of March 1871 and recorded in the Clerk's Office of the County of Madison on the 30th day of March 1871 at 11 o'clock AM in Book 123 of Deeds at page 347. And this deed is intended to convey to the said Sarah H. Brown all the land and premises which was conveyed by the said Sarah H. Brown to the said Cora V. Marvin by deed bearing date March 13th 1893, and recorded in the Clerk's Office of the County of Madison on the 26th day of March 1894 at 2 o'clock PM in Liber 187 of Deeds. And also all water rights which were conveyed to said Cora V. Marvin by said deed are hereby conveyed to said Sarah H. Brown. Possession of said premises to be given on or before the 16th day of April 1894. And the said parties of the first part hereby sells and conveys to the said Sarah H. Brown all the personal property which was transferred to the said Cora V. Marvin by the aforesaid deed from Sarah H. Brown to the said Cora V. Marvin. With the appurtenances and all the Estate Title and Interest therein of the said parties of the first part. And the said Cora V. Marvin and C. Laverne Marvin do hereby covenant and agree to and with the said party of the second part her heirs and assigns that the premises thus conveyed in the quiet and peaceable possession of the said party of the second part her heirs and assigns they will forever Warrant and Defend against any person whomsoever lawfully claiming the same or any part thereof..."

Recorded: May 17th 1894, 2PM."

Taking a closer look at that document again: That was just A year after. The important things I saw here that changed were listed below. A dissection for a better understanding is merited.

First, when Sarah H. Brown contracted the agreement, the only name mentioned was Cora V. Marvin. A year after, when Cora V. Marvin returned the document, another name came up. This is C. Laverne Marvin, Cora's husband.

Second: The willful transfer of Sarah H. Brown's personal effects and the Estate to a chosen person, in exchange for the care, an aging woman would need as she progress towards the sunset was launched. This type of planning is no different with what we have today. Indeed, there were what they called the "Old Ladies' Home" even then. I believe it would be a good guess to say that such Programs would have their disadvantages, and issues, in the same manner that what we now call "Nursing Homes" have theirs today. Would it not be correct to say here that the reason these facilities are now regulated is because of the challenges and difficulties that have arisen from the experiences there. So, Sarah H. Brown wanted to remain in her Home until her death. I have a strong affinity with this very practical, very visionary woman. This is unfortunate that the relationship established with the Marvin Family did not deepen enough to see through Sarah H. Brown's deathbed. It only lasted a year and a month, as can be deducted from the dates on the agreements [13 March 1893 to 10 April 1894].

Third: The fact that the House had been generating revenue tells me that Sarah H. Brown possessed an Entrepreneurial Spirit. The Musicals and Performances held in Brown Hall attest to this use of the House as a Venue. Also, I am inclined to think that the Performance Poster advertising for the Georgetown Hall would really have been in the Brown Hall. The Town may have acted as liason for these performances, especially if the permits would have been issued by the Town, it would have made sense to broker the venue as well.

Fourth: Sarah H. Brown have always used the South Front Room.

Fifth: The water rights[19]. The "Spring" that developed into a resource viable enough to commercially power the economy of a community.

Sixth: The fact that she worried about the appropriate repairs and upkeep of the House in a will, is another factual evidentiary record that this gentlewoman was looking ahead in the future.

Seventh: Also, the fact that she cared about her clothes, the burial part of her dying, as well as "just in case if every income fails", she would like to make sure that Cora V. Marvin can have the opportunity to devise a brilliant way to take care of her wishes and be able to execute the responsible actions regarding the House and the estate.

Query: What a story. I wonder How this ended this way, and Why?

---

[19] Madison County Leader and Observer Morrisville, NY Thursday Morning April 4, 1912 .Twenty - Seventh Year No. 43 : Georgetown. "Floyd Currier of Hamilton was in town Monday collecting the water rent for the Crystal Springs Water Company."

20. The Walk to the Sunset with Sarah H. Brown.

A very introspective, contemplative walk. Just like the one you go to and be held hands with on the beach, yes, a white sand shore. Walk up to a drumlin, a hillock, a breezy knoll.

Of course, you, dear readers can add more of her. That is the reason for the space left here, for you.

✍

We can all add something here, to make the story a lot more colorful. Thus when you find the occasion to visit us, there would be more things to share back to the House; to the Site; to the Memories; to the Spirit of Making a Positive Difference One Person at a Time. By then, it is with utmost high hopes that the aspirations to propel this project of Conservation & Preservation would have moved past the Initial stages of Rehabilitation. It is unfortunate that at the moment of this writing, that stage of defining the perimeter is at a standstill. The complex layers of challenges stumbled upon in the installations of cornerstones to mark the physical / literal ground in acreage, based on the provenance deeded / titled / recorded and copies henceforth shown here, have not found the right ears, audience, and professional experts to correctly identify this History according to the veracity of facts at hand. The real story need be celebrated as a viable tool of economic advancement instead of inciting fraudulent distortions. Honesty still counts.

A simplified trace of where the four (4) property parcels of the Brown Estate.

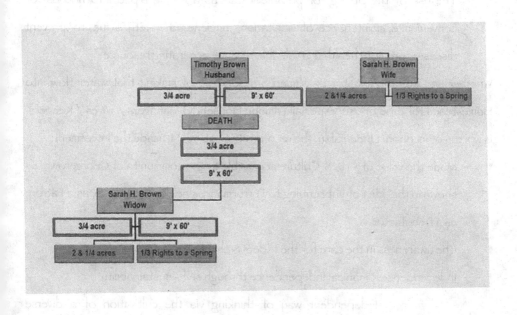

Plate 42   Tim & Sarah H. Property Accounts

21. Her Contribution

* The continuation of the burying ground, we now call that the business of Memorial Grounds

* The use of the Spring for potable water: as a lifeline piped into houses for convenience, maintenance of sanitation, hygiene, a safety issue to prevent diseases, promote health & a valuable revenue generating resource.

Whether she was the initiator or played a minor part of making that water flow into Homesteads for ease of use; especially among Household Managers / Wives / Keepers, is worthy of mention. Undeniably, the records show, Sarah H. made the investment.

* Made the value of Arts & Culture accessible to the community of Georgetown, as shown in the idea of subscribing to Performances held in the House: as a Patron, as a Benefactor

* The awareness in the care for the Elders & the Aging

* Independence: Financial Independence through self - sustainability

Independent way of thinking via the cultivation of a diverse mindset

* Decisive action - recognized the opportunity when the opportunity presented itself

* Sound Judgement - the woman's intuition in sensing a good investment; and the instincts to find a wonderful mate in life, for a lifetime.

In both emotional and practical risk taking, she's not only brave but had a knack for choosing stellar stocks. Obviously a very astute feel about these things.

* Provided the Inspiration for a Magnificent House, their Home, Her Home.

Part VIII. Income Generating Property

From Sarah H. 's covenant document that have the terms of a Will, we now conclude that these couple put priority in the value of revenue generation. The properties they had invested on were not just there to be admired and provide comfort in the every day existence of sleeping, cooking, entertaining. These wonderful comforts enjoyed under the roof of the Structure to be their House and Home had also served the purpose of a source of income to finance everything that happened under it, in it, within it. Brilliant! Sheer Genius. This is what is called income from rents. From the Town Hall; there must have been a lease agreement? Funded, constructed, actualized the building of a magnificent structure from seemingly ordinary material; is any Person's Dream, realized. The hopes of collecting revenues to finance the secured stability of any person's golden years is just about every individual goal, as well. I take it every one can agree to that?

So why are people of today surprised at the notion of Self - sustainability as an overarching Goal for the house in this Project? Do people in today's modern generation, hard of comprehension that it had been done? It can be done. Is the mindset - by the township, by the county or regional? Income generation is the only way to be relevant. The establishment of a solid source of funds without relying on grants, exemptions, and alms to finance programs that would render Historic sites, Museums, or any venture relevant, and constantly evolving as the changing times is the key to Relevancy, and staying germane? Are we feeding the entitlement standpoint that Everybody wants to use the facility without any responsibility of shelling out funds? Even the use of the grounds at government Parks charge admission, and permits or stickers that one pay for. Do not forget there is such a thing as schedules, and hours of operation!

IX . A Multi - Use VENUE; A Function Hall:

1893, the will of Sarah H. Brown confirmed that usage of the Structure generated income. The following excerpted, and transcribed record of a business incorporation is an example of that use. A multi - purpose function hall, for gatherings, meetings, conferences, or as the Town Hall. Was there a plan to turn the most decorative structure in town to be the Town Hall? Cazenovia did. One thing factually sure: this showed that the House fiscally self - sustained.

This meeting was held at the Brown Hall, Village of Georgetown, NY.

The Formation of Hillside Cemetery

1882, February 16	Liber Miscellaneous B p.262
Notarized: 18 February 1882	Recorded: 23 February 1882 at 3PM

The following met at Brown Hall. Re: formation of the Hillside Cemetery Association:

John Q. Hawks	Joseph Neal	Charles Smith	Wm. W. Hare
Astron Neal	Orville Mack	Geo S. Carver	Allan Drake
Theron Drake	H.W. Atwood	Frank Drake	Chas Foster
W.B. Morey	Scoville Upham	L.W.Brown	Milton D. Allen
Beuf Peckham	Daniel Havesiu		Orlando Dutton
Otis H. Whitmore		Frank E. Whitmore	

Minutes:

1. John Q. Hawks, Chairman - elect
2. Frank E. Whitmore, Secretary
3. That there would be 9 Trustees

   First Class: Allen Drake, L.E. Beach, Frank Whitmore

   Second Class: John Hawks, L.M. Brown, Frank Drake

   Third Class: E. U. Brown, B. Peckham, Orville Mack
4. First Monday of February, fixed date of Annual Meeting
5. Subscribed & Sworn: Albert C. Stanton, Justice of the Peace

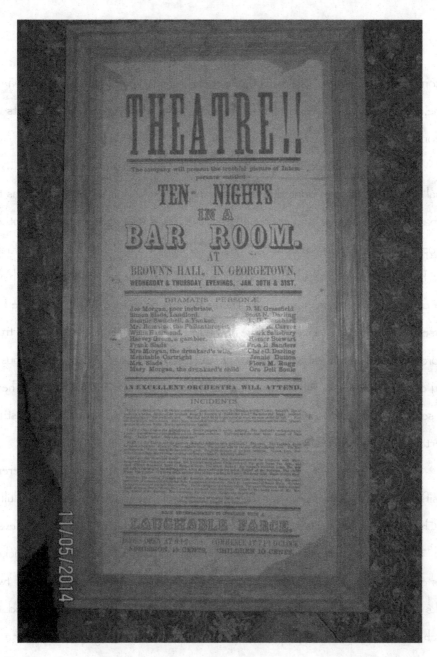

Plate 43-0174   Playbill

X. Performing Arts at the House

To continue on the same facet as to the use, and function of the House other than a Home, we have been privileged to have a visual of the following records of events to reinforce this Income Property Philosophy factually.

The House was used as a performance center for the Arts, and Musicals. The actual presentations were printed in the following playbills. If I may be so daring as to compare these enjoyment, and appreciation of the Arts in Georgetown to that in other metropolis like NYC, may not be farfetched imaginings of a wannabe scribe. The facts are in here courtesy of a dearly beloved lady amore E.E[20]. The advertising Posters have most of what can be seen in a Playbill. They show the necessary information. See for yourself, as pictures were taken from the now framed original documents. Finally, A true Record of civility, of cultural patronization as were performed in this Magnificent House. They did have live music; full orchestra at the House, for such entertainments! There was seating arrangement even. Hmm. Comparative to a box, on a real Theater style entertainment venue?! Yes, and it is not Free either.

The Admission was for twenty - five cents. Seating comes in different classifications. Thirty - five cents for the Reserved, and that was not just for the Adults, the Children, too. Does this not tell you how refined the tastes of these people even then. The business of it was very well coordinated, as shown by the advanced ticket sales date of" 15th April, 1882, 9PM at the Post Office," it announced. That was two weeks notice. Well, that would be equivalent to an Apple unveiling of today. A product launch for a new gadget, a toy; a promotional release where fans stay up all night for a

---

[20] I am leaving her in a climactic shroud as she deserve more than just a mention in a footnote.

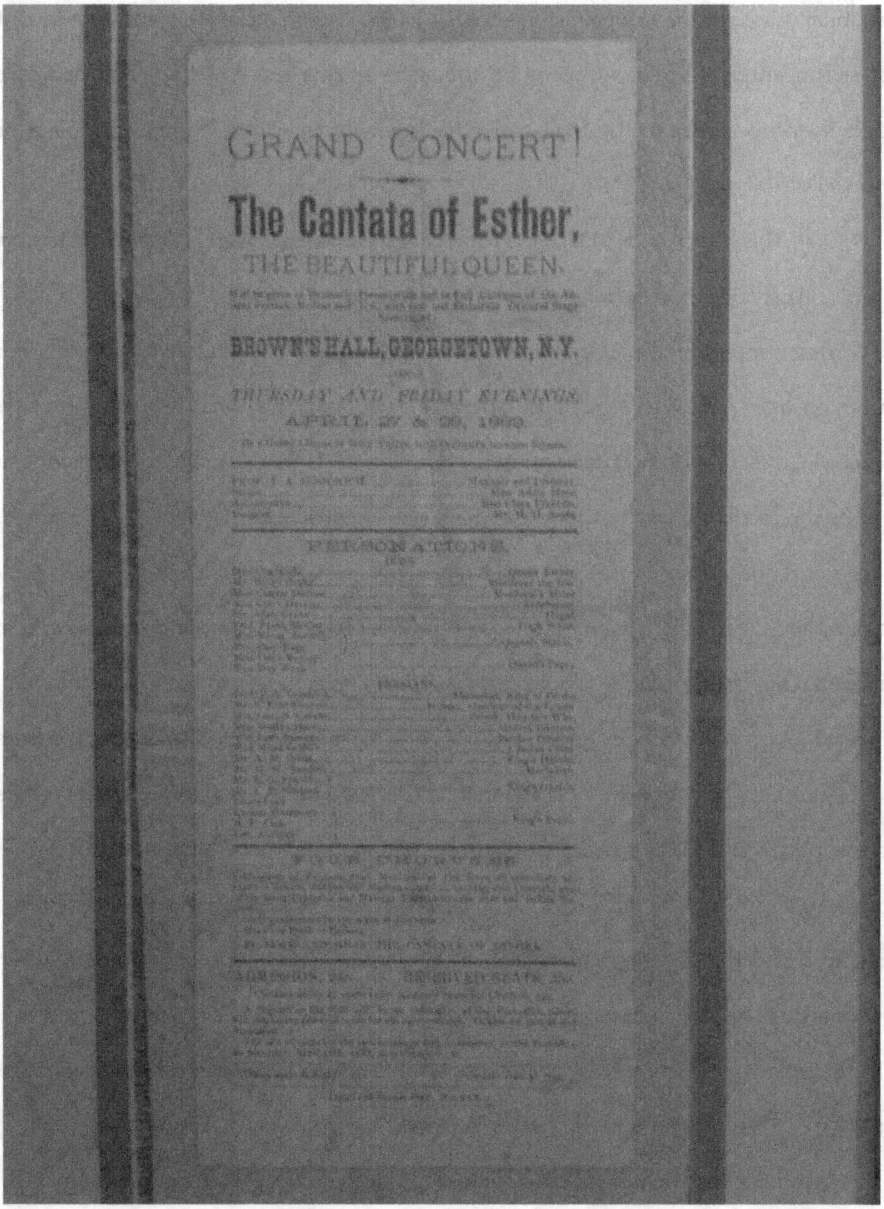

Plate 44-0723   April 27 & 28, 1882

A Grand Concert: "The Cantata of Esther, the Beautiful Queen".

new album or video; the opening of a show or musical; even a book signing of a favorite best selling writer. The crowd would be the same as one see how the many dedicated people lined up to get to the Malls prior the opening for Black Friday Shopping; but maybe a little bit more tame.

Only, this happened in 1882! In a town called Georgetown, NY! People had to come on foot, by carriage, horse, buggy?, Or an automobile?.

What happened to the appreciation of the Arts, and high culture TODAY? Where can we go from Then, to Now, and Where are we going forward? Why obstruct this Project of Conservation & Preservation for the House? Is this just sheer Prejudice? How many of the locals go to the Opera, or to a live Theatrical Performance? Or even just plain go out, and meet new people, and try new things? Or maybe let these new people, and new things, come here even for a momentary visit to enrich our panoramic view, spice the day to day grind of life?. Those little visits can go a long way to open tolerance in diversity that promote deeper understanding. Discernment that lead to productive lives.

Another interesting live performance, a real Musical the way I look at it. The play had five parts, and with an accompanying live orchestra. The bill announced it as "Ten Nights in a Bar Room" at Brown's Hall, in Georgetown. The only thing missing here was the year, it had the date as 30th & 31st of January, a Wednesday & Thursday evening performances. Another observation worthy of note, at least on my part was that most of the people that participated or performed in these playbills were familiar local last names.

I wonder if the theater guild was literally from the town, or the neighboring city, or if there was an actual outfit of an MGM / Hollywood type production business localized here. A CNY version. I have seen other performance posters / handbills, but do not have

Plate 45-0288   The Square Piano

either the Brown Hall printed on it, or an indication that the Acts were held in the Brown Hall. Some had the handwritten venue as the Brown Hall. Because the venue part was handwritten in pencil, and the authentication of this type is not within the scope of this compiled work at the moment; mention of them in existence is what I can say here. There was one that printed the Georgetown Hall as the venue. This one makes me strongly be inclined to surmise the notion that the House was used either in the Town Hall Capacity, and / or used for purposes the Town Hall had contracted with. It would be helpful to recall how Sarah H. Brown itemized that function in the 1893 agreement terms, as an income source. Yes, dear readers, it is okay to flip to that Will again, a few pages back.

This one handbill printed a performance that went with the title "Grand Pageant of American History, given by the Georgetown Auxiliary of the Red Cross, Town Hall, Georgetown, NY the 24th of November 1917". On this particular production, Alice Stevens played the part of Priscilla. Elwin Stevens, as one of the Darkies. Mrs. Elwin Stevens on the piano. The rest are mostly last names we all are familiar with as local residents, even to this generation.

So, I am connecting that the square piano may have something to do with Bertha as a musician. I would not hesitate to surmise that even Alice, and Julia could have played as well. That was the standard in that era. I can remember it still was, during my time, and I am on the Modern Era. If the three elder women picked that instrument, then Frances may well have been.

If all these deductions fail, the fact that there were Musicals performed there, the piano was an important necessity. Anyhow, Yes, let it be documented here too, that the square piano is there. More about the Piano in the works, and would soon be shared.

Please have patience.

22. The Sarah H. Brown in all of Us.

The Devoted Lover,

An Entrepreneur,

A Sound Investor,

A Strategic Speculator,

A Fashion Icon,

The Modernist,

A Brilliant Woman of Substance.

There cohabited these qualities inherent in every individual human being, of every race, in every nation around the world. There maybe more in each one, as different experiences, and environmental factors mold each one, unique in every way, not one the same as the other, but mirror one another. Factor all these with whatever gender orientation a person is inclined to be. The innate qualities of a Positive nature is ingrained in the DNA of humankind. Let us therefore make this an opportunity to share, in the Spirit of Giving back. Re - awaken the sleeping giant of a trait named "Respect" for one another. A call to shine the light through the Truth of the Facts, in all Honesty, with Integrity in the Story of the History of this Woman as the real driving force behind this Magnificent Structure. Immortalize the true American Spirit of Making a Positive Difference wherever we are. The Woman behind the Man. The Great Person of a Man behind -

The Woman.

Brave, Daring, Beloved. Adored, & Respected by A Partner that built her a Home as a Shrine for her. A token of Love.

XI. The Union of Timothy & Sarah H.BROWN

Plate 46-0546   The Brown Estates

1864 - 1895

The end of an era of the First Owners.

23. Chain of Ownership:

General Obligations Law defines "estate & interest in real property include every such estate and interest, freehold or chattel, legal or equitable, present or future, vested or contingent". Title 1 § 5-101.2.

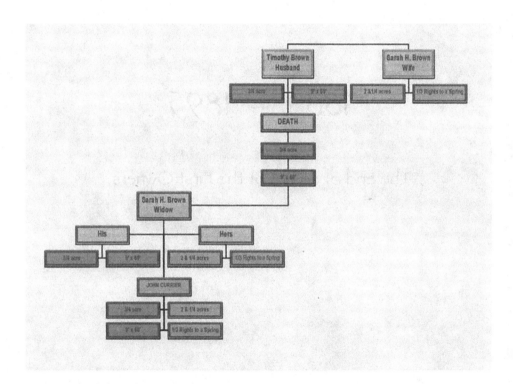

Plate 47 From Timothy to Sarah to John Currier: A Trace.

"Conveyance includes every instrument, in writing, except a Will, by which any estate or interest in real property is created, transferred, assigned, or surrendered". GOL Title I § 5-101.1.

Plate 48- 0559 Sarah H. Brown to John Currier, 1895

XII. Part B. The Curriers:

JOHN CURRIER

Carriage, Sleigh & General Repairing and Painting

GEORGETOWN, N.Y.

———

Note: Above information taken from the Business Advertisement found in the 1803-1905 Georgetown Horse and Wagon Days, Muller House, The Old Muller Hill House Booklet.

24. John[21]

1895, June 01 Sarah H. Brown to John Currier and Arvilla L. Currier, his wife
$800.00 Liber 188 p. 159

"... All that tract or parcel of Land, situate in the Village of Georgetown...aforesaid deeded to her by Timothy Brown May 5th 1885 Recorded in Madison Co. Clerk's Office May 14th 1885 9 o'clock AM in Liber 163 page 155. Described and bounded as follows: viz. on the North by land owned by the Baptist Church, East by land formerly owned by Mary M. Ellis. On the South by land formerly owned by Russell Whitmore. On the West by the center of the highway, containing three - fourths of an acre more or less. And being part of Lot (91) Ninety one of said Town. Also all that tract or parcel of land deeded by the Trustees of the First Baptist Society of said Town to Timothy Brown on the 15th day of August 1882, and recorded in the Office of the Clerk of Madison on the 5th day of August 1884 at 11 o'clock AM in Liber 161 page 20. Also that tract or parcel of land deeded by Zinah H. Moseley, Milton D. Allen and Mary his wife, Isaac Fletcher and Mercy his wife to Sarah H. Brown on the 22nd day of March 1871 and recorded in the Clerk's Office of the County of Madison on the 30th day of March 1871 at 11 o"clock AM. in Book No. 123 of Deeds page 347. Also all the rights and privileges in and to a certain Spring of water which was conveyed to the said Sarah H. Brown by deed from Hiram N. Atwood & wife, and George Curtis & wife, and recorded in the Clerk's Office of the County of Madison on the 14th day of March at 9 o"clock AM in Liber 162 of Deeds page 140. To which said deed reference is hereby made for a more particular description of said water rights."

..recorded: June 26th 1895, 9AM.

Note: In this sales transaction, the encumbrance of the said mortgage was not mentioned.

---

[21] A blood relationship of the Currier's to Sarah H. Brown, a hearsay as of this writing.

25. Mortgage JtoF

From Sarah H. Brown to John Currier, there was no written mortgage on the Deed of sale for $800.00. Following the chain of ownership, It is worthy of note here that when John Currier sold the Brown Estates to Floyd Currier, there was an apparent Encumbrance from John Currier back to Sarah H. Brown. That lien was reflected in the deed of sale from John Currier & Arvilla, to Floyd Currier.

Here it is, excerpted from the deed of <u>John Currier to Floyd Currier</u>.

1897, December 06 Liber 192 p. 267

"...And this conveyance is made subject to a certain Indenture of Mortgage this day executed by the parties of the first part to said Sarah H. Brown to secure the payment of the sum of three hundred and fifty dollars as therein specified which said party of the second part hereby assume and agrees to pay as part of the purchase price of said premises. With the appurtenances, and all the state, Title and Interest therein of the said party of the first part and the said John H. Currier & Arvilla L. Currier parties of the first part do hereby covenant and agree to and with the said party of the second part, his heirs and assigns that the premises thus conveyed in the quiet and peaceable possession of the said party of the second part, his heirs and assigns they will forever Warrant and Defend, against any person whomsoever lawfully claiming the same or ay part thereof, except said mortgage...." ...recorded: December 8th 1897, 1:20AM.

Compare this with the annotation from the 1898 deed of sales of Floyd Currier to Chauncey G. Stevens. This is a wonderment that baffles me:

Why would a debt to an old widowed woman not be prioritized before anything else?

What happened to the income from the estate as the will mentioned?

The income from the water rights that was piped - in, even then?

How did Sarah H., who would be very frail at this point had managed?

26. Mortgage FtoC

Shown here in transcribed format for ease of reading is how this annotated encumbrance had evolved in description, from John to Floyd and Floyd to Chauncey. It was excerpted from the deed of sale between Floyd Currier to Chauncey Stevens.

1898, October 31 Liber 199 pp. 490-91

"...And this conveyance is made subject to a certain Indenture of Mortgage executed by John H. Currier and wife to Sarah H. Brown on the 6th day of Dec. 1897 to secure the payment of the sum of $350. as therein specified and upon which there is now owing $319.77 which said Mortgage the party of the second part assumes and agrees to pay as a part of the purchase price of said premises. With the appurtenances, And all the estate Title and Interest therein of the said parties of the first part, And the said Floyd Currier does hereby covenant and agree to and with the said party of the second part his heirs and assigns, that the premises thus conveyed in the quiet and peaceable possession of the said party of the second part his heirs and assigns will forever Warrant and Defend against any person, whomsoever lawfully claiming the same or any part thereof. Except, by virtue of said Mortgage. ..."   ...recorded: December 5th 1898. 3PM

Points of Analyses:

1   John Currier owed Sarah H. $350.00 dated 6th day of Dec. 1897[22]

2   1898, October 31 Liber 199 pp. 490-91 recorded: December 5th 1898. 3PM
     Same date John Currier sold the Brown Estates to John Currier

3    $319.77 was left out unpaid

4    $30.33 had been paid off, by installment

5   That John Currier via a sales transaction transferred this debt to Floyd Currier.

---

[22]Floyd to Chauncey deed of sale, 1898, Oct. 31 Liber 199 pp. 490-91 Recorded. Dec. 5th 1898.3PM

This annotation on the deed informs the reader that John H. Currier & wife Arvilla L. Currier owed Sarah H. Brown the amount of $350.00. That Floyd Currier [current owner per this deed of sale] would assume that mortgage. If the payment came from the purchase price of $500.00, this left John and Arvilla Currier, $150.00 to pocket as part of the proceeds in this particular deed of sale transaction, when Floyd Currier assumed that responsibility when he bought the Property.

Now, let me be the devil's advocate here: if these gentle people would have taken the time to have paid off the mortgage first, which was and is the usual way of doing business, in a more honorable fashion, then and especially now, why then was this encumbrance still an impediment by the time Floyd sold the property to Chauncey? This would have meant that this debt had not been squared of yet. True?!. What ever transpired here as to the WHY, and HOW COME, is open to conjecture, and I would not do so. The point of all these is to just present the facts. If along the course of further research, we happen to come along any factual explanation on this, then it would be worthwhile revisiting this puzzling issue again, to base the deductions on more factual evidence.

Suffice it to point out that at the time of the buy out transaction made possible by our more modern luminary figure Alice Stevens, this encumbrance was no longer there. To end this page at a happier note, that would have been thank you to dear Daddy: Chauncey G. Stevens.

Questions to start an interesting brain - storming and more fact finding investigative searches: The death of Sarah H. Brown?? When? Where? How? Was she with a Family member, or a close Friend, or alone in a Home for the aged? Facts, authentic one only, please. Verifiable. Those that can withstand scientific scrutiny.

Plate 50-0564   John Currier to Floyd Currier, 1897

27. Floyd[23]

1897, December 06 from John Currier & wife Arvilla L. Currier to Floyd Currier
for $500.00 Liber 192 p. 267

"...all that tract or parcel of Land, situate in the town of Georgetown...and being all of the premises deeded to Sarah H. Brown by Timothy Brown May 5th 1885 and recorded in the Madison County Clerks Office May 14th 1885 at 9 o'clock AM in Liber 163 page 155 described and bounded as follows: viz. On the North by land owned by the Baptist Church & Society East by land formerly owned by Mary M. Ellis. On the South by land formerly owned by Russell Whitmore. On the West by the center of the highway. Being part of Lot No. 91 of said town containing three fourths of an acre more or less. Also all that tract or parcel of land deeded by the Trustees of the First Baptist society of said town to Timothy Brown on the 15th day of August 1882, and recorded in the Clerks Office of the County of Madison on the 5th day of August 1884 at 11 o'clock AM in Liber 161 page 20. Also that tract or parcel of land deeded by Zinah H. Moseley, Milton D. Allen and Mary his wife, Isaac Fletcher and Mercy his wife to said Sarah H. Brown on the 22nd day of March 1871 and recorded in the Clerk's Office of the County of Madison on the 30th day of March 1871 at 11 o"clock AM. in Book No. 123 of Deeds page 347. Also all the rights and privileges in and to a certain Spring of water which was conveyed to the said Sarah H. Brown by a deed from Hiram N. Atwood & wife, and George Curtis & wife, and recorded in the Clerk's Office of the County of Madison on the 14th day of March at 9 o"clock AM in Liber 162 of Deeds page 140, to which said deed reference is hereby made for a more particular description of said water rights. And this conveyance is made subject to a certain Indenture of Mortgage this day executed by the parties of the first part to said Sarah H. Brown to secure the payment of the sum of three hundred and fifty dollars as therein specified which said party of the second part hereby assume and agrees to pay as part of the purchase price of said premises. With the appurtenances, and all the state, Title and Interest therein of the said party of the first part and the said John H. Currier & Arvilla L. Currier parties of the first part do hereby covenant and agree to and with the said party of the second part, his heirs and assigns that the premises thus conveyed in the quiet and peaceable possession of the said party of the second part, his heirs and assigns they will forever Warrant and Defend, against any person whomsoever lawfully claiming the same or ay part thereof, except said mortgage...recorded: December 8th 1897, 1:20AM."

---

[23] A relation to John Currier: fact verification pending, still hearsay as of this writing.

Note: This deed informs the reader that John H. Currier & wife Arvilla L. Currier owed Sarah H. Brown the amount of $350.00, and that Floyd Currier [now current owner per this deed of sale] would assume that mortgage payment from the purchase price of $500.00. This leaves John and Arvilla Currier, $150.00 to pocket as part of the proceeds in this particular deed of sale transaction.

Uncertainties mirrored again:

What happened to this encumbrance as of repayment status to Sarah H. Brown before death, or after ?? Also, what was this IOU for? Was the sale price not fully squared off by John Currier? Was it about the use of something? Lease, or rental money owed? The water rights use?

Interesting Facts that connect to MR. Floyd Currier:

1   Liber 2070 p. 252 Bottom part of 2nd paragraph: "... At all times reserving all water rights & privileges formerly deeded or conveyed to Mrs. Ella Bartlett, B.T. Miner, Henry Saunders, the Crystal Spring Water Company & others."

2   Third paragraph: " The above described premises are the same as those conveyed by Floyd Currier and wife to B.T. Miner 1912 March 23 Liber 249 p. 489. "

Note: B.T. Miner died 1923, March 16 Last Will bequeathed the above to Edson R. Miner, nephew.

Queries:

1912, March 23 Liber 249 p. 489 This water rights would not be the same water rights that was Sarah H. Brown's 1/3, would it? Floyd Currier just sold Chauncey G. Stevens in 1898, October 31 Liber 199 pp. 490-491, remember? More on this as we follow the maze.

XII. Part B. The Curriers:

1895 ~ 1898

FLOYD CURRIER,

Funeral Director and Embalmer

ESTABLISHED 1896

Both phones - Bell and Newton.   Also Telegraphic Communication

Georgetown, N.Y.

Note: Above information taken from the Business Advertisement found in the 1803-1905 Georgetown Horse and Wagon Days, Muller House, The Old Muller Hill House Booklet.

Plate 51-0572 Floyd Currier to Chauncey G. Stevens, 1898

28. Is this the Revenue Generated from the 1/3 Rights to a Spring?

MADISON COUNTY LEADER AND OBSERVER MORRISVILLE, NY THURSDAY MORNING APRIL 4, 1912. TWENTY - SEVENTH YEAR NO. 43. Georgetown

- "Floyd Currier of Hamilton was in town Monday collecting the water rent for the Crystal Springs Water Company."

So many questions, so many data, factual ones that are parts, and pieces that even in their incomplete form show a picture as complex as a mural representing a diverse lifestyle, that even our generation fail to upstage. It is the hope that through the compilation of these facts, the community can come together to pay due homage, and respect to the ancestors that have done nothing except live lives that were demanded of the generation that was.

The brilliance of those lives intertwined, left us all with the shell of what a marvel those events were. The actions, the decisions, the choices that were made then, we now harvest to enjoy, and continuously benefit from. Why can we not acknowledge them.? They may not have been perfect. The ones that were, we honor; the ones filled or tinged with errors - acknowledge. Then maybe we can try to understand.

As, civility had grown in more advance & modern present day: Why can we not try to rectify? What We do now - our actions, decisions, and choices would be the story the future generations would render History. Let us therefore all join hands in making that story, one that would continue the positive aspects of that Journey, our Human Ancestors had started, whose path already been paved; and if not at all be able to Conserve & Preserve what was left of that Legacy, at least be able to acknowledge what once were? All in the efforts to Respectfully Commemorate that History Truthfully, accurately, in open honesty, integrity, dignified, as the facts present themselves.

29. The Georgetown Water System &

The Crystal Springs Water Company

What connections, correlations and secrets got buried, were buried and still are buried beneath the Company name?

TIDBITS from a collage of newspaper clippings shared by anonymous:

1926 Georgetown Reservoir had a collapsed Dam made of earth, the water was completely drained.

1952 Georgetown water system known by the name Crystal Springs Water Co., was started by E.W. Cuyle and Floyd Currier who since had moved to Hamilton, NY.

Of late, this was ran by E.W. Andrus, who frequented Florida in the winter and began the process the formation of a water district run by the 87 users of the system.

1996 A $450,400 Federal Department of Housing & Urban Development grant was received by the town.

1997 The 125,000 gallon steel water tank replaced the in - ground concrete tank, paid for from the grant.

1998 Under the leadership of Town Supervisor Russell Hammond, the replacement well was discovered on the land owned by Georgetown Fire Department.

Oh well, so the group of users, some 87 or so from Main Street felt it would be for the improvement of their quality of life to move the commercial use of the Spring. Still, as responsible entrepreneurs, the first order of business would be either to own via procurement or lease via contracts of agreements the use of this commodity. Where are the documentations of ownership for this very lucrative and well operated system? 1/3 undivided Rights to the Spring. The story of the goose that laid the golden eggs befit this particular story.

30.   Chauncey[24]

1898, October 31 Floyd Currier & Lilian E. Currier to Chauncey G. Stevens

$700.00   Liber 199 pp. 490-91

"...Witnesseth that the said parties of the first part, in consideration of the sum of Seven Hundred dollars (700.00) to them duly paid, have sold, and by these presents do grant and convey to the said party of the second part his heir and assigns. All that Tract or Parcel of Land, situate in the Town of Georgetown County of Madison and State of NY, and being all the premises deeded to Sarah H. Brown by Timothy Brown May 5th 1885 and recorded in the Madison County Clerks Office May 14th 1885 at 9 o"clock AM in Liber 163 page 155 described and bounded as follows viz. On the North by lands owned by the Baptist Church & Society. East by lands formerly owned by Mary M. Ellis. On the South by land formerly owned by Russell Whitmore. On the West by the center of the highway being a part of Lot No. 91 of said town containing 3/4 of an acre more or less. Also all that tract or parcel of land deeded by the Trustees of the First Baptist Society of said town to Timothy Brown on the 15th day of August 1882, and recorded in the Clerks Office of the County of Madison on the 5th day of August 1884 at 11 o'clock AM in Liber 161 page 20. Also that tract or parcel of land deeded by Zinah H. Moseley, Milton D. Allen and Mary his wife, Isaac Fletcher and Mercy his wife to said Sarah H. Brown on the 22nd day of March 1871 and recorded in the Clerk's Office of the County of Madison on the 30th day of March 1871 at 11 o"clock AM. in Book No. 123 of Deeds page 347. Also all the rights and privileges in and to a certain Spring of water which was conveyed to the said Sarah H. Brown by a deed from Hiram N. Atwood & wife, and George Curtis & wife, and recorded in the Clerk's Office of the County of Madison on the 14th day of March at 9 o"clock AM in Liber 162 of Deeds page 140, to which said deed reference is hereby made for a more particular description of said water rights. And this conveyance is made subject to a certain Indenture of Mortgage executed by John H. Currier and wife to Sarah H. Brown on the 6th day of Dec. 1897 to secure the payment of the sum of $350. as therein specified and upon which there is now owing $319.77 which said Mortgage the party of the second part assumes and agrees to pay as a part of the purchase price of said premises. With the appurtenances, And all the estate Title and Interest therein of the said parties of the first part, And the said Floyd Currier does hereby covenant and agree to and with the

---

[24] Son of Albert Stevens. Wife Julia, daughter, Alice; son Elwin married to Bertha Spaulding; bore infant daughter Frances, the granddaughter Chauncey never met.

said party of the second part his heirs and assigns, that the premises thus conveyed in the quiet and peaceable possession of the said party of the second part his heirs and assigns will forever Warrant and Defend against any person, whomsoever lawfully claiming the same or any part thereof. Except, by virtue of said Mortgage. ..."   ...recorded: December 5th 1898. 3PM

Note: On this transaction, the deed of sale to Chauncey G. Stevens from Floyd and wife Lilian E. Currier, notice the change of status of Floyd Currier, who a year ago when he bought this property was single and now had a wife. Also, Floyd Currier was not able to make good on his promise to square away the Mortgage of John Currier to Sarah H. Brown. The $350.00 Mortgage amount was now reduced to $319.77 which meant that only $30.23 was remitted. This brings to mind the following questions:

1. During John H. Currier & Arvilla to Floyd Currier deed of sale= $500.00
   Of this amount, how much was deducted to pay Sarah?
   If only $319.77 was deducted from the Mortgage amount of $350.00, then was the $500.00 sales price, the amounted direct income for John H. & Arvilla Currier?

2. Why was the Mortgage not cleared away first, before John H. & Arvilla received the proceeds from the sales transaction?

3. Now that Chauncey G. Stevens had acquired the Sarah H. Brown Property, would she be paid in full in the Mortgage amount still owed her?

4. Was it Chauncey that paid off this encumbrance to Sarah H.?

5. Where was Sarah H. Brown all these time?

___

???? 1912 : Why is Floyd Curried the person collecting the Water Rents? On what Capacity; Authority?

Part XIII.   The Stevens

The Stevens Family were a very well off family as shown on the property holdings; close knit as presented in the complex webbed network of heirs and inheritances read amongst the records looked into, and chanced upon, in eureka moments. A very interesting, enlightening informative cache of beautiful bits of scenes almost like Downton Abbey style, Georgetown, NY version. Here's a sample.

ALBERT STEVENS

Liber 168 pp.511-512   1884, December 02
                            Surrogate Court: 17 September 1887
                            Recorded: 16 September 1887

Mr. Albert Stevens had five children namely:
Sybil Green married to Reuben Green
Mary L. Gilbert married to Jay Gilbert
Martha Baker married to Lafayette W. Baker
Albert Stevens, Jr.
Chauncey G. Stevens

We have now just been introduced to the next key character in the saga of the Brown Estates. Chauncey G. Stevens. The above data were from the Legacy of Mr. Albert Stevens. We can easily deduce here that Chauncey was one of the named son in this document, and that he had siblings mentioned above. It also meant that his father Albert had left him some property.

Who really is Chauncey G. Stevens?

The best that I can quickly share to you dear readers is the chart of his family blood lineage here. The information illustrate the siblings and the relationships formed from there; it is unfortunate that as of this writing, the maternal side need some work. Data gathered did not show what was the name of his mother.

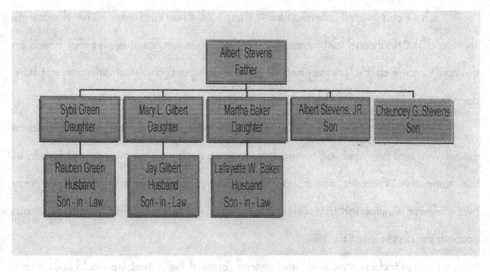

Plate 52 Understanding Chauncey's roots.

It is fascinating to see documents that showed those interrelationships played out in the distribution of inheritances: real cash, property and much more. Here's a tidbit to whet the taste buds of history buffs in people. From George Stevens Will, that you will see later on, we can deduce that Chauncey's sisters were blessed with what were his niece & two nephews:

Sybil Stevens - Green & Reuben Green: Bert Green

Mary L. Stevens - Gilbert & Jay Gilbert: George Gilbert

Martha Stevens - Baker & Lafayette W. Baker: Clara Baker

31. Death 2

Chauncey was the second son of Mr. Albert Stevens. He had a brother named Albert Stevens, Jr., and three other sisters named Sybil, Mary, and Martha. When they all came of age, the sisters got married and brought forth children of their own.

Chauncey himself married Julia; they had Elwin and Alice. The documents showed that Chauncey's vast interests extended to Canastota. It is my belief based on the court orders that Chauncey met his creator unexpectedly. That Julia may not have been that ready to step into his big shoes is apparent in this document here.

The transition from beloved stay at home wife, caring for two growing children even if very well provided for, to suddenly assume both roles of mother and father; at the same time takeover major business dealings, and transactions can be very overwhelming. Compound that with the mourning, and remember, we have to take into account the dynamics of the time.

Even in today's standards and general terms of living, that life would still be very hard. We maybe luckier in our generation as we can now avail without much stigma of the assistance of a shrink, and or feel like on vacation, and go to Rehab for a few weeks. Back then, this may not be as easy even for a woman of steel tenacity, and rock hard strength.

Plate 53-0525   Grief on the Death of Chauncey G. Stevens.

32. Heirs & Inheritance:

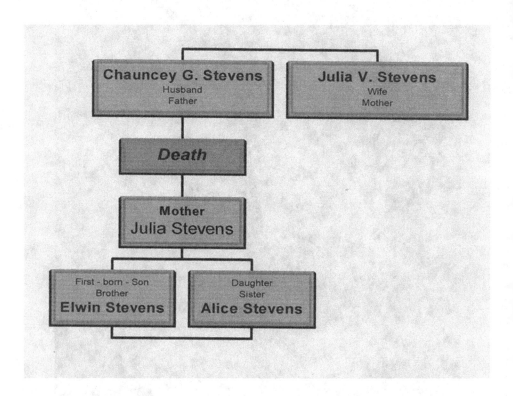

Plate 54   The Death of CGS

33. His Accomplishments & Contributions:

Two beautiful Children: Elwin

                                  Alice

Beloved wife: Julia

Provider: vast landholdings

Sound Investor: real estate

Owner: of a Magnificent House, a Home

The unfortunate, untimely demise of Mr. Chauncey Stevens transformed the lives of the people that took the responsibilities of taking good care of the Brown Legacy and moving that forward. The well grounded children of good character, and will of steel to continue their lives in the directions they had been as we see them from our generation, and from the lenses we now have proved that he was hardworking. A committed father, I may surmise.

That would have been really hard for the children. To experience first hand the loss of a parent: who was the pillar of strength, power and financial stability would have been devastating. To numb themselves in the longings for the sweet wonderments the presence of a father accord a home that render it safe from the wolves of the world - suddenly gone? I cannot put the feeling into words. There's no salve found, I'm sure.

This kind of helplessness, words are not fit to describe. I cannot. I would not. The loss so great, that for any child to power up, and take the world head on, squarely on little shoulders - is the testament of true blue bloodline. I am positive genetics played a huge part on that. Most of all, in finding a partner, a friend, a wife, that carried on was the greatest asset marked by his sound choices, and decisions. To Chauncey, Salute!

1898 - 1986

The STEVENS

The Stevens - Cossitt

34. Mrs. Chauncey G. Stevens: Julia V.

Devoted Wife   Mother of Elwin & Alice

Mother In - Law to Bertha   Grandmother to Frances.

Occupation: Seamstress / Dressmaker[25]

The next page showed a legal document denoting that by 1906, Julia was a widow, with two children; a boy and a girl. What was going on in the world out there? Yes, out of Georgetown. It would really be helpful to have a wider panorama that would ensure a more open perspective of what it would have seemed like - to have lived, and thrived in their generation. First, there was the San Francisco fire of 1906. There was the electric cars, and MR. Bell had phones ringing. No electrification as of yet, thus the whalers of New England dominated the market of illumination. Candles, and candlesticks, my dears. Gas lamps for streetlights? Fashion would be of the Victorian era influences, and changing. Those kinds that we may classify today as long gowns. Petticoats and tight laces, gloves; Yes. Heels not showing. Adamantly so. Cobblestone streets? How did they walk? Interestingly enough, with chaperones.

A farmer's wife, she was. Or should I say, a landowner's wife.? I see her as synonymous to the soccer Mom. With two school aged children, why not? Also, as the mistress of her home, she would have a flower garden, an herbarium of sort for her delicious homemade cooking, went with the women of her church and other Ladies' Society. Since she was registered as a seamstress or dressmaker, she would be equivalent to the Coco Chanel Georgetown, NY version. A career woman & a mother, a single parent with a vocation.

---

[25] Census

To you dear readers, if the slight skepticism to my romantic notions keep tugging on your sleeves, pardon me. A little indulgence, please. Here are the facts, please do take great considerations to read between the lines too.

1906, September 18 Julia V. Stevens, widow of Chauncey G. Stevens $1.00
                    of the Town of Georgetown, County of Madison, NY
                    to Grove S. Thompson, Village of Canastota, MadisonCounty, NY
                    Liber 222 pp. 79-80

"..Witnesseth that the said party of the first part in consideration of the sum of One Dollar ($1.00) to her duly paid, has sold, and by these presents, does grant and convey to the party of the second part, his heirs and assigns, All that tract or parcel of land situate in the village of Canastota, County of Madison and State of NY described as follows: Being lots Nos. 10,11,12,13,14,15,16,17,18 and 19 described and designated on the map of "Lands of A. and E. Stroud", 38 lots, Canastota, Madison Co. NY. Which said map have been heretofore filed in in Madison Co. Clerks Office. Said lots No. 10,11,12 and 13 are each four rods front & rear in width on Pleasant Street, and eight rods deep extending Northerly from said Pleasant Street said Lots 14,15,16,17 and18 are each four rods front and rear in width on Stroud Street, and one chain and 87 links deep extending Easterly from said Stroud street. Said Lot No. 19 is four rods front and rear in width on Hickory St. and twelve rods deep extending Southerly from said Hickory St. and lying just Easterly of, and adjoining Lots 16,17, and 18. Together with all and singular the hereditaments and appurtenances thereto belonging...

...And the said Julia Stevens for her and her heirs executor and administrators does covenant, promise and agree to and with the said party of the second part, his heir and assigns, that she has not made love, committed, executed, or suffered any act or acts, thing or things whatsoever whereby or by means whereof the above mentioned and described premises, or any or any lot or parcel thereof, now are, or at any time hereafter shall or may impeached, charged or incumbrance in any manner or way whatsoever...

...recorded: May 11th, 1907. 11AM"

Note: I wonder if this was a typographical error, or was there something about the law in 1906 that not making love was a part of the soundness of this transaction transfer?

1906, September 18   Elwin H. Stevens et al. (by ADM) $500.00 only

"...Between Elwin H. Stevens and Alice C. Stevens of the Town of Georgetown County of Madison and State of NY, infants under the age of twenty one years by Julia V. Stevens their Special Guardian of the first part, and Grove S. Thompson of the Village of Canastota, County of Madison, State of NY, of the second part, Witnesseth as follows: Whereas a Petition was made heretofore presented to the Madison County Court on behalf of the above named infants praying for a sale of the right, title and interest of the said infants in the premises in said petition mentioned and hereinafter described; upon which petition an order of the Madison County Court was made at a term thereof, held at the Judges Chambers in the Village of Cazenovia County of Madison, NY. bearing date the 20th day of August, 1906 appointing Julia V. Stevens above named, the Special Guardian of such infants with respect to these proceedings, upon his filing the bond therein required and said bond having been duly filed and said Court having on the 27th day of August 1906, made further order that it be referred to a Referee to inquire into the merits of the application, and examine into the Truth of the allegations of said petition, etc.; and whereas said Referee did on the 30th day of August 1906 report his opinion thereupon together with the testimony taken by him therein, and after an examination of the matter an order of the said Madison County Court was made at a term thereof, held at the Judge's Chambers, in the Village of Cazenovia, County of Madison NY. bearing date the 31st day of August, in the year 1906, wherein it was among other things in substance ordered, that said Referee Report be confirmed and the said real property be sold; that the above named Special Guardian of such infants be authorized and empowered to contract for the sale and conveyance of all the right, title, and interest of the said infants in such estate, subject to the approval of the Court, for a price not less than that specified in the Referee Report mentioned in said order: and upon the terms and conditions therein mentioned; and that said sale, with the name of the purchaser, and the terms and conditions of said agreement, be reported to the Court, under Oath, before the conveyance of such premises be executed. And whereas, the said Special Guardian, pursuant to said last mentioned order, contracted for the sale of the said right, title and interests of said infants in the said premises upon terms and in the manner authorized by said last mentioned order, with Grove S. Thompson of the Village of Canastota County of Madison and State of NY for the sum of Five Hundred Dollars

($500.00), that being the highest sum offered for the same, subject to the approval of the Court; and thereupon the said Guardian made his report under oath, of such agreement to the Court, pursuant to the requirements of the last mentioned order, upon which another order was made at a Term of said Court held at the Judge's Chambers in the Village of Morrisville County of Madison NY. bearing date the 17th day of September 1906, confirming such report, and among other things approving and confirming such sale, directing the same to be carried into effect, and ordering the said Guardian to execute, acknowledge and deliver a deed of said premises to said party of the second part upon his complying with the terms on which by said agreement, the same was to be delivered and whereas said party of the second part has fully complied with the said terms, Now, therefore, this Indenture witnesseth, that the said party of the first part, by Julia V. Stevens, said Special Guardian as aforesaid pursuant to said several orders, and in pursuance of the Statute in such case made and provided, and also for and in consideration of Five Hundred Dollars ($500.00), to her duly paid, the receipt whereof is hereby acknowledged, have bargained, sold, granted, released and conveyed, and by these presents do bargain, sell, grant, release and convey unto said party of the second part, and to his heirs and assigns forever, all the right, title, interest, claim or estate of the said infants, parties of the first part, of, in and to all that tract or parcel of land situate in the village of Canastota, County of Madison, State of NY, described as follows: Being lots Nos. 10,11,12,13,14,15,16,17,18 and 19 described and designated on the Map of "Lands of A. and E. Stroud, 38 lots, Canastota, Madison Co. NY." Which said map have been heretofore filed in Madison Co. Clerks Office. Said lots No. 10,11,12 and 13 are each four rods front & rear in width on Pleasant Street, and eight rods deep extending Northerly from said Pleasant Street said Lots 14,15,16,17 and 18 are each four rods front and rear in width on Stroud Street, and one chain and 87 links deep extending Easterly from said Stroud street. Said Lot No. 19 is four rods front and rear in width on Hickory St. and twelve rods deep extending Southerly from said Hickory St. and lying just Easterly of, and adjoining Lots 16,17, and 18. With the appurtenances thereto belonging to have and to hold the same, unto the said party of the second part, his heirs and assigns forever...."   ..recorded: May 11th, 1907. 11AM

Note: This particular transactions in 1906 for the Family of Chauncey G. Stevens left a remarked discomfort in me.

35. Julia, Elwin & Alice

From the preceding factual documents attached, we have a glimpse of what life was when the foursome turned threesome. Julia - the beloved wife, a dutiful mother, a woman of means. The thought provoking question is: Did the situation became the catalyst to bring out of her, the business acumen that her husband possessed? The first born son Elwin was still a minor. Alice a child. Two children to raise on her own. Julia would be what we now call a Single Parent. A single mom. Now, take a hold of yourselves. No conjectures, just imagine. This was the earliest part of the 1900. 1906. The Victorian era had just been fading away, may not have completely. Check it out yourselves, be interactive with me. Yes, take a hold of that history book. Google it if you have to, it is quicker. What was going on then? Fashion, money issues, social mores and cultural hips and hip nots. What is very unshakeable testamentary to the truth was how these family of Chauncey came out as Winners in the long saga of their Lives.

Fact 1 MUSIC   the power of Music.

Fact 2 LOVE   the power of Love

Fact 3 Community   the power of "It takes a village ..."

Fact 4 Church   there were at least 4 Churches in Georgetown then

Fact 5 Family   the Stevens Family was a tight knit one, and very well funded

Fact 6   Goals, Aspirations, Ambitions

Fact 7   Elwin Stevens was announced in a news article clip to be planning to enroll in an automobile engineering school in Geneva, that would be the same as being in the field of IT today, as the automobile was in its infancy at this time.

A.   The news clip

1909, January 28, Madison County Leader and Observer, Morrisville NY
Georgetown: January 27
"Elwin Stevens has gone to Geneva where he intends to enter a school of automobile engineering".

B.   The Theater Handbill

This substantially authenticate the power of Visual & Performing Arts in the healing of anything that ails human beings.

1917, November 24th This one handbill printed a performance that went with the title "Grand Pageant of American History, given by the Georgetown Auxiliary of the Red Cross, Town Hall, Georgetown.

On this particular production:

Alice Stevens played the part of Priscilla.

Elwin Stevens, as one of the Bluecoats.

Mrs. Elwin Stevens on the piano.

The rest are mostly last names we all are familiar with as local residents, even to this generation.

Notes:

It is demonstrated here that by 1917, Elwin Stevens had:

reached the age of majority

taken on a bride, Mrs. Elwin Stevens

Also, that the family was engaged in the Community, interested in Music and the Arts.

This practice follows in the footsteps of Mrs. Sarah H. Brown.

I wonder what had become of Mrs. Chauncey Stevens?

36. The Stevens Clan

GEORGE D. STEVENS

The Will of George Stevens detailed the distribution of his assets. In this document, Minnie S. Stevens was the name of his wife. This gave us the information that Elwin Stevens was set to receive $60.00 Then, the hierarchy of heirs:

Liber 278 p.27   Drawn: 1916, February 12   Probated: 31 July 1925   Recorded: 27 August 1925
wife Minnie Stevens
Matthie Baker 1/5 ,Mary G. Miller 1/5

if she dies before him, & he dies:
3/5 divided into the following five people, share & share alike -
Minnie Frost, Lydia Stevens, Jessie Dunham, Sarah Butler & Alice Stevens

Notice here that by this time, Chauncey was not mentioned.

Data to be taken: 1906 Lydia Stevens was already a widow.

This division and recording of the will was in the year 1925.

The upcoming events before 1925 would be sad yet opened new beginnings as well.

By the year 1906, Elwin & Alice had lost a father named Chauncey

Elwin had reached the age of Majority as by

1912, Elwin was already married

1917, Elwin as Head of the Family sold off a parcel to W. Trass, but by

1920, Elwin's young wife Bertha, would attend to their holdings

1925, Elwin had preceded George Stevens in meeting his Creator.

Note: This is to bring additional material to establish the fact that the Heirs of Chauncey were never neglected by the Stevens Family.

Plate 55-0575   First - born Son: Head of the Family

37. Elwin H. Stevens

Here's a clip from what can now be construed equivalent to the who's who gossip column in the newspaper, and what one can read over Twitter, Facebook or Instagram Today. Elwin had planned to enroll at the automobile engineering school in Geneva, I wonder if this was realized?

1907, January 10 Madison County Leader and Observer Georgetown
Edward Givens and MS. Ada Andrews Nursing Injuries from Accidents
January 08 - While Arthur Ellis, Edward Givens, Carl Elmer, Elwin Stevens and Clyde and Earl Buckingham were returning from Georgetown Sunday on a hand car over the new Otselic Valley railroad the car left the track near D.W. Taylor's with the result that Givens received a dislocated shoulder and all the rest sustained more or less serious bruises.

1909, January 28, Madison County Leader and Observer, Morrisville NY
Georgetown: January 27
Elwin Stevens has gone to Geneva where he intends to enter a school of automobile engineering.

Note: It is my belief that this type of career would be the most lucrative then, as the up and coming trend of transportation technology / innovation is the automobile. It would have been like the IT in the era of Computers and Cyber - optic Communications.

Also, Elwin was set to receive $60.00 from the Will of MR. George D. Stevens[26], as set forth in Liber 278 page 27. This document was:

 Drawn: 1916, February 12   Probated: 31 July 1925   Recorded: 27 August 1925

---

[26] a relation on the Stevens side of the family

Plate 56-0574   Elwin & Bertha, newlyweds, 1912.

MADISON COUNTY LEADER AND OBSERVER MORRISVILLE, NY THURSDAY MORNING APRIL 4, 1912. TWENTY - SEVENTH YEAR NO. 43 **Georgetown**

- "Mr. and Mrs. Elwin Stevens have moved into the house on West Street recently vacated by Mr. and Mrs. H. R. Perry"

Note: This article would confirm that by 1912, Elwin had reached the age of majority, married and moving into another house to create a home. Whether he was just married or on a honeymoon is for the imagination until the actual factual document verify as to the very date of the wedding. Until then, what we have here, as to his marriage is a very intelligent deduction based on the fact that his wife Bertha was able to dispose of the assets that belonged to him after he died. On those records, Bertha assumed the responsibility of the Guardian to Frances. Since Julia was Elwin's mom; Alice his sister; Bertha his wife, then this Frances, an infant was his daughter. These deductions are not mythical. By the process of elimination, it is Scientific to say that the conclusions arrived are based on accepted recorded data. The only thing missing was the actual date which would be on the marriage record. More about this family soon.

MADISON COUNTY LEADER AND OBSERVER MORRISVILLE, NY THURSDAY MORNING MAY 16, 1912. TWENTY - SEVENTH YEAR NO. 49 **May 15**

- "Mrs. Elwin Stevens has been spending a week with her parents, Mr. and Mrs. Charles Spaulding, in Sauquoit".

Note: Here we meet Elwin's in - Laws. From this information, we can figure out that Mrs. Elwin Stevens was Bertha Spaulding. The Spaulding family lived in Sauquoit, which would have meant that they had moved to Georgetown, as the later deeds showed. Would it be safe to infer at this point that they moved to be near their daughter?

Plate 57-0526   In - Laws

This particular sales transaction of Elwin to Mr. Trass is of importance as this specific parcel, and its description would come full circle in the over - all picture of the story, of the History of the Brown - Stevens - Cossitt Land Acreage Legacy.

1917, October 26   from Elwin H. Stevens, and Bertha M. his wife,
                    Julia V. Stevens, Alice C. Stevens Georgetown, Madison, NY
                    $300.00   Liber 250 p. 384
                    to William Trass, Georgetown, Madison, NY

"... being part of Lot 91...bounded as follows, Viz; Beginning at a stake on the North West corner of the lot, on B.E.Ross South line running then Easterly along B.E.Ross South line about 199 and a half feet to a stake, thence in a southerly direction about 323 feet to a stake, thence in a Northerly direction 309 feet on the East line of the old Cemetery to the North east corner of said Cemetery, thence West about 9 feet, thence Northerly about 97 feet to the place of beginning, containing about two acres of land be the same more or less."

"Reserving therefrom a strip of land thirty feet wide deeded to the Otselic Valley Railroad Co. running across said lot from North to South, for and in consideration of the amount paid by the party of the second part, the parties of the first part agree to pay all damages that the Otselic Valley Rail Road Company or their successors to the above described property." ..recorded: October 30th, 1907, 9 AM.

Note: Take extra good look on the reserved portion of this land sale transaction. 30' wide strip of land was deeded to the Otselic Valley Railroad, running North to South. This very same parcel of land deeded here by Elwin Stevens to William Trass was then turned over by MR. Trass to Leemon Ray Cossitt. More of this at the latter pages of the book.

38. The OTSELIC VALLEY RAIL ROAD

SYRACUSE DAILY JOURNAL LAST EDITION VOL.LIII.-NO.184 WEDNESDAY AUG. 4, 1897

BINGHAMTON INTERESTED: BUSINESS MEN LOOK WITH FAVOR ON THE PROPOSED OTSELIC VALLEY RAILROAD. Binghamton, Aug.4 1897 -

The Binghamton Board of Trade is becoming interested in the proposed Otselic Valley Railroad, which would extend from this city to Madison County. It is probable that a special meeting of the board will be called on some evening the last of this week for the purpose of discussing this project and trying to determine what steps can be taken to go by way of Castle Creek instead of running parallel to the Delaware, Lackawanna & Western as far as Whitney's Point.

Several business men of this city are interested and it is thought that the project will soon surmise definite shape. It is understood that capitalists living at the upper end of the proposed route are ready to help build the road; and the farmers along the way are said to be enthusiastic over the subject, many of them having offered to donate the right of way, and some of them being ready to assist in the grading of the line.

General Edward F. Jones and the other members of the board of trade believe it will be possible to interest Binghamton business men so their northern neighbors can be met halfway in the effort to build the line, which would practically open up a new country and could not help but be of great benefit to this city. They are anxious that everyone who is interested in the subject will attend the meeting which will be called later.

Note: Now, this news article was from 1897. If we back track on the Plank Road abandonment and Company dissolution record, and connect that event with this OVRR, was the same route used? Was this a repurpose of that right of way?

1865, July 19 Recorded: 21 July 1865 The Georgetown and Otselic Plank Road Company filed a dissolution. Book 2 of Registry of Incorporations.

OTSELIC VALLEY RAIL ROAD COMPANY CERTIFICATE OF INCORPORATION:

1906 October 01 Certificate of Incorporation Filed: Recorded on 08 Oct. 1906

Instrument # 1906- 00000015 Seq. 1- 3

This incorporation document attests to the fact that the news articles are based on written, recorded facts, that we can all still review at this generation. We owe our gratitude to the taxpayers that funded the people that maintained, and still do take care that these documents be made available for use today in their truest forms, accurately.

The following compiled copied news articles from the digitized newspaper / micro film version brought forth by the humanitarian efforts of gargantuan proportions that understanding be made more available in today's technological reach, and the kindness of MR. Tryniski, Fulton, NY. The website being www.fultonhistory.com.

1906, October 04 Madison County Leader and Observer Georgetown Trolley Road

The Otselic Valley Railroad Company who wants to operate a surface road from South Otselic, Chenango County, to Georgetown Station, Madison County, a distance of twelve miles, was incorporated Monday with a Capital of $120,000. The principal office will be located at South Otselic. Among the directors are B.F. Gladding, E.J.Stack, M.K.Perkins, D.W. Crumb, R.R. Brown, all of South Otselic.

Note: Was this title an issue of rhetorical semantic? Was this Trolley Road one of the purposes this right of way had been used?

1906, October 25 Gleaner News of DeRuyter

Building the Otselic Trolley destroyed this issue: the order for the long legal did not come until last evening and it must go in this week or the road be blockaded.

1906, November 15 DeRuyter Gleaner South Otselic News Happenings of the Past week at the Burgh

Nov. 18 - It is expected that the grading for the Otselic Valley Railroad will be completed from the station to Georgetown Village tomorrow. Rails will be laid at once. Will Brown joins the construction gang Wednesday.

1907, January 17 Thursday. The Cincinnatus Times Vol.09 Number 33 Cincinnatus, Cortland County, NY. L.D. Blanchard, Editor

The Otselic Valley Railroad - At a special meeting of the Directors of the Otselic Valley Railroad Co., held at their office at South Otselic, NY., on Jan.09,1907, the following resolution was unanimously passed.

Whereas, W.F. Wenright was elected at a regular meeting of the Board of Directors of the Otselic Valley Railroad Co., to the Office of General Manager and whereas he has been guilty of misconduct and has violated the trusts reposed in him, in that he has conducted the business of the Otselic Valley Railroad Co., in a careless negligent illegal and improper manner, in that he has through his mismanagement and misconduct ruined the financial credit of the corporation, it is therefore Resolved, that the said W.F. Wenright be and hereby is removed from the office of General Manager of the said Otselic Valley Railroad Co.,for cause, and that all his powers, and duties as such hereby revoked.

It appears that for some time, the directors of the Otselic Valley Railroad Co., have been dissatisfied with the management of the company's affairs by Mr. Wenright, with above action as the result. It is only fair to Mr. Wenright to say that he is absent at the present time & therefore is not in a position to defend himself. It was also voted to discontinue work on the railroad for a time until the affairs of the company are straightened out.

The directors are very pleased with the progress made on the construction, and with the grading nearly half completed, a third of the track laid, and the right of way nearly all provided for, there appears no doubt but the road will be completed this summer. - Otselic Valley News.

1907, January 24 Madison County Leader and Observer Morrisville NY
Georgetown Station
Work on New Railroad to be Resumed Feb. 1st - Apparent lack of Funds
Jan. 21 - Messrs B.F. Gladding, C.H. Woodly and Frank Jackson came up the new line of railroad from South Otselic the other day and gathered in the surplus tools etc., that were left scattered along the highways and hedges by the workman.

Work on the Otselic Valley railroad was suspended two weeks ago for various reasons, the principal one being that there were no funds in sight with which to pay the workmen. It is predicted however, that on or about Feb.1st matters will be so arranged that the work can be pushed to completion, if so desired by those who are most nearly connected with the undertaking.

1909, January 28, Madison County Leader and Observer, Morrisville NY
Georgetown: Who owns the O.V.R.R. Rails?

January 27 - An attempt is being made by the New York Central people to remove the rails from the right of way from the defunct Otselic Valley railroad. When the road was built two years ago the rails were shipped subject to a sight draft attached to the bill of lading. but the wily " Capt." Wenright succeeded in laying them without making payment. The railroad company had to settle and therefore claim the rails. An attempt is also being made by the stockholders of the road to stop the work.

1911, July 20 Thursday DeRuyter Gleaner Vol. 33 No. 45 $1.50/ yr
Local Views of Interest to the Summer Visitor

The orders issued by Judge Lyon requiring certain parties to testify before the Referee Eugene Clinton concerning the property and affairs of the Otselic Valley Railroad Company, was affirmed by the Appellate Division and the first hearing was held at Cazenovia Friday.

1911, September 28 Thursday DeRuyter Gleaner Page 7
County Tax Sale Georgetown

Description of lands in the town of Georgetown Madison County assessed in the 1910, Otselic Valley Railroad bounded and described as follows: North by the NY Central Chenango Branch R.R. the same being 30 feet east and west, east by all lands and village lots upon said railroad to a highway running east and west from Brown School house to Phillips' Mills, south by the said highway 30 feet west by all lands and village lots on said railroad the same being 5 and 1/2 miles roadbed

tax.................$117.50

1912, April 04 Thursday Morning Madison County Leader and Observer Morrisville, NY
Twenty - Seventh Year No. 43

• What appears to be the last chapter in the more or less stormy career of the famous Otselic Valley railroad is about to be written. The receiver, Eugene Clinton of Norwich has contracted for the removal of the rails with Edward Andrus of this place.They are to be sold for old iron.

1912, May 16 Thursday Morning. Madison County Leader and Observer Morrisville, NY. Twenty-Seventh Year No. 49

May 15

• The right of way and steel of the famous Otselic Valley railroad will be sold at public auction at the depot on Saturday, May 18th, by the receiver, Eugene Clinton of Norwich.

1912, May 28? Thursday Morning

Madison County Leader and Observer Morrisville, NY Thursday Morning May 2ε, 1912 Twenty-Seventh Year No. 50

GEORGETOWN OTSELIC RAILROAD

Partially Completed Line of Defunct Company Sold at Auction

Of the latest procedure in the affairs of the Otselic Valley Railway Company, and which have been in the courts for several years, or since the project died aborning, through the promoter of the road absconding, our Georgetown Station Correspondent writes:

Public sale of the Otselic Valley Railroad property was made at this point on Saturday by the receiver, Eugene Clinton, Esq., of Norwich. After closing out the rails, the right of way was sold to the highest bidder the aggregate amount for both sales totaling $4,500. A proposition was then made to combine both sales and bid on the whole in a lump, with the result that the property was sold for $4,740 to Louis Sarachan, representing the Rochester Iron and Metal Company of that city. Besides Eugene Clinton and Judge Straton of Norwich, and Judge M.H. Kiley of Cazenovia, there were men representing various interests from Rochester, Syracuse, Cazenovia, Hamilton, South Otselic, Utica. Thus ends the dreams of the dreams of the promoters of this deal, whereby many a poor man was badly taken in, besides some others with ample funds to fall back on. The sale of the Otselic Valley Railroad property will not be considered final until confirmed by the courts having jurisdiction over the matter. Local interests were well represented at the sale.

Says our local correspondent: "The right of way, rails and all that remain of the defunct Otselic Valley railroad were sold by the receiver, Eugene Clinton at the depot here Saturday, to the Rochester Iron and Metal company for $4,740. Several parties here and at South Otselic are heavy losers in the company, chiefly through the operations of Capt.' Wainright who promoted the road."

Of the sale and future prospects of the enterprise, Monday's Utica Press has the following:

"Nathan & Kowalsky of this city are among the purchasers of the South Otselic Railroad, which was sold at Georgetown, Madison county, Saturday. The sale was made by Eugene Clinton of Norwich, one of the receivers of the railroad company. The road was sold for about $5,000. The railroad purchased has been in the hands of receivers for the last two years. It was the plan of the promoters of the road to make a steam connection between Georgetown, Madison county and South Otselic. The company secured rights of way over 14 miles and made payments to about 40 farmers for land required for the construction of the line. In all, about $40,000 was put into the construction work and securing the necessary land, but the company went into the receiver's hands before the road was put into operation. For the last two years, the receivers have been in charge of the road waiting with the hope that some way could be devised to put the proposed line in operation. However, they soon tired of this game, and the road was offered for sale at public auction. The highest bid was made by A.E. Nathan of this city. Besides Nathan & Kowalsky, the purchasers included Louis Sarchan of Rochester, and Horton Brothers of Syracuse. Last evening, Mssers. Nathan & Kowalsky said that they had no plans as to the future management of the company, nor had they determined when the effort to set the line in operation would be made."

The news clips were arranged in the chronological dates and years of appearance. By the raw articles themselves, and without further elaboration, I feel that they sanctimoniously tell the complete picture. I believe that by the readers reading them first hand here as if in a scrapbook, there can be higher possibilities of being transported to the era that once was, and be immersed in the experience.

Let the imagination be in a creative mode to lift the Spirit of making a positive difference. In one's own life, with others, for others. The ripples would radiate bigger and wider. Think of the many lives that would be touched, constructively changed, economically modified, and wonderfully transformed. Let us live up to the Spirit of Giving, sharing, of moving forward. From the ashes of failures, we can all learn not to repeat them, and keep the hope active. Alive.

Again, the question of: Is this why the plank road is not in the map nor part of the taxed description of the parcels of this Site? As an exemption?

In the quest for an answer to why the rest of the deeded descriptions are not accounted for in taxation maps; and being threatened to be totally unaccounted for in the commissioned land survey; the inevitable cross referencing of what the Law that guide the privilege of property ownership say is consulted.

Here is one of the many NY laws and regulatory measures to protect the integrity of property investments and safeguard from the age old trickery practiced by those people that subscribe to fraud, forgery, land grab, robbery and other forms of making the lives of those individuals aspiring to be responsible, law abiding citizens difficult.

RPTL § 489 - dd. *Exemption of railroad real property from taxation*

1   Subsidized railroad real property shall be exempt from taxation. The exemption shall be granted each year only upon
(a) application by the owner of said property on a form prescribed by the commissioner and
(b) Submission of proof as may be required by the commissioner that the property is subsidized rail road real property. The application and proof shall be filed with the appropriate assessing authority on or before the appropriate taxable status date, with copies thereof simultaneously filed with the commissioner and the department of transportation.

2   Bridges, viaducts and other similar structures constructed on or after January first, 1959 as the result of the creation, pursuant to article 12-B of the highway law, of a new highway, street, or roadway shall be exempt from taxation. No assessment of any bridges, viaducts, and other similar structures lengthened or reconstructed on or after January 01, 1959 as the result of the widening, relocation, or reconstruction of an existing highway, street, or roadway pursuant to article 12-B of the highway law, shall be increased by reason of such reconstruction or relocation, not withstanding the provisions of any general, special, or local law to the contrary; provided, however, that the assessment on the original portion of such bridges, viaducts and other similar structures may be varied in accordance with the changes made generally in assessments on other local real property. Whenever any new construction of property is exempt pursuant to the provisions of this subdivision and the provisions of subdivisions of subdivision 6 or 7 of this section, such property shall receive the exemption provided by subdivision 6 or 7 of this section.

Note: There is a whole topic on laws that governed railroads: dispersal, repatriation, repurposing, lease, sales of the rights of ways. For this particular instance; the Otselic Valley Railroad Company was a locally owned company that intended to connect with the already running Georgetown Station 3 miles or so from the 4 cornered Main St.

39. ROW: Rights of Ways

1944, April 26 Liber 339 pp. 19 - 23 Edson R. Miner & wife, Luella Miner to Harold J. Evans:

This particular deed is crucial when it comes to the legacy of Leemon Ray Cossitt to the House. This is brought here in this chapter and may be construed as too early, but there is no such thing as too early to talk about rights of way. It is important then, today, and in the successive years in the future. This would pop its very important head again when you come to ask for Occupancy Minimum and Maximum.

This is particularly directly proportional and related to this ROW and square footage. The following excerpted descriptions of ROW[Right of Way] allow for the two parcels of Leemon Ray to be accessible being situated in a land locked position. The Ingress and Egress were then provided for here allowing passage but not ownership of the land tract. 1947, Land parcel of 1 & 1/2 acres, from Harold J. Evans and the 1939 Land parcel of 2 acres that had the remnants of the Otselic Valley Railroad, & Plank Road histories.

"... Also all that right of way and easement situate in the Town of Georgetown, County of Madison and State of New York, briefly bounded and described as follows: "
1919,   Description 1

A   "... Being a right of way with wagons, teams loads and machinery, automobiles and all farm vehicles and loads along the easterly side of the lands deeded by Arthur J. Yale & wife to Alfred Moore by deed dated on the 21st day of June, 1919."
B   "... Said right of way to be open at all times."

1920,   Description 2
A   "... Being the ROW with wagons, teams, loads & machinery, automobiles & all farm vehicles & loads along the westerly side of the lands deeded by Delia E. Andrus to first parties..."

[in this case Edson R. & Luella Miner who was now at this point 1944 was transferring it to Harold J. Evans]

1920, June 02 Liber 255 p. 370 Recorded: 1920 Aug. 20 Delia E. Andrus to Edson R. &
Luella Miner

B   "this ROW to be used in common by all parties to this instrument and none of them to blockade the same or permit vehicles to remain therein so as to impede the ROW of the others. The ROW hereby conveyed is to be exercised by second parties only between the buildings on the premises of first parties as they now stand and the westerly side of first parties."

1921,   Description 3

A   "The ROW hereby conveyed extends from the highway no. Of first parties premises to the lands of second parties lying south of the premises of first parties and may be used by second parties at any and all times but conveys no title to lands and conveys only the right of way, privilege and easement as heretofore described, to and from the highway and the lands of the second parties."

B   "Being the same premises conveyed by W. F. Woodman, Lottie A. Woodman & Clarence A. Parker to B. Treat Miner & Edson R. Miner, 1921 Aug. 19 Liber 259 p. 327."

1921,   Who is this ROW for?

" The lands over which ROW & easement is conveyed is of the following dimensions, viz: three cornered in size 9 feet on the south side and running to a point on the north side and taken from the S.E. Corner of the lands deeded to Moore by Yale by the deed aforesaid,
the distance on the west side to be 99 feet and on the east side a very little less and this right of way is to be exercised by second parties only over the three cornered parcel above described the right of way so conveyed not extending to the highway north of the premises deeded to Moore by Yale but only 90 feet from the south side thereof. Being the same premises conveyed by Alfred Moore and wife to B. Treat Miner and Edson R. Miner, etc.1921, Aug. 19 Liber 268 p. 146."

Note: So from the above descriptions, are ROWs now sinking as true evidence as to the advancement of thinking, foresight for progress of the people of old? To the point that we have not even come close. Why? That right of way is in question. It is missing.

Here is a copy of the law so you can have them at your fingertips while you read this work. Please feel free to double check and add to this on this Site's upcoming legitimate blog space, and or vital traditional mail or in person. Especially, when we open the site.

RPL Article 9 Recording Instruments affecting Property
§ 335-a   Easements of Necessity

The owner of any lot, plot, block, site of other parcel of real estate being a subdivision or part of a subdivision of any larger parcel or parcels of real property shown upon a map of said parcel or parcels of real property and its subdivision or subdivisions, filed in the office of the county clerk or of the register of deeds of the county where the property is situated, prior to the sale or conveyance of such lot, plot, block, site or other parcel, or subdivision thereof by the seller thereof, upon which map any road or street is indicated or shown as giving access to or egress from any public road or street to such lot, plot, block, site or other parcel of real estate thereon indicated or to any part thereof, sold or granted after such filing, and the owner of any lot, plot, block, site or other parcel of real estate, <u>the conveyance whereof shall specifically give the right of access to or egress from the same by any private road or street over lands belonging to the maker of such conveyance and which road or street is described in such conveyance, may, when necessary to the enjoyment of the lot, plot, block or site or other parcel of real estate so sold or conveyed and when the same is not bounded by a public road, lay, beneath the roads or streets indicated and shown upon such map or described in such conveyance as giving access to or egress from any public road to such property so sold or conveyed as aforesaid, wires and conduits for the purpose of supplying the said property with electric light and telephone service.</u> Such wires or conduits shall be laid only on condition that the private roads or streets on which the owner has the right of access to or egress from such property shall be restored as nearly as possible to their original condition and that the person or persons entitled to the fee of such private roads or streets or having an easement over the same shall be compensated for actual damage occasioned by laying of such wires or conduits.

Nothing herein contained shall be deemed to affect in any manner lands acquired by the city of New York for the purpose of construction or development of its water supply system.

Add, L 1923, ch 785, eff May 24, 1923.

Note:

This is for the Ingress and egress: ROW. I have placed this copy of these laws to lay credence to the thoughtful act of respect I had bestowed to the adjoined property owners by communicating the interest of asking where the boundaries are, if there is a possibility I can have access of having the delivery trucks of materials, tools and workforce be able to use the rights of way, much more to double check where the heart of the people would be regarding this Site. As the attuned reader can probably discern, these things did not go very well.

RPAPL § 881.   *Access to adjoining property to make improvements or repairs*

When an owner or lessee seeks to make improvements or repairs to real property so situated that such improvements or repairs cannot be made by the owner or lessee without entering the premises of an adjoining owner or his lessee, and permission to enter has been refused, the owner or lessee seeking to make such improvements or repairs may commence a special proceeding for a license so to enter pursuant to article four of the civil practice law and rules. The petition and affidavits, if any shall state the facts making such entry necessary and the date or dates on which entry is sought. Such license shall be granted by the court in the appropriate case upon such terms as justice requires. The licensee shall be liable to the adjoining owner or his lessee for actual damages occurring as a result of the entry. Add, L 1968, ch 220, eff Apr 11, 1968.

Note: This reinforces the ROW on RPL Article 9 Recording Instruments affecting Property § 335-a Easements of Necessity.

Remember Natalie Wood in " Splendor in the Grass?" This movie have parallels with the story of this site. At the end of the movie, Natalie came back to her parents home in the same town to see the boy Buddy once more, to check whether the sparks of young love is still there.

This parallel can be the developmental stage for this Site to be in. From the unique vantage view, as an owner of a beautiful human masterpiece; as the barefoot and neophyte Museologist; as the Educator and a Student of Life: this is the chance for everyone concerned that have or are having interests in this site to either welcome the Truth of the facts, and have them be immortalized on the ground up; or continue the miserable depressed mood of the Town as is.

That other choice is to continue what you have been doing which places you in the wrong side of that authentic history, the facts of which I have pieced out here for your convenient perusal. You then create a new truthful history attesting that you chose to be in that wrong side of History by keeping this Truth, erased, defaced, replaced. In short, you impeded, halted and stopped the progress of the truth in exchange to have your personal vested interests be served. That is fraud, forgery, lying, cheating, being deceitful, stealing. Check for your selves.

While that is totally different from repurposing the site. Before you can repurpose, you have to take account stock, lock, and barrel of what was there. This truth is the stock, lock, and barrel. That is what inventory is. This is therefore what can be the catalogue raissone for this Magnificent Masterpiece. The acreages are the canvass. An adept registrar is taking stock, at your service. Your skills and assistance to ensure that quality check is in place is necessary, Asap. Thank you.

40.　Elwin & Bertha with Frances

Plate 58- 0525　The Elwin Stevens' Family

Resurreccion Dimaculangan

Timeline Trace:

1906   Under the Administrative Role of his Father's Landholdings
            with the Guardianship of his Mother, Julia.

1907   Accident at the hand car on the OVRR.

1909   Goal to attend the Geneva School of Automotive Engineering.
            Mrs. Elwin Stevens played the piano in a Play at the House.
            Played a role as one of the " Darkies" in a Play at the House.

1912   Mrs. Elwin Stevens visited her parents for a week stay.

1917   Land Sales to MR. William Trass.

1920   Mrs. Elwin Stevens was acting the role of Head of the Family.
            Elwin Stevens would have been in a permanent meeting with his Creator.

1925   Set to receive $60.00 from the Will of MR. George Stevens[27]. Mrs. Elwin
            Stevens & daughter Frances would have received it by then.?

Frances: what happened to her? Did she live a life equivalent to any that had lost a father at a very young age? Were there descendants of her still living today in Georgetown? If there were: I wonder what they feel about the buy - out? Do they have misgivings being that all these happened when she was a baby, and if so how were these emotions demonstrated? If not, and if they are interested in sharing their story, this would be a wonderful way to start a conversation, and to have their up close account of their end of the story come full circle with the deeded records. History based on facts.

In the meantime, the reminder that all the personalities and characters whose stories intertwined with the six deeds of Historic Site 06000160 would have their own platform of exposure after the completion of this Project. Contributors, welcome.

_____

[27] Liber 278 p.27

173

Plate 59-0528   Julia Stevens' Family

41. Death 3

Again, another widow too early, too young, too soon, and a very infant daughter to be left without a father. Now, we have all the female characters together - in mourning.

Julia just lost her husband, now her son.

Alice lost a father, now her only brother.

Frances, an infant lost a father.

Bertha had a very precarious situation to handle, if she was not careful.

The fact that Bertha was able to act as the next in line to Elwin showed that she stepped up for the position and came out a winner? The winning part of each individual is quite not the scope of this book for analysis at this point.

That Bertha was able to handle the situation on the level, and with strength, and determination, as the up close examination of the documents revealed, have to suffice for now.

Let's take a look back, and have a moment of Silence for the family then, and the families that Today, in our generation experience the same; are in the same situation, or had been in similar circumstance. Today, we remember and take account the blessings that were brought by the lives lived, by the people that had walked the Journey in the celebration of human life ahead of us.

42. Heirs & Inheritance

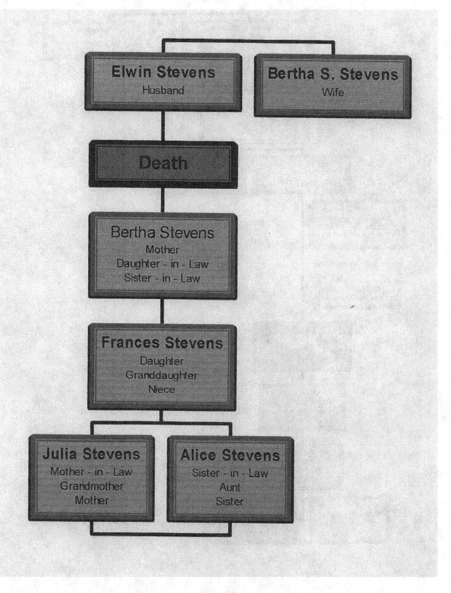

Plate 60   The Death of EHS

Understanding how the Chauncey G. Stevens Family evolved into the Elwin H. Stevens Family: and moving forward. The Interrelationship chart at a glance:

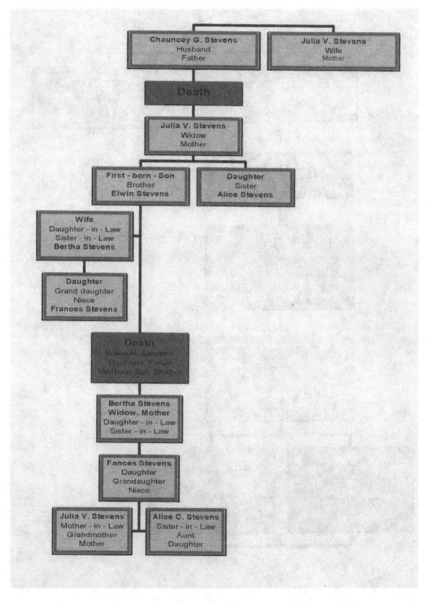

Plate 61 Charting Two Deaths

OWNERSHIP TRACE

The Rigours of Life Changing Decisions when faced with CrossRoads in the Nineteen - twenty.

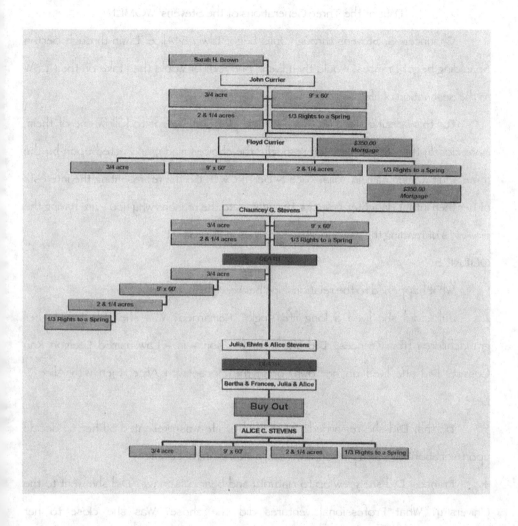

Plate 62 Charting 7 Transfers, 3 Deaths

Sarah H. To Alice

43. Bertha & Frances, with Julia & Alice

Four of the Three Generations of the Stevens' WOMEN:

Chauncey G. Stevens through Julia begot Elwin & Alice. Elwin through Bertha Spaulding begot Frances. Would they live in one roof or would they take on the NESW as the destination of life?

For this specific story, in this historical platform, we got to follow one of them, more closely than the others. Interestingly, the choices made, and acted upon by the three adult women namely Julia, Alice & Bertha, with Bertha representing the interests of her then infant daughter Frances, brought us to the reasons why you - are having the privileges of reading these wonderful story lines in this format.

QUERIES:

1   What happened to the relationships between these relations?

2   Julia: did she lived a long life single? Remarried? Was she able to see her grandchildren from Frances? Did she meet the son - in - Law named Leemon Ray Cossitt? Did she lived on her own, or in the House with Alice, then with Alice & Lee?

3   Bertha: Did she remarried? What kind of life was presented to her to decide upon, vocation wise, as a person, a woman, a mother in that circa?

4   Frances: Did she grew up to maturity and bear offsprings? Did she went to the University? What Professional ventures did she chose? Was she close to her Grandmother Julia, and aunt Alice? Does she have living descendant today?

5   Alice: would be mentioned in the context of House / Estate ownership, and as part of the quest to clear the acreage inheritance of the Magnificent House.

Plate 63-0530 Three Women & A Baby: Mourning

44. Mrs. Elwin Stevens[28]: BERTHA

Bertha was the Daughter of Mr. & Mrs. Charles J. Spaulding[29], originally of Sauquoit, NY. Records showed land holdings[30] of Charles J. Spaulding adjoined the Chauncey G. Stevens' Estate.

1912, Bertha Spaulding & Elwin Stevens had moved to the house vacated by Mr. & Mrs. H. R. Perry on West Street. That was in April. By May that year, Mrs. Elwin Stevens spent a week with her parents.

1920, was a very important year for all the central characters of this Story of Owners for the Magnificent House. Records of deeds dated August 28 of this year were acted upon by the four female Stevens': devoid of Elwin which had been Head of the Family. For Bertha to have had taken that role meant that Elwin had submitted his Earthly presence on a permanent leave of absence. Sad as that may, there were then four more lives to move the cause of making a positive difference, and funds could not hurt to have at every one's disposal. This is especially true with a child in tow. The scenario, a mother & sister in law. A young mother & her infant daughter. Where to live? How to move on? Case in point: Dispersion of Assets. By the heir & inheritance hierarchy; through the documents available and excerpted in the many pages here, we realize fully that Bertha assumed the role of Head of the family as the spouse of Elwin, and the mother of his heir.

---

[28] Madison County Leader and Observer Morrisville, NY Thursday Morning April 4, 1912. Twenty - Seventh Year No. 43.

[29] Madison County Leader and Observer Morrisville, NY Thursday Morning May 16, 1912. Twenty - Seventh Year No. 49.

[30] refer to Liber 883 pp. 190-191 first paragraph.

Two land sales transactions happened that year, 28 August. One of them was the crux of the climactic backdrop of why we have the story that we currently have.

Plate 64-0665 A Young Widow & a Baby

45. Assets & Dispersion

1920, August 28 Bertha Stevens, individually and as Special Guardian
of Frances Stevens, an infant; heirs at law
Julia V. Stevens, *Alice C. Stevens*, next of kin of
Chauncey G. Stevens, all reside at Georgetown, Madison Co., NY
to **B. Treat Miner, Edson R. Miner** for $1, 500.00 Liber 262 p.192

"... Also another piece or parcel of land being part of the Southeast quarter of Lot 91 in said Town and bounded as follows: Beginning at the south east corner of Wm. P. Hare's Village lot thence to the South East corner of lands formerly owned by Wm. Way, Thence Westerly along the south line of land formerly owned by said Wm. Way and George W. Harris land to the center of the highway. Thence Southerly along the center of the highway to the North line of Harriet Curtis land, Thence, Easterly along the North line of said lot to the North east corner of said lot. Thence Southerly to the South East corner of Harriet Curtis lot, thence Easterly to the place of beginning, being the Village lot formerly owned and occupied by Moseley & Hare...

...Excepting and always reserving from the above described land a certain piece or parcel situate on lot No. 91 which is fully described in a certain deed made by Ebinezer Moseley to Zinah J. Moseley and Wm. W. Hare dated Sept. 26th. 1850, and recorded in the Clerk's Office in Madison County on the 11th. day of Nov. 1850 in B.O. of Deeds at page 516, said land being the Village lot on which the dwelling house and barn originally stood containing one rood and eleven and 2/10 rods of land..."

Note: A bundled land sales of lots 92, 91,104. Lot 91 exception, Check the BO. p. 516, please! Division of property to move lives forward. This is a story in itself.

XIV. The 1920 Buy - Out:

1920, August 28   from Bertha Stevens, individually and as Special Guardian
of Frances Stevens, an infant
Julia V. Stevens, *Alice C. Stevens*, heirs at law and next of kin of
Chauncey G. Stevens, all reside at Georgetown, Madison Co., NY
to **Alice C. Stevens** for $700.00 Liber 262 p. 276

"...described as follows: being all the premises deeded to Sarah H. Brown, May 5,1885 and recorded in Madison County Clerk's office May, 14th, 1885 at 9 o' clock A.M. in liber 163 at page 155, and bounded on the North by lands owned by the Baptist Church Society, Esat by lands formerly owned by Mary M. Ellis, on the South by lands formerly owned by Russell Whitmore; on the West by the center of the highway, being a part of lot no. 91 of said town containing three fourths of an acre of land more or less.

Also all that tract or parcel of land deeded by the Trustees of the First Baptist Society of said Town to Timothy Brown on the 15th day of August, 1882 and recorded in the Clerks Office of the County of Madison on the 5th. day of August, 1884 at 11 o'clock A.M. in liber 161 at page 20.

Also all that other piece or parcel of land deeded by Zinah J. Mosley, Milton D. Allen and Mary his wife, Isaac Fletcher and Mercy his wife to said Sarah H. Brown, on the 22nd day of March 1871 and recorded in the Clerk's Office of the County of Madison on the 30th day of March, 1871 at 11 o' clock A. M. in book no. 123 of deeds at page 347.

Also the rights and privileges in and to a certain Spring of Water which was conveyed to the said Sarah H. Brown, by a deed from Hiram A. Atwood, and wife, and George Curtis and wife and recorded in the Clerks Office of the County of Madison on the 14th day of May, 1885 at 9 o'clock A.M. in liber 162 of deeds at page 140 to which said deed reference is hereby made for a more particular description of said water rights."...

Notarized 28th Aug. 1920. Recorded: 01 October 1920, 9 AM

Note: This brilliant move of Alice is best understood in the context of what goes on in the 20's at large.

So many things went on. If by the 1912, Elwin had married Bertha, and was able to enter into business transactions by the 1917, then we can deduce that Alice, the younger, and only sister would be in her age of majority by the 1920 as well. Still, if we consider the time, how women were treated, and what accepted roles they had undertaken to move within the dictates of Society then: It is my belief that there were difficulties.

Nevertheless, if we put these challenges with in the bounds of Georgetown, NY, that may not be as hard. Especially, the Stevens were highly regarded, and with their recorded landholdings, can be construed even in today's standards as prominent citizens of the area. Such is the wide angle I perceive this story of Alice Stevens.

Of course, every character brought forth here can be further discussed in their own merits and I do not have to be the only one. This Project was embarked upon with the wholesome intent to inspire others to share factual records for further understanding, and cross fact checking of the True Story.

Meanwhile, the topic here is the accounting of the collected, collective acreage inheritance of this Magnificent Structure. Let us stay in focus, and center our attention to the actions of the people that made this Structure the point of our discussions here.

Through the virtue of marriage, the sister in - law Bertha took over the role of the spouse, which is the brother of Alice. As head of the family, the issue of fiscal sustainability was foremost. With a child, a mother in - law, and a sister - in law: the division of interests had to be resorted and moving on forward be planned at best. The shares for the House as part of the property to be divided was at hand.

How do you divide the home that Alice, and her mother lived on into 3 shares? The third share now had to be shared into two, as Elwin's share goes to Bertha his wife, and then of course daughter Frances. The answer? Liquidation. To sell.

Plate 65-0522   Alice Stevens

If you are the one living in the comforts of a beautiful home, would you not try to continue doing so? What recourse? Buy out the ones that needed the liquid share of the solid asset. This was what Alice Stevens did. Anyhow, all of them can still live under the same roof.

The point of interest now is: Did the four of them live under one roof after Elwin died? Remember, Bertha had a very wholesome family as well.

What roles could the Spaulding family may have played in the lives of their young widowed daughter and beautiful grand daughter? To deduce all the positives here:

They doted on Frances.

They comforted Bertha.

Had Bertha embarked on a Career? Remember she was an accomplished musician - a pianist. She had performed in the Theatrical Production. What about Alice? Did she go to College, or the University? Julia? Apart from the management of the Household that got extended, did she pursue any other professional or Personal life goals? Frances? Did she grow up and carried on the legacy of the Stevens and the Spaulding Family?

What happened to these people after? Any one can continue the story from here. Meanwhile: Let us take a look at the document transcribed. A really good look.

These documents dated the same and completed the same time tell of different parcels that should not be confused about.

The changing of the Guards. Yes. I consider this move of Alice Stevens to be as that. The next generation of Stewardship to the House and the Estate.

Alice had the foresight to know that she was not only taking on the property of her father Chauncey, but the History of the Town entwined with the Legacy of the Brown Estates as well.

What is $800.00 in the 1920's?

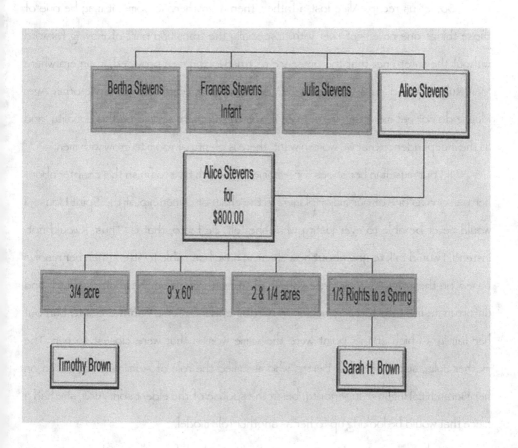

Plate 66 An investment with Historic Resonance.

The sound waves still felt strongly today.

XV. Alice C. Stevens[31]

So, let us recap. Alice lost a father, then a brother. To some, it may be one of those things one never get over with. Especially the transition part of moving forward without the safety net that the presence of trustworthy men provided, in an era where Men Ruled. Period. This was the generation trying to wean out of the Victorian Age. Please do not get me wrong here. Even if women say there should be this equality, and all the independence that we women want, there is plenty of room to grow with men.

If I put myself in her shoes for a moment, enough time to finish this chapter about her persona as one of our major players in the chain of ownership of the Spirit House, I would never be able to ever justify what she felt, de facto, that is. Thus, I would not. Instead, I would talk to you about how she may have been able to strengthen her resolve based on the tragic circumstances she had to go through by these unexpected, and unfortunate life transforming incidents. Factual evidence? She had the gall to buy out her family - which at this point were the same women that were closest to her. The mother Julia, sister - in - law Bertha who assumed the role of Administrator based on her hierarchical legatee superiority, being the spouse of the eldest son. Also, she had a niece that would be looking up to her as another role model.

This buy - out move is seen as a mark of great faith from all the other women, her mother and her sister- in - law. Indeed, the faith on her is apparent as to the following:

1   a very well placed vote of confidence to Alice,

2   and for Alice, a strong indicator of inner will of steel.

---

[31] A buyout move, a legal strategy; a very ballsy decision, from a Woman of great courage.

Even I, find that strategy remarkably brilliant. These elements were windows to the dynamics that swirled around her persona, and still is, as I read her today. This decision showed her to be a true blue blooded woman of substance. She knew what she want, she knew how to get them. Her priorities are clear, crystal. Am I seeing the DNA of Chauncey G. Stevens, the spirited and well landed gentry, an entrepreneur?!

We see here that she was decisive:

had foresight	sound judgement
strong resolve	well - placed faith in herself to carry on

Plate 67-0464 Daddy's Girl

XVI.   The Marriage

By now, we all know what she brought on the table when she partnered with Mr. Leemon Ray Cossitt. It was a fact that he was a widower, from Hamilton. He had landholdings in Georgetown. His business brought him there. After the death of the spouse, as the norm dictated, he would have gone through mourning with his children. This was expected then, even today. Although men were allowed a lot more leeway in everything during that time, as a key person in the community, I am sure he moved in the society with great consideration of the mores, and traditions. If it was not about himself, then surely for his children, as a role model, and as a successful entrepreneur. Then, Life went on.

So, the beauty and allure of a beautiful woman drew his attention. Big deal. What is there not to like in that circumstance? The courtship happened. The wedding, the ceremony, the romance. Here we are. The love story. I appreciate good ones. Even if any one person reading this is such a skeptic, kindly indulge me on this. There are no perfect people, nor perfect relationships. Correct. Taking an up close, and personal look on the facts of this union, the landholdings grew. The records said so. That is positive. With any venture rendered successful, there always were the positive machinery of support behind them. To this, everyone can agree.

From the Brown estate that Alice invested on, this union with Mr. Lee Cossitt expanded the landholdings of Alice with an additional two more land parcels. Remember the 1917 Elwin Stevens to William Trass sales transaction for two acres? The next change of hands for that property was William Trass to Leemon Ray Cossitt in 1939. This property adjoins the property of Alice that came from the Brown's. That is even more positive. This is construed as an expansion. A merger of landholdings.

Plate 68-0532 Leemon Ray & Alice

XVII. Leemon Ray Cossitt

♡♡♡♡♡♡♡♡♡♡♡♡♡♡♡♡♡♡♡♡♡♡♡♡♡♡♡♡♡♡♡♡♡♡♡♡

The man, I would not know. There are relations still around. They would be the better people to talk about him. As the human being behind the pages of the documents that had been archived and dusted off to be presented here. Here's few words choice words.

Lee & Lee

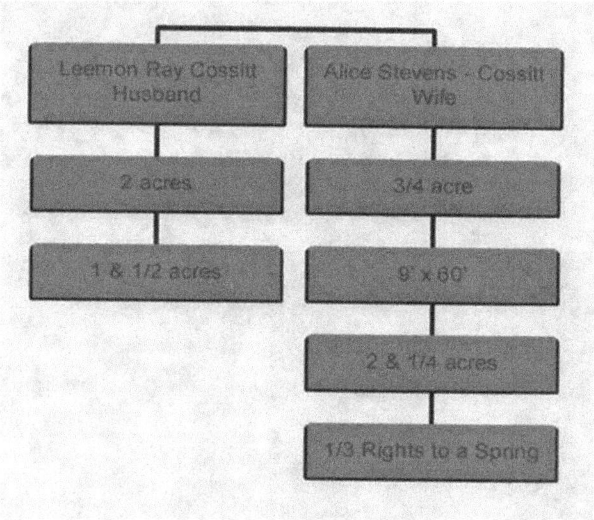

Plate 69   Solid Asset Inventory

There's Wisdom that come with the chronological maturation. Born out of experience came Honor & Respect bestowed to the woman that he married, and cherished. Alice in turn, found refuge, comfort, security in the arms; the strong arms of the man that filled her soul. What more to say that the deeds would not impart if the readers feel his presence in between the pages?!.

♡♡♡♡♡♡♡♡♡♡♡Merger☂of☂Landholdings♡♡♡♡♡♡♡♡♡♡♡♡♡

Plate 70-0624 Husband & Wife

XVIII.Parcel ONE of Mr. Cossitt's acreage legacy

An Inheritance. The one of two Land Parcels added to the Financial Assets' Story of the History of the House. The metes & bounds description is even to the .5 of a foot precision. The riveting story of a journey of this 1939 land purchase came back full circle to a Steven in 1955, via a love story that need be told and retold; not expunged. This chapter aim to Take a look at both of them, side by side by going over each one in comparison with some other land parcel descriptions that threatened to throw confusing details to the recorded, clear provenance of these two inherited land parcels of the Magnificent House - as a result of that Love Story shared by Leemon Ray & Alice. The final recording of that romance was deeded within the pages of the legal documents these land parcels came with, and upon which the couple based the sustenance of their lives on. It would be a total injustice to the sacrilege of LOVE, if their story be forever trampled.

1

A Microscopic Examination of the Leemon Cossitt Heritage, as added to the acreage inheritance of the Magnificent Structure owned by Timothy & Sarah H. Brown, then Alice Stevens - Cossitt.

2

If one would take the time to put the two deeds together, which was literally done here for a comparative fact check, and examine if you can decipher any differences, as the word descriptions had evolved; then cooler heads would prevail to better ably rationalize the truth. Here's the backtracked chain of that piece of land from MR. Trass, and how the detailed nuances can be unraveled that shed light to what transpired then.

Plate 71-0582   William Trass to L.R.Cossitt

46. A Microscopic Study of: Mr. Cossitt's acreage legacy: Parcel ONE

This parcel came full circle. It originated from 1917, Elwin Stevens to Mr. Trass. Then, twenty - two years after - in 1939, Mr. Trass sold it to Mr. Cossitt. Here it is:

1917, October 26   from Elwin H. Stevens, & Bertha M., his wife;
                    Julia V. Stevens, Alice C. Stevens Georgetown, Madison, NY
                    $300.00   Liber 250 p. 384
                    to William Trass, Georgetown, Madison, NY

"... being part of Lot 91...bounded as follows, Viz; Beginning at a stake on the North West corner of the lot, on B.E.Ross South line running then Easterly along B.E.Ross South line about 199 and a half feet to a stake, thence in a southerly direction about 323 feet to a stake, thence in a Northerly direction 309 feet on the East line of the old Cemetery to the North east corner of said Cemetery, thence West about 9 feet, thence Northerly about 97 feet to the place of beginning, containing about two acres of land be the same more or less...

Reserving therefrom a strip of land thirty feet wide deeded to the Otselic Valley Railroad Co. running across said lot from North to South, for and in consideration of the amount paid by the party of the second part, the parties of the first part agree to pay all damages that the Otselic Valley Rail Road Company or their successors to the above described property." Recorded: October 30th, 1907 at 9AM

So, did any one see any modifications on the descriptions? NO? Yes? If so, you can scribble them here and let us compare what we noticed ourselves, with what you have. If you did not see any, go over the pages again, please. That way, we can be interactive. Two heads are better than one. The more sets of eyes the better, and a space was left here for you:

—

—

—

From 1939 to Mr. Cossitt's death in 1954, it was 15 years he had possession of this farm, unto this day, this parcel had always been Mr. Leemon Cossitt's legacy to Mrs. Cossitt and to her assigns thereafter via legitimate land sales & transfers. Please do check it out here for a comparative look.

1939, June 27 Between William Trass to Leemon Ray Cossitt $250.00 Liber 330 p. 421
      Recorded 27 October 1941, 10:30 AM

"...All that tract, piece or parcel of land, situate in the Town of Georgetown, County of Madison, State of NY, described as follows: Being a part of Lot 91 of said town and bounded as follows: Beginning at a stake on the northwest corner of the lot now or formerly owned by Mrs. Fred Currier (formerly Ross) south line; running thence easterly along said Currier south line about 199 1/2 feet to a stake; thence in a southerly direction about 276 feet to the corner of lands formerly owned by H. H. Whitmore; thence in a westerly direction about 323 feet to a stake; thence in a northerly direction 309 feet on the east line of the old Cemetery to the northeast corner of said Cemetery; thence west about 9 feet; thence northerly 97 feet to the place of beginning, Containing about two acres of land be the same more or less....

Reserving therefrom a strip of land on the northerly end 65 feet wide on the west line and tapering 58 feet on east line..."

<u>Discerned Changes:</u>

The description from when Elwin Stevens worded this parcel, to the time MR. Trass described the same parcel, the following differences stand out:

A   1   The Reserved Portion ran North to South

       2   The reserved measurement is 30' wide

       3   The length of the reservation spanned the length of North to South

B   1   Reservation became East and West

       2   Reservation taken from the North end of the parcel

       3   The width and length changed

       4   65' W tapered to 58' E

46.1 Red Flags:

This parcel of land was rendered exception on the deeds of Harold J. Evans to the Miners, to the Chapin, to the current owners. MR. Cossitt procured, this one from MR. Trass. Surely, Integrity, Honesty and Transparency had been practiced then, as much as those traits are still valued today.?.

How can any owner miss these parcels for their own, or even as part of their own?

1990, August 07 Deed Image 3 of 6 Under Parcel Two it said:

"... beginning at the Southeast corner of the land (now or formerly) owned by L.R. Cossitt, and extending North from the line of the so - called Burgess farm at that point; along the East line of Village properties (now or formerly) owned by L.R.Cossitt, Frank L. Brown and Josephine F. Brown, his wife, Lyn D. Trass and..."

Book 0914 page 098. This parcel was used as a reference point. And so are these documents that repeated the same: 1

977, March 21 Mortgage Book 421 p.28 (Image 3 of 6) Digitized Format in Country Rec.

1977, March 21 Book of Deeds 697 p.741 (Image 3 of 6) Document digitized in County

46.2 Red Flags:

Second, this parcel is landlocked. How in the world was this farm land been used for lumber timber production, hauled the produce from the low lying flat land up to the higher ground? How were they transported, and which right of way was used?

Where did I get this information of lumber? That was the information given me by everyone I spoke with earliest of the " pre - ownership" data collection. Here is the legally accepted factual documentation for that ROW:

46.3 Red Flags:

Note: Again, This is the parcel that Leemon Ray Cossitt bought from William Trass. Mr. Trass bought this parcel in 1917 from Elwin Stevens. This particular parcel had been used as a monumental point of reference in the adjoined farm as shown in:

1990, August 07 Deed Book 0914 page 098, Image 3 of 6 Under Parcel Two it said:

"... beginning at the Southeast corner of the land (now or formerly) owned by L.R. Cossitt, and extending North from the line of the so - called Burgess farm at that point; along the East line of Village properties (now or formerly) owned by L.R.Cossitt, Frank L. Brown and Josephine F. Brown, his wife, Lyn D. Trass and..."

Book 0914 page 098, worded that this is owned by L.R Cossitt. Also found in the following digitized recorded documents:

1977, March 21 Mortgage Book 421 p.28 (Image 3 of 6) Digitized Format in the County Records. Charles D. Chapin & Elaine Mortgage to Leon E. Chapin & Ruth C.

1977, March 21 Book of Deeds 697 p.741 (Image 3 of 6) digitized format in the County Records. Leon Chapin & Ruth C. Chapin to Charles D. Chapin & Sarah Elaine.

Both documents above mentioned this Cossitt Parcel as the point of reference, cited as a monument for the land that was described. A boundary point. L.R. Cossitt's land was made the referenced point. How much more clearer one need, to lay off someone else's land, unless there is the sinister intention to bully, oppress, & practice prejudice?

This particular piece of land was used as a monumental reference point for the adjoined land. What could possibly be the rationale by this farmer, a key person in the community to claim that which does not belong to him by lawful property title / deeded ownership, by moral values, and if one would take his words of "never really cared about this Site"? Why the hostility of ripping the habilitation containment barriers, and having the commissioned survey put the pins in what is starkly clear land not belonging to him?

The Continuing Saga of Deceit, Cover - up, and a Spider web of Intrigues Continue. Should efforts in the Spirit of Making a Positive Difference be now Welcomed in Peace, to totally Rest these Inconsistencies to their irrevocable, irreversible END? These lies are too heavy a burden to be kept a rolling towards the future. Let us hold hands together and wash them off, sanitized the clean in an amiable, civilized, truthful legal fashion worthy of being marked HISTORIC.

STEP !:   Bring them all into the Open to be Oxidized.

STEP 2:   Recognition of the Errors and Omissions are crucial to:

STEP 3:   Identification of the ERRORS or INCONSISTENCIES.

STEP 4:   CAUCUS, this is where a DIALOGUE happens

STEP 5:   Airing of Grievances, Fears, and Concerns

STEP 6:   ANALYTICS, bringing everything into Perspective

STEP 7:   Finding WAYS to Bring them into the Plan

STEP 8:   ACTUALIZE the Conceptual Design addressing all PERSPECTIVES

STEP 9:   CARRY OUT the DESIGN

STEP 10:   Account the RESPONSIBILITIES

STEP 11:   CREDITS of Merits

STEP 12:   The Historic Site is OPEN for Revenue Generation & Service, to fund the CONSERVATION and PRESERVATION of the Structure and it's Legacy.

Bring them into the Open. So we can all understand one another.

Here are more articles clipped from the digitized version of the newspaper:

1946, October 11 Friday. The Cortland Democrat, Cortland, NY. Page Four Cincinnatus.
- 40 Years Ago - The Otselic Valley Railroad Company was incorporated with capital stock of $130,000. The proposed line was to run from South Otselic to Georgetown Station on the E.C. & N.

1911, September 28. DeRuyter Gleaner Page 7 County Tax Sale
- Description of lands in the Town of Georgetown County of Madison assessed in the year 1910 Otselic Valley Railroad bounded and described as follows: North by the N.Y. Central Chenango Branch R.R. the same being 30 feet east and west, east by all lands and village lots upon said railroad to a highway running east and west from Brown School House to Philips' Mills, south by said highway 30 feet west by all lands and village lots on said railroad, the same being 5½ miles roadbed.

<u>Why is the Otselic Valley Railroad of importance under the Heading "L. R. Cossitt?"</u>

I hope the readers remembered Elwin Stevens, and the role he played as the first born son after the demise of his father Chauncey Stevens. First born is not just a title and long words to be used to drag the pages along, but to express the importance of responsibilities the First Born have on their shoulders. The expectations, and the will to fill the boots of the father. There was pride in it then, and still so today, even if the father never made it home or have left the home. Elwin Stevens took the administrative stance in the estate and landholdings of his family when he turned the age of Majority.

There was the record of a sales transaction for two acres to William Trass with an annotation for a reserved portion. This was the same two acres that Leemon Cossitt bought from William Trass. Only this time, the reservation description annotated had evolved. It is interesting to take a microscopic look on the issue of Reservation from the Northern side of this property that is the "Ross' South line". For by the time Mr. Cossitt had the deed, there was no clear mention of what the Reserved portion was intended for. It was just that - Reserved.

Adjoining land owners and their representation, including the commissioned initial survey did not reflect, or should I word it here as "did not want to disclose" what that reservation was for. Multiple inquiries about it returned a shrug, a rolling of the eyeballs. Thus the tenuous back - search of the chain of ownership was embarked on. The legal responsibility to know what that reservation was for, and the goal of ensuring accurate Historical Documentation based on facts, merited this in - depth look. It was for the

"Otselic Valley Railroad".

The Railroad. This was the big secret, no one seemed to remember anymore. I wonder why? Is the over 100 yrs. old pain of the business gone bad still unoxidized? Can we find it in our hearts to open up for something positive to come out of that pain? Is growing up with wisdom from the past, long overdue? Improve lives instead of the pervasive practice of deceit and lies that get compounded with fraud and cover - ups. Wallowing on deep seated bitterness is bad. This is the truth that is as clear as the sun in the sky. Even mourning for the dead expires. We build memorials instead, to heal the pain. Join me in having those memorial markers installed without any air of negativity.

Anyhow, what I am accounting for are the deeded land acreages that lawfully, morally belonged to the House. This price had been paid for fair, and square. Let this Project move forward and you will see how all of you would have given yourselves the favor of having given a Project of Making a Positive Difference, a chance to touch your life, and one other life at a time.

WHAT happened to the Rights Of Way (ROW) after the purpose intended had outgrown itself? Of course, every legal question needs a competent legal Professional that goes by the title Lawyer, Attorney or Esquire. What I have here is the lay person's understanding of what the NY Blue book and other Books on Law explanations have made me understand. Such is the situation, and the perspective that I am writing these, about this topic here. Take them with a grain of salt. PLEASE Consult a very Competent Lawyer that specialized in the specific area of the issue in question. This my view based on the NY Law on the use of ROW. First the following elements have to be cleared:

1   method of acquisition

      1.A   legal procurement

      1.B   imminent domain

      1.C   donation, for the service and betterment of the public

      1.D   lease

2   This particular case of the Otselic Valley Rail Road Company had the Right Of Way (ROW) auctioned off.

      2.A   the Company can only auction what they owned via

          2.A.1 legally paid for procedure, straight bought out process

          2.A.2 not quite straight forward if by imminent domain

          2.A.3 return, Repatriation if terms of donation had a clause for it

          2.A.3.1 if total donation, unconditional gift without question, the Co. then gets to ownership mode (lawyers needed; in all the above cited scenarios anyway, to CYA - cover your ass, lawfully)

47. ROSS' SOUTH LINE: Trass' & Cossitts' NW Line

A small incision on the 1939 land purchase of Leemon Cossitts' description here merit an in depth look at where it is, to try to understand why is this land parcel and its measurements are being blurred on the taxation documents, and map. Then being totally unaccounted for in the commissioned survey, and ballistically being "word of mouth" thrown out there, as part of the next door farmer's land; or that he owns it.

<u>Ross South Line & Wm. P. Hare Lot, One & the Same:</u>

To trace the lineage of this line, a back search on the adjoined land ownership and titles had been made as well. It is inescapable. The end of Ross' South line is the start of Trass' & Cossitt's . The NW corner of the property, where the description is saying the parcel starts. See for yourselves how the descriptive details were written and how that very same description started to take a circuitous wording. Please notice the year when all the very roots of the problems enveloping this Historic Site's property started swirling its course. Compare that questionable part with all the other efforts to undermine the Brown - Stevens - Cossitt legacies as laid out within the other chapters here, and you may be surprised or not, how the occurrences all fall into the same range of timing.

Yes please, take out that sharpened pencil, the compass, grid lined paper, a protractor, and start drafting. You may as well contribute to the efforts being brought up here. If you do, please feel free to send it to the Project with all the information to credit you with. With our sincerest gratitude, on its way in advance.

For now, here is the order of people that owned the property from the time this 1917 & 1939 Deed of Leemon Ray Cossitt was drawn. The documents selected here reflect the chronological era of ownerships and the changes that occurred on that adjoined piece of land, documented to be Ross'.

1913, December 19   Luella H. Perry To Eunice F. Lamb Liber 240 p. 73 for $155.87

"... Being part of Lot No. Ninety - one (91) in said Town and situate in on the east side of the highway leading from the Village of Georgetown to Otselic and bounded as follows, viz: On the West by the center of the highway, on the North by lands of Herbert J. Brown and lands formerly owned by Milton D. Allen, on the East by lands formerly owned by Mary and Milton D. Allen, on the South by lands formerly owned by John Currier and Hiram Atwood. Being the same premises owned by Wm. P. Hare at the time of his decease.

Containing by estimation one acre of land be the same more, or less.

Reserving a strip of land (30) thirty feet wide deeded to the Otselic Valley Rail Road Company used for that purpose only.

This deed is given subject to certain Mortgages held by Zilpha Mack, George Griffith and E. F. Lamb,   Possession to be given March 31st 1914."

1913, December 19   Eunice F. Lamb & Addie E. Lamb, wife To

Benjamin E. Ross & Effie U. Ross, wife.

Liber 240 p. 74 for $1.00

"... Being part of Lot ninety one (91) in said Town and situate on the east side of the highway leading from the village of Georgetown to Otselic and bounded as follows, viz: On the West by the center of the highway, on the North by land of Herbert J. Brown and lands formerly owned by Mary and Milton D. Allen, on the East by lands formerly owned by Mary and Milton D. Allen, deceased, on the South by lands formerly owned by John Currier and Hiram N. Atwood. It being the same premises owned by WM. P. Hare at the time of his decease, containing by estimation one acre of land be the same more, or less. Reserving a strip of land thirty feet wide (30) deeded to the Otselic Valley Rail Road Company used for that purpose only.

This deed is given subject to certain mortgage held by Zilpha Mack, George Griffith and E. F. Lamb.

Possession to be given March 31st 1914."

Note: Herewith attest to the confirmation of the OVVR print media account and vice versa. It may not have had the operational capacity of the railroad boom as it was cut short, but indeed the path for it was secured. The cooperation of the land owners were documented on a clause just as the RPL[real property law] stated that "agreements, encumbrances etc., should be made in writing and be part of the conveyance document".The true, real, and authentic deeds do not lie.

1924, March 15   Benjamin E. Ross and Effie U. Ross To J. Fred Currier

Recorded: 1924, March 24 3:00 PM $ 2,000.00

"... viz., Being part of Lot No. Ninety one (91) in said town and situate on the east side of the highway leading from the hamlet of Georgetown to Otselic and bounded as follows: viz: On the west by the center of the highway, On the north by land of Herbert J. Brown and lands formerly owned by Mary and Milton D. Allen; on the east by lands formerly owned by Mary and Milton D. Allen, deceased, on the south by lands formerly owned by John Currier and Hiram N. Atwood. Containing by estimation one acre of land, be the same more, or less. Reserving a strip of land thirty feet wide (30) deeded to the Otselic Valley Rail Road Company used for that purpose only.

Being the same lands deeded by Ernst D. Perry to Luella H. Perry, by her to Eunice F. Lamb and by Lamb and wife to first parties by deed recorded Liber 240 of Deeds at page 74 Madison Co. Clk's Office Dec. 20th 1913 (thirteen)

Excepting and reserving the use and occupation of said premises to and including the 31st day of March 1924 (twenty - four)

While the instrument includes all fixtures and property that is properly termed real estate except an engine and a bench in the shop which are the property of H.J. Brown and are excepted and reserved from the operation thereof."

1986, December 27   Josephine C. Davenport to Ray C. Simmons

Recorded: 1991, September 30   Liber 937 p.231 for $ 1.00

"... All that tract or parcel of land in Great Lot 91, Village and Town of Georgetown, County of Madison and State of New York, bounded as follows: Beginning in the center of the road from Georgetown to Otselic (New York State Highway No. 26) 114.0 feet northeasterly of the intersection of the centerline of the road with the northeast line of the Georgetown Church

Cemetery and running North 38 degrees 46' East along the center of the road 84.0 feet to the southwest corner of land sold to William Dale by Ivor and Ruby Phillips in 1962 (Book of Deeds 602 Page 223) thence South 51 degrees 14' East along the southwest line of Dale and over a steel pin at the east edge of the sidewalk (36 feet) a total distance of 384.2 feet to an iron pipe; thence South 8 degrees 33' West 97.2 feet to a steel pin on the north line of land sold by Edwin Stevens to William Trass in 1917 (Bk Deeds 250 page 384) thence North 51 degrees 14' West along the north line of Trass (250/384 and 252/190) over a steel pin at the east edge of the sidewalk (379.4 feet) a total distance of 415.4 feet to the place of beginning; containing 0.75 acre more or less.

Being and hereby intending to convey all that tract or parcel of land conveyed by Camilla Moore Brown to Charles H. Davenport and Josephine C. Davenport on December 19, 1963 and recorded in the Madison County Clerk's Office on January 6, 1964 in Liber 609 of Deeds at Page 534.

1992, January 28   Ray C. Simmons to Lyle G. Mason

1992, January 30   Liber 944 p.246 for $1.00

"...All that tract or parcel of land situate in the Hamlet of Georgetown, Town of Georgetown, County of Madison, State of New York, being part of Lot 91 in said Town and being more particularly bounded and described as follows:

Beginning at a point in the centerline of State Highway Number 26/80 at the northeasterly corner of a parcel of land heretofore conveyed to Slocum by deed recorded in the Madison County Clerk's Office in Book of Deeds 699 at page 457, said point also being northeasterly along said centerline, a distance of 114.0 feet from the northeasterly corner of the Georgetown Church Cemetery; thence N 39 48' 35" E along said centerline of Route 26/80, a distance of 84.00 feet to a point therein, said point being the northwesterly corner of a parcel of land heretofore conveyed to Dale by Deed recorded in the Madison County Clerks's Office in Book of Deeds 602 at page 223; thence S 51 14' 00" E along the southerly line of lands of Dale, a distance of 363. 98 feet to the southwesterly corner thereof; thence S 08 33' 00" W a distance of 97.20 feet to an iron pipe at the southeasterly corner of lands of Slocum (699/457); thence N 51 14'00" W along the easterly line of lands of said Slocum, a distance of 414.42 feet to the point of beginning.

Being and intending to convey all that tract or parcel of land granted by Josephine C. Davenport, December 27, 1986 to Ray C. Simmons and recorded at the Madison County Clerk's Office in September 30, 1991 in Liber 937 of Deeds at page 231.

Subject to easements and restrictions of record."

Let us see what the law says about surveys and maps. The verbatim quote of section 381 of the Real Property Law was transcribed using underlined fonts to highlight the particular points of interest, that directly pertain to the issue about why the Ross' South line was, and is a critical point of reference here. It is a fact that one end of any figure or shape stretched or snipped out can decide the difference as to the outcome.

The stretching and the snipping would be the deciding factors whether the original shape would be retained or take a new form. When we talk of numerical figures or what is appropriately termed metes & bounds description; especially in today's technological advancement; should we be not better of in tracking and finding the exact whereabouts of the parcels described? As any competent Surveyor would, as this RPL section says?

RPL Article 12 "Section 381. Survey, map or plan to be filed

There shall be filed with the registrar a survey, map or plan of the land title to which is sought to be registered, which shall be made by a <u>Competent Surveyor</u> and shall be subject to the Approval of the Court, and which <u>shall clearly show the exact boundaries of the land and its connection with adjacent lands and adjoining neighboring streets or avenues, and all encroachments, if any, and all other facts which are usually shown by Accurate Surveys.</u> If *any adjacent land is already registered*, the <u>survey must Properly Connect and Harmonize with the Survey of Such Previously Registered land.</u> There shall be attached to such survey, map or plan, and filed with it, an affidavit of the surveyor by whom it was made, that it was made by him personally or under his immediate supervision and direction; that it is a survey, map or plan of the property described I the petition of the official examiner's report of title, and that according to the best of his knowledge and belief said property is included in the boundaries shown on such survey, map or plan, without any encroachments or improper erections, except as follows: (stating and describing any encroachments or improper locations of buildings, fences, or other structures). After the original registration of any parcel of land, a new survey, map or plan of compliance with the provisions of section 334 and section 335 of the RPL, as amended, and chapter 620 of the laws of 1926. *The filing of such a new survey, map or plan shall outline the registered portion of the property, shall be noted as a memorial on the certificate of title to which it relates, and thereafter the land or any interest therein shall be transferred or encumbered by reference to it; in the event that the old description is used, reference must also be made to the new* *map.* Add, L 1909, ch 52, amd, L 1929, ch 575, eff July 1, 1929. Amd, L 1991, ch 640, § 3, eff Jan 1, 1992."

Note: Notice the italicized sentence in this section. Is this how whoever is or are behind this fraudulent act intend to reduce the size of this Brown-Steven - Cossitt Estates trying to do? From the survey, change the acreage description of the six parcels of deeded property?

As has been sporadically noted along the pages of this entire book, every crucial detail of this saga are still being followed thoroughly, to bring Justice to the Truth of this Story; and To ensure that this story remain as authentic as to the Historical standards of assignations that were designed to be. This is in consonance with the belief that the only way to set the issues of discord in the community for which this particular piece of Art still stands today with this unfortunate backdrop, is to set the records that had been straight all these years be so continuously be, instead of being messed with, even before I had my name connected to it. That is very evident in the story popularized if you google about this site. That was also the same story stamped with the approval of historicity. Not labeled accordingly as myth as it should be, just looked at the application form. How was this farce trumped the truth beats me. The very reason this work took the format and the language that you are reading at the moment. It should be so obvious that this story had been treated horrendously by they very individuals that we would have expected to be trusted, to be trustworthy, to be honest, to protect and to grant that the facts not be blurred.

This is also an appeal to those that have still retained their unbiased senses and sensibilities: Surely one cannot just trumped the use of deeded documents in the conveyance of real property? Because if this is happening today, as I feel it should not be - there would be one or two or a couple more that had the same experience?

Would that not be a societal problem? That a responsible community would want to take on as a community cause to stop and not let happen?

I was given hearsay information that when city people buy land and for this particular hearsay of a story say : 9 acres on deeded description. When surveyed, this situation turned out around 5 acres or so. When that new city landowner moved out, the very same land was bought by a local folk, then the 5 acred surveyed land, then became the 9 acred deeded description as originally worded and described in the deed.

Is this problem sanctioned by the Culture that permeates this Region or just this County, State or USA wide?

Am I to understand that learning is thrown out the window for land grab?

What happened with plain old reconciling math sentences with number sentences?

Surely, that is as basic as Air?

I turned to Mr. Lincoln on what he thinks about this; given that he would have seen this during his lifetime though cut short: 1809- 1865. He spoke from the print words, and I am privilege to be able to read, and comprehend. I wish we can share such to the people as shown by the print words in their Deeds. If only they would read? Or the people that can, please assist?

"A capacity and taste for reading gives access to whatever has already been discovered by others.
It is the key, or one of the keys, to the already solved problems.
And not only so, it gives a relish and facility for successfully pursuing the yet unsolved ones."

A.Lincoln

Here are a few quotes from Mr. Abe Lincoln, that I believe befit the thematic issue about the land issues from the adjoined landowners that are currently sitting on the area in question; as well as the people behind the offices of the agencies that are tasked to be governing bodies to protect:

"I am not bound to win, but I am bound to be true. I am not bound to succeed, but I am bound to live by the light that I have. I must stand with anybody that stands right, and stand with him while he is right, and part with him when he goes wrong."

"Nearly all men can stand adversity, but if you want to test a man's character, give power."

"Fellow citizens, we cannot escape history."

The question is: Which side of History are you on?

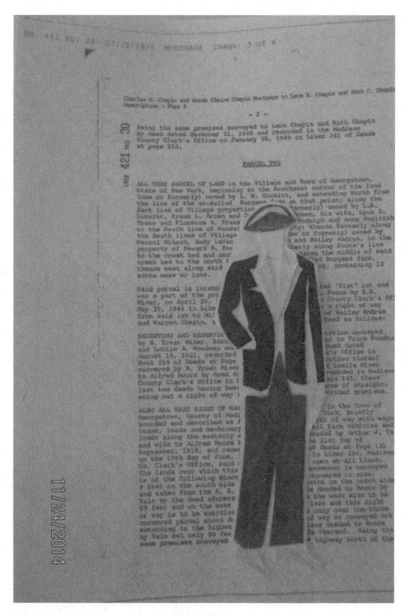

L. R. Cossitt Parcel One Still Used as a geo-positional monument for adjoining lands.

Plate 72-0263 Liber 421 p.30 Deed Description Parcel Two of that adjoined land Parcel; Changed Hands.

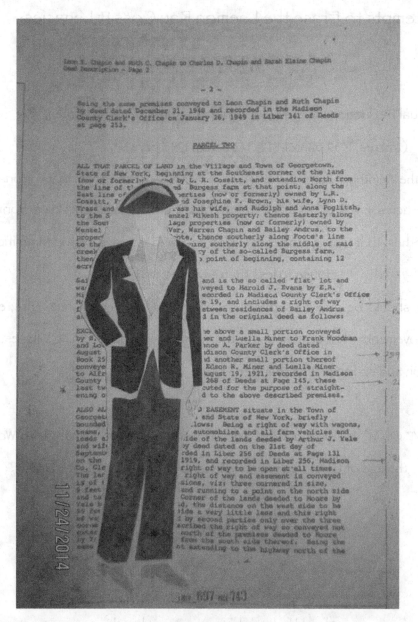

Leon E. Chapin and Ruth C. Chapin to Charles D. Chapin and Sarah Elaine Chapin
Deed Description - Page 2

- 2 -

Being the same premises conveyed to Leon Chapin and Ruth Chapin
by deed dated December 31, 1948 and recorded in the Madison
County Clerk's Office on January 26, 1949 in Liber 141 of Deeds
at page 213.

PARCEL TWO

ALL THAT PARCEL OF LAND in the Village and Town of Georgetown,
State of New York, beginning at the Southeast corner of the land
(now or formerly) owned by L. R. Cossitt, and extending North from
the line of the so-called Burgess farm at that point; along the
East line of the properties (now or formerly) owned by L.R.
Cossitt, F____ and Josephine F. Brown, his wife, Lynn D.
Trass and ____ass his wife, and Rudolph and Anna Poglitsh,
to the S____ enzel Mikesh property; thence Easterly along
the Sou____ lage properties (now or formerly) owned by
Wenzel ____Var, Warren Chapin and Bailey Andrus, to the
proper____ote, thence southerly along Foote's line
to the ____uing southerly along the middle of said
creek ____y of the so-called Burgess farm,
then____ point of beginning, containing 12
acre____

Sai____ and is the so called "flat" lot and
wa____veyed to Harold J. Evans by E.R.
Mi____corded in Madison County Clerk's Office
M____e 19, and includes a right of way
f____tween residences of Bailey Andrus
a____d in the original deed as follows:

EXC____e above a small portion conveyed
by S____er and Luella Miner to Frank Woodman
and Lo____nce A. Parker by deed dated
August ____dison County Clerk's Office in
Book 25____d another small portion thereof
conveyed____ Edson R. Miner and Luella Miner
to Alfr____ugust 19, 1921, recorded in Madison
County ____268 of Deeds at Page 145, these
last tw____cuted for the purpose of straight-
ening o____d to the above described premises.

ALSO AL____ EASEMENT situate in the Town of
Georgeto____ and State of New York, briefly
bounded ____lows: Being a right of way with wagons,
teams, ____, automobiles and all farm vehicles and
leads al____ide of the lands deeded by Arthur J. Yale
and wif____y deed dated on the 21st day of
Septemb____rded in Liber 256 of Deeds at Page 131
on the ____1919, and recorded in Liber 256, Madison
Co. Cle____right of way to be open at all times.
The ler____ right of way and easement is conveyed
is of t____sions, viz: three cornered in size,
9 feet ____and running to a point on the north side
and ta____Corner of the lands deeded to Moore by
Yale b____d, the distance on the west side to be
so fee____ide a very little less and this right
of wa____d by second parties only over the three
corne____scribed the right of way so conveyed not
exten____north of the premises deeded to Moore
by Ya____from the south side thereof. Being the
same ____t extending to the highway north of the

11/24/2014

____ 697 ___743

L. R. Cossitt Parcel One Used as a geo-positional monument for adjoining lands.

Plate 73-0262 Liber 697 p.743 Deed Description Parcel Two of that adjoined land Parcel.

Attempts to Erase the Leemon Ray Cossitt Legacies:

WHY?

Factual Deduction 1: Because it would merge the Cossitt Estates,

(2 acres, 1939 parcel + 1 & 1/2 acres, 1947 parcel),

with the Timothy & Sarah H. now Alice Stevens - Cossitt Estates that comprised:

(3/4 acres + 9' x 60' + 2 & 1/4 acres + 1/3 Undivided Rights to a Spring.)

Together, that would render the inherited land acreage of the Magnificent

House to less than seven acres.

That should be able to support the House in it's maintenance, care, even

improvements, that would benefit the entire Town, the adjoining Villages, the

region and so forth! What happened?

WHY? Oh WHY I even have to ask WHY in the Modern Ultra - Tech World:

the age of GPS; huge parcels of land can be unaccounted for????

Let us take a real close up on the documents and their inconsistencies!

The old fashioned way, so we can adopt the

Correct measures and move this Site Forward.

XIX. Parcel TWO of Mr. Cossitt's acreage legacy

An Inheritance. The second Land Parcel added to the Financial Assets Story of the History of the House. Let us review. There were two titled parcels from Leemon Ray. One was procured in 1939, the other in 1947.

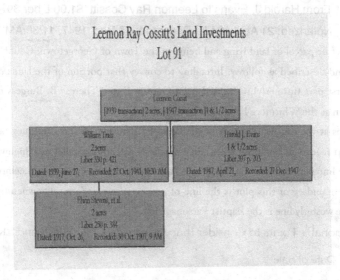

Plate 74 Year 1939, Leemon Cossitt, 1947

Today, this two land parcels are land locked, I wonder why? Not one person was helpful in allowing for the passage of delivery trucks for the placement of materials to the area within the property to be easily accessed for the ongoing habilitation work. The following records were stumbled on via intensive research.

1944, April 26 On the Record found in Liber 339 pp. 19-23 Madison County Clerk dated 1944, May 25, at 10 AM between Edson R. Miner and wife Luella Miner to Harold J. Evans. These rights of ways, usage, locations, and descriptions are eye openers.

48. A Microscopic & Detailed Look: Parcel TWO of Mr. Cossitt's legacy.

An Inheritance. The second Land Parcel added to the Financial Assets Story of the History of the House. There were two titled parcels from Leemon Ray. One was procured in 1939, the other in 1947. Below was the one procured in 1947. The actual description was lifted off the actual deed.

1947, April 21 From Harold J. Evans to Leemon Ray Cossitt $1.00 Liber 397 p.203
Notarized: 21 April 1947   Recorded: 27 Dec. 1947, 11:30 AM

"... All that tract or parcel of land lying and being in the Town of Georgetown, County of Madison, State of NY and described as follows: Intending to convey that portion of the lands owned by the party of the first part (formerly) purchased from Gordon F. and Theresa B. Burgess on March 30, 1947 and known as the Whitmore Farm, described as follows:
Said plot begins at the southeast corner of the Baptist Parsonage lot and continues easterly on the same course 241 feet to an iron post; thence in a northerly direction parallel with highway No. 26 for 267 feet to the line between the said Whitmore Farm and properties owned by Leemon R. Cossitt. The northerly boundary of this plot is the line of property now or formerly owned by Leemon R. Cossitt and the westerly line is the Baptist Parsonage lot..."

Noted Questionable Points to Consider that can cause CONFUSION and ERRORS:

A	1	Date of Sale
	2	The measurements
B	3	Baptist Parsonage as the Monument Point of Reference Cited
	4	This brings this Parsonage on the East Side of Rte.26
	5	East side Location Contradicted by the Deed from Otis H. Whitmore to the Trustees of the Baptist Church
	6	East side Location supported by Taxation Documents
	7	The Question of WHY?

See for yourself the factual evidences worded in the Wagner Deed here excerpted. Do compare, please. This comparison would address the following glaring similarities that can be used to confuse and switch identities of the parcels even at the very best of intentions. Attention to details can be easily be dropped, such already happened in this case:

48.A Leemon Cossit's Second Parcel Compared with WAGNER's PARCEL:

1947, April 21 from Harold J. Evans to Charles Wagner $1.00 Liber 395 p.253-5.
Recorded: 17 November 1947. 10:30 AM

"... Said parcel is bounded on the west by the center of the highway known as Route 26; on the south by lands owned by Archie C. Coye for a distance of 230 feet along a line between the two properties; thence in a northerly direction 275 feet in a line parallel with the center of the said highway; thence westerly parallel to the dividing line between Coye and this parcel a distance of 230 feet to the center of said highway Route 26..."

1957, June 11 Liber 539 p. 353-5 The aforementioned parcel was then sold by Charles Wagner to MR.& MRS. L. Chapin, in 1957. Recorded: 11 June 1957. This parcel can still be traced as an exception on the current deeds of the adjoined land to this Historic Site. Also noteworthy is the fact that the current taxation map does not show this piece anymore, as well.

1   The measurement of 241' Cossitt 's South line, versus the 230' of Wagner's.

This particular metes and bounds description for this particular piece of land bought by Charles Wagner should not be confused with the similarity of the numerical footage measurements of the L. R. Cossitt parcel, bought the same day from the same MR. Harold J. Evans.

Why am I bringing this topic here?

It was one snagged challenge in the survey. A very ugly experience for me, and these inconsistencies are still there. These are presented here, in an effort, to totally, eliminate, any sliver of a chance, of having the measurements be superimposed on either parcels.

To Delete any cause of confusion or mix up. You see, land descriptions are the fingerprints of the land parcel. Each should be individually custom fitted to the land piece. To stamp out fraud, duplicity, that can lead to costly lengthy legal procedures. Besides, for the simple reason of Peace of Mind that the property one invested in is truly one's own. Let is be a lesson for others too.

A call to action for those professing to be Professionals in the Measurements of Land Acreages to be more detail oriented, in the goal of making a Positive difference in the lives of Property Owners through Efficiency, Accuracy, Neutrality to Protect the Integrity of the Science and Math Procedures used in the Field of Surveys.

A look at what the NY Law on properties have to say about this:

"Section 381. Survey, map or plan to be filed

There shall be filed with the registrar a survey, map or plan of the land title to which is sought to be registered, which shall be made by a <u>Competent Surveyor</u> and shall be subject to the Approval of the Court, and which <u>shall clearly show the exact boundaries of the land and its connection with adjacent lands and adjoining neighboring streets or avenues, and all encroachments, if any, and all other facts which are usually shown by Accurate Surveys.</u> If *any adjacent land is already registered,* the <u>survey must Properly Connect and Harmonize with the Survey of Such Previously Registered land.</u>

We lifted this sentence from this Deed dated 1946, September 19, on Liber 375 p. 131 - 136.

"Also excepting and reserving therefrom on the east side of the public highway, about one - fourth of an acre of land occupied by the Baptist Society of said Town for a parsonage."

1/4 on the East side of Route 26, where is the actual deed for this? Liber 375 p. 131 - 136 was an annotation or clausal exemption; from the bulk deed. Was this a subdivision out of that deed? What happened to the other separately deeded parcels that are merged?

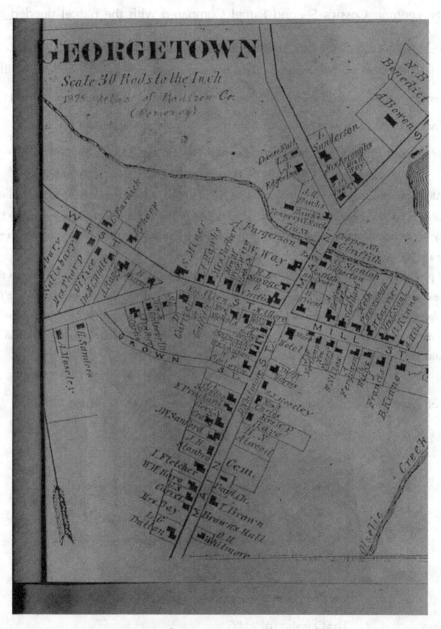

Plate 75- 0742 Map 1875

Picture taken and accessed from the Madison County, NY, Records.

48.B Leemon Cossit's Second Parcel Compared with the parcel deeded by Otis Whitmore & Asociates to the The Trustees of the First Baptist Church:

There were two titled parcels from Leemon Ray. One was procured in 1939, the other in 1947. Below was the one procured in 1947. The actual description was lifted off the actual deed again, and placed here for a second comparative study:

1947, April 21 From Harold J. Evans to Leemon Ray Cossitt $1.00 Liber 397 p.203
Notarized: 21 April 1947   Recorded: 27 Dec. 1947, 11:30 AM

"... All that tract or parcel of land lying and being in the Town of Georgetown, County of Madison, State of NY and described as follows: Intending to convey that portion of the lands owned by the party of the first part (formerly) purchased from Gordon F. and Theresa B. Burgess on March 30, 1947 and known as the Whitmore Farm, described as follows:

Said plot begins at the southeast corner of the Baptist Parsonage lot and continues easterly on the same course 241 feet to an iron post; thence in a northerly direction parallel with highway No. 26 for 267 feet to the line between the said Whitmore Farm and properties owned by Leemon R. Cossitt. The northerly boundary of this plot is the line of property now or formerly owned by Leemon R. Cossitt and the westerly line is the Baptist Parsonage lot..."

Noted Questionable Points to Consider that can cause CONFUSION and ERRORS

A	1	Date of Sale
	2	The measurements
B	3	Baptist Parsonage as the Monument Point of Reference Cited
	4	This brings this Parsonage on the East Side of Rte.26
	5	East side Location Contradicted by the Deed from Otis H. Whitmore to the Trustees of the Baptist Church
	6	East side Location supported by Taxation Documents
	7	The Question of WHY?

49. Baptist Parsonage: West side

This time, the Repeat Study is for a Comparison to pinpoint the accuracy of the location of the referenced monument cited on the deed, the First Baptist Church Parsonage. The correct, accurate, and truthful location of the Parsonage will determine the exact measurements, and geo-positional placement of this second Cossitt parcel. Below is an excerpt.

1877, March 09   From Otis H. Whitmore to Charles W. Smith, F.E. Franklin et al. Trustees of the First Baptist Church of Georgetown $1300.00 Liber 139 p. 364 Recorded: 14 March 1877 at 1PM

"...part of Lot 91...beginning in the centre of the highway leading from the village of Georgetown to Otselic and at a point in direct line with the North line of Russell Whitmore's home farm now owned and occupied by him thence South 35° west along the centre of said highway sixty - two and one half 62 & 1/2 links thence South fifty - five degrees east 2 chains and 50 links thence North 35° east on a line parallel with the centre of the highway aforesaid one chain & 25 links thence North fifty - five degrees west 2 chains & 50 links to the centre of the aforesaid highway thence South 35 degrees West along the centre of said highway 62 & 1/2 links to the place of beginning containing fifty rods of land more or less..."

Notes:

According to this deed, supported by the Gillette 1859 Atlas adaptation, the Parsonage's location would be on the West side of Rte. 26. How was it, that by the time Leemon Ray Cossitt bought the parcel in 1947, April 21 From Harold J. Evans for $1.00 as found in Liber 397 p.203, Notarized: 21 April 1947 and Recorded: 27 Dec. 1947, 11:30 AM; the description referencing the Baptist Parsonage, which in 1947 to today had sat on the

East side of Route 26 should in actual, physical location be on the West side of that highway all these years? What happened here?

A couple of things are necessary to be clarified for the story of this Historic site to be narrated truthfully. This critical step would affect every effort on the physical ground. This include the halted, if not the visible dramatic slowed rate of advancement that the Project can cover, to move forward. On the surface, this can be construed as a loss, but I strongly believe that doing the right thing to make things right is the first step to the a stronger foundation of human relations based on integrity, whose corners must never be cut off, shortchanged or ignored.

This is the investment not measured in any monetary units. This is the only type of investment that do not makes sense in dollars, and cents. To some, maybe. It would be easy to sweep under the rug, so to speak. Yet no one wants to have the barrier along the tree line be left alone until this issue is fixed. As to why there would even be an issue baffles me; the documents for this site is intact. The Hostility. The code wall of silence, and the covert hatred in overt ways! Thus, I beg to differ on the point that this deemed difficult and complex issue, is of no import. This is the most consequential issue of all, regarding the real Historical Story of this Site. That include the legacy of any one that touched or had been touched by the documents hereunto revealed. Whether that touching was positive or not, unfortunately. Without ironing these hitches that pertain to any land issue, challenges or questions, the overarching Goal of Making a Positive Difference would not make sense and cents either. Thus, before we can really advance here, even on the story of history, I have just got to subject, to put through, the other land parcel MR. Leemon Ray Cossitt left his wife MS. Alice Stevens - Cossitt to further Scientific and Mathematical scrutiny. This is the best time to correct all the errors and make a positive thing out of something full of not so positive ingredients. This is the challenge that can produce the Best of Results. We all need all the Help we can. All the prayers and encouraging thoughts, as well.

Have faith, you would appreciate all these trouble in the long run. It would be called Accuracy in this Specific History. History Founded on the Premise of the Truth based on Facts. Authentic Facts, subjected by Fire, that is.

From the Brown era to the current state of affairs, there were and are six legally accessioned parcels that came with the House. Out of the six, two parcels came from MR. Leemon Ray Cossitt. Let us make an effort to allot an unhurried time to give an intense close up look at these two separate parcels.

The DISSECTION:

1   Take into account the deed Date of sale was year 1947.

This was a more recent land parcel acquisition. 1947 compared to the 1877 location of this designated Parsonage. The Baptist Parsonage was used as a monument reference here.

2   The highway leading from the village of Georgetown to Otselic is State Rte.26. This goes North & South. At present, the actual site currently receiving that Baptist Church Parsonage designation sits on the East side of Highway State Route 26. The Taxation documents, the people that occupy the House, and are key leaders of the church and the Historical Society claim this to be on the East side of the Highway.

What is going on here?

3   The Otis H. Whitmore Deed for the Baptist Parsonage said otherwise. (Yes, please read it again, that was the reason it was placed here). Fact Check. The location was, and had always been on the West side of Rte. 26. Also check the Gillette map documenting the same. This was attached here, too.

50. Baptist Parsonage: East side

1   Now here, if everybody stood firm on the premise of Honesty and Integrity, then taking Mr. Otis Whitmore's deed description for the parcel procured by the Church, it is easy to understand that this parcel was, and is on the West side of Rte. 26. This meant on the right side, if one is traversing the highway going South. Take that then, as the truth when MR. Harold J. Evans (key leader of the Town in his era), used it as the reference point for Leemon Ray Cossitt's land, the Cossitt's parcel would start right on the current location of the Parsonage. The East side of the highway, or the Left side if going North on Rte. 26.

2   Why then, would this particular parcel and the structure now being referred to as the Baptist Parsonage, be where it is now? Here is a document that bespoke of a parsonage on the East side of the Highway.

From Liber 363 pp. 56-61 dated 31 March 1946 from Maud J. Upham to Gordon F. Burgess. Quoted here directly from p. 62, second paragraph:

" Also excepting and reserving therefrom on the east side of the public highway, about one fourth of an acre of land occupied by the Baptist Society of said Town for a parsonage."

This was repeated exactly the same on Liber 375 pp. 131-136 the same deed transferred by Gordon F. Burgess to himself - Gordon F. Burgess and wife Theresa B. Burgess. Quoted here directly from p. 132, second paragraph:

" Also excepting and reserving therefrom on the east side of the public highway, about one fourth of an acre of land occupied by the Baptist Society of said Town for a parsonage."

3   The Transfer of the actual deed measurements on the literal ground 1947 deed to Leemon Cossitt can then be followed from this notation of exception from the aforementioned deeds of the Burgesses. Still, why were the metes and bounds measurements for this parcel undermined and not used in the surveys? Then, we still have the questions of what really happened here? A noted exception from another deed saying east versus the actual deed for the parsonage with descriptions on the west and that very well reinforced by the maps and atlases of the period. Questions and confusions can be prevented. Descriptions and Land measurements are the finger prints of each land parcel. Attention to details are immensely important, and cannot be overemphasized.

4   Issue of Possession questions and hostilities

        4. a. The adjoining farmland claiming ownership by possession, WHY? HOW? By mistake, lost in translation? This highway Rt. 26 was mentioned on the top paragraph on this page as well. So how can any one make any mistake whatsoever in the interpretation of these deeds?

        Here is an excerpt from his Deeds.

1990, August 07 Liber 0914 p. 097 Image 2 of 6 Under heading Parcel One, Second Paragraph: "All TRACT OR PARCEL OF LAND, lying and being in the Town of ... bounded and described as follows:..that is located or situated on the east side of the highway known as Route #26 and running between Georgetown and Otselic...containing approximately 175 acres of land, be the same more or less.

        ...Said lands being bounded (now or formerly) as follows: On the North by the Baptist Parsonage, Lee Cossitt, Harold J. Evans and Ransom Eaton, bounded on the east by Douglas Campbell and perhaps one other land owner, on the on the South by Douglas Campbell, Donald Campbell and Archie Coye, bounded on the west by the aforesaid highway..."

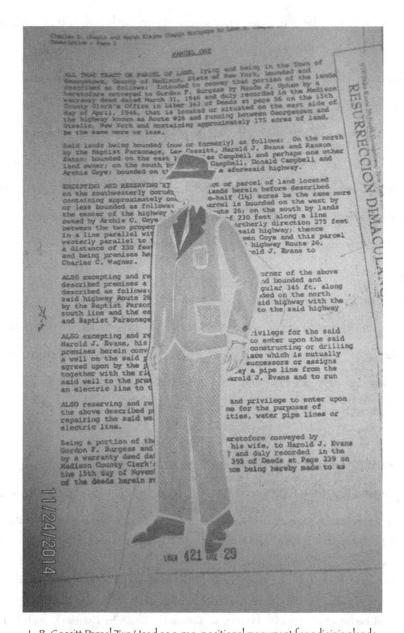

Charles B. Chapin and Sarah Elaine Chapin Mortgage to ...
Description - Page 2

PARCEL ONE

ALL THAT TRACT OR PARCEL OF LAND, lying and being in the Town of
Georgetown, County of Madison, State of New York, bounded and
described as follows: Intended to convey that portion of the lands
heretofore conveyed to Gordon F. Burgess by Maude J. Upham by a
warranty deed dated March 31, 1946 and duly recorded in the Madison
County Clerk's Office in Liber 363 of Deeds at page 56 on the 15th
day of April, 1946, that is located or situated on the east side of
the highway known as Route #26 and running between Georgetown and
Otselic, New York and containing approximately 175 acres of land,
be the same more or less.

Said lands being bounded (now or formerly) as follows: On the north
by the Baptist Parsonage, Lee Cossitt, Harold J. Evans and Ranson
Eaton; bounded on the east ... as Campbell, Donald Campbell and
land owner; on the south b... Campbell, Donald Campbell and
Archie Coye; bounded on t... e aforesaid highway.

EXCEPTING AND RESERVING al... ct or parcel of land located
on the southwesterly corner... lands herein before described
containing approximately on... e-half (1½) acres be the same more
or less bounded as follows:... arcel is bounded on the west by
the center of the highway ... ute 26; on the south by lands
owned by Archie C. Coye ... f 230 feet along a line
between the two proper... rtherly direction 275 feet
in a line parallel wit... said highway; thence
westerly parallel to ... een Coye and this parcel
a distance of 230 fee... highway Route 26,
and being premises he... old J. Evans to
Charles C. Wagner.

ALSO excepting and re... orner of the above
described premises a ... d bounded and
described as follows:... gular 345 ft. along
said highway Route 26 ... ded on the north
by the Baptist Parson... aid highway with the
south line and the ea... to the said highway
and Baptist Parsonage

ALSO excepting and re... rivilege for the said
Harold J. Evans, his ... to enter upon the said
premises herein conv... constructing or drilling
a well on the said p... ace which is mutually
agreed upon by the p... successors or assigns
together with the ri... ay a pipe line from the
said well to the prem... arold J. Evans and to run
an electric line to t...

ALSO reserving and re... and privilege to enter upon
the above described p... me for the purposes of
repairing the said we... ities, water pipe lines or
electric line.

Being a portion of th... eretofore conveyed by
Gordon F. Burgess and ... his wife, to Harold J. Evans
by a warranty deed da... 7 and duly recorded in the
Madison County Clerk'... 395 of Deeds at Page 239 on
the 15th day of Novem... ce being hereby made to as
of the deeds herein r...

11/24/2014

LIBER 421 PAGE 29

L. R. Cossitt Parcel Two Used as a geo-positional monument for adjoining lands.

Plate 76-0264 Liber 421 p. 29 Deed Description Parcel One of that adjoined land Parcel.

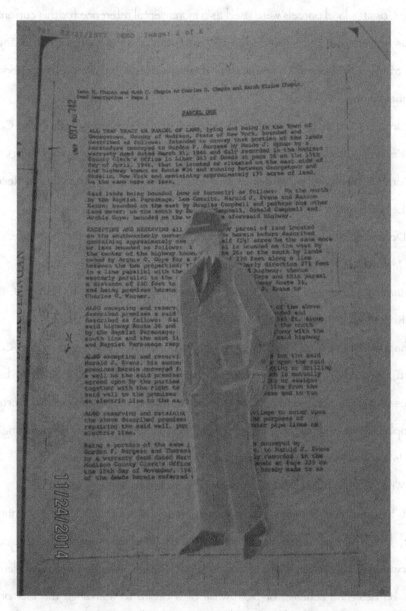

L. R. Cossitt Parcel Two Used as a geo-positional monument for adjoining lands.

Plate 77-0261 Liber 697 p. 742 Deed Description Parcel One of that adjoined land Parcel.

Mr. Lee Cossitt's land parcels were used as a monumental reference for this current and previous farmers own land. Worded to be "excepted", too. Is it or is it not in English? Lost in translation? Here are a few more of the same deeds that denoted exception and referential point:

1977, March 21 Mortgage Book 421 p.28 (Image 2 of 6) Digitized Format in the County Records. Charles D. Chapin & Elaine Mortgage to Leon E. Chapin & Ruth C.

1977, March 21 Book 697 p.741 (Image 2 of 6) digitized format in the County Records. Leon Chapin & Ruth C. Chapin to Charles D. Chapin and Sarah Elaine.

1948, December 31 Liber 341 p. 253 Harold J. Evans to Leon & Ruth Chapin Recorded January 26, 1949 at 11 AM

1947, March 30 Liber 395 p. 239 Gordon F. Burgess & Theresa B. to Harold J. Evans Recorded: 15 November 1947 at 9 AM.

What happened? WHY? HOW? What is going on in this Town, and in the County Property, Records, Treasury, Assessor, Mapping? Is this FRAUD legitimized by the agencies that are supposed to protect that Constitutional right to Property, Liberty, for the People? Do we not call the taking of something that is not one's own as Stealing?

Is it not a Crime? Punishable by Law?

WHY had this type of action or decision resorted to, if this is what it is?

Honest to goodness answers that are mature, lawful, mathematical & scientifically cogent, based on accurate documentation with Integrity is what this Project of Conservation & Preservation of History, is about. Please, if by any mistake, calculated or not, by designed scheme, or plain whim of a desire to rearrange the lots on this subdivision #06, would somebody please give a mature, legally acceptable rationale as to the WHY?

51. A Priori ipso Facto:

From the description excerpted, we can deduce the following:

A: Location of the Deeded Baptist Parsonage was switched.

1877, actual title of actual parcel description places the site on the West Side; 1946, 1947 documents excepted reference placed the site on the East side for 1/4 acre.

B: Identity Switch.   Identical metes & bound land descriptions are susceptible to confusion, errors and thievery in property, resulting to disputes. Thus the extreme importance of vigilance to details. Mathematically, Scientifically. The issue is tackled head on here. For Prevention. My apologies if these feel redundant to you. This is an effort to achieve clarity, as the circumstances call for.

B.a   Ensure that the exact measurements on the Cossitt deeded descriptions are followed, so as not to be confused with the measurements used in what was Charles Wagner's parcel from Harold Evans. Both were deeded on the same year, date, within the same Lot 91, and in space proximity. Wagner parcel was not shown on the tax map is not helping clarify, instead, add to confusion that lead to more mistakes.

B.b   This deed is not defined nor depicted in accordance to the worded description. While the numerical measurements were laid in the map, the location points of start and end do not match the deed cited references. WHY?

B.c   L. R.Cossitt's two parcels, and the parcels of other owners, were used as monument reference points by the current adjoining land deed descriptions. Why then are the adjoining farmers taking possession of these land acreages?

C: Ingress & Egress. The ROW worded on the adjoined deeds up to the current ones. What happened to it? Why are difficulty and oppressive action better, than doing the right thing because it is the right thing to do? Can somebody educate me on this???

On MY end of this situation; WHY am I trying to Right the Wrong?

BECAUSE it is the RIGHT thing to do:

So we can try to find a lawful, acceptable way to correct these errors that would be fair, decent, and beneficial to everybody. Not to mention the release of stress, anxiety and the removal of the threat of always looking over one's shoulder, for fear of being caught red handed. So we all would have some kind of closure, a very permanent finality. So we can all make a positive headway towards our individual Goals of lasting stability.

Lastly, if nothing move anyone to reason, at least lend credence on the NY State Historic Landmark Signage standing by the sides of the highway, even if by itself it has its own questionable issues. There are at least four of them that not one Government Office can account as to which agency spent tax payers dollars having that installed. Isn't this something??

Some kindness, so as the deeds of the dead would have some justification, even. Whatever antidote, or amendments chosen for each individual case, would be custom fit to ensure that every one get their rights counted. Just a little break, for the house, for the Spirit of making a positive difference.

We would not want to throw people out of Homes. Nor prevent people and the public from enjoying this marvel of human endeavor, the House of Magnificent Craftsmanship. What this is about is the enjoyment of the site that adhere to the standards of civility, safety, responsible use, and accountability in purpose. The funds to improve, maintain, pay taxes, even volunteers for which many have expressed desire to share, surely the liability insurances cost money, time cost money, materials cost money. We all know that! Do these things really need to be spelled here to be heard and be clearly understood? Is this not part of common sensibilities that daily operations do, incur costs, in dollars and cents; and thus need be appropriated in budgetary terms.

Not one stepped up the plate to take this cause, nor had any one given back. As far as the 411 low down of the Wilson Era, not very kind words were abundantly brought to my ears and would not be dignified here. Those are taken as cautionary tales for me and became part of the purpose for this endeavor. One thing that stood out, was that there was not one person I had the privilege of communing rallied behind the efforts to keep the true and authentic heritage of the site. If that was so, I would not be in the predicament that I am with this format and platform, nor would the site be in the stage of gutted-ness amidst the controversies, lies, coverup and obliterated story of History.

Please, this is a civilized country the last time I checked. Let us not make this high expectation of civility be trashed away because of a few personal misguided vested interests placed front and center. We should all advocate improving the quality of lives for every one. That includes the ones we like or not, for Humanity is not about liking or not liking. Let this site and the legacy of old be for unification, for inclusion, for innovative mindsets that would trample tunnel vision.

Humanity is about Benevolence. One does not have to be a millionaire, or billionaire nor be royalty to partake of this quality. This is the human emotion exercised by organisms that possess Superior Brain Configuration. The Homo Sapiens.

Surely, oxidizing these dark clouds hanging over the Town is better than dragging these controversial toxicities along for another 30, 60 years moving slowly forward? Another generation of lying, deceit, silence, pain, hurts, prejudice; every thing imaginably uncivilized, is this the better choice?

52. Death 4

How many times can a woman, even of towering strength be tested to mourn for a loved one in all her lifetime? This is the third male presence removed from Alice's life. Her father, her brother, then her husband. That is, for us to recall that she outlived her mom, her grandparents - grand pa Albert Stevens, her uncles too. Remember George Stevens? This man provided for Alice, Julia and Elwin in his will. If you can read these without squirming nor quizzically squinting, then you are comprehending. It is a good sign for me. It means that you are reading. You are remembering the characters here.

Thank you.

Then again, is experiencing death not a testimony of a life lived to the fullest? To live is to love. With love comes joy, and happiness. For those feelings to be appreciated, the contrasts should be experienced as well. Thus, pain, suffering, and death. These emotions come with life. How did MRS. Alice Stevens Cossitt carried on?

1   Take stock of MR. Cossitt's legacy

This meant taking care of the inheritance. That meant trying not to think of the heart aches, and head aches. If she can remove the headaches, the better. The story gets to be more interesting as I pored on the documents left behind by these interesting people.

2   Community Sharing (more on this, later)

To help us all understand the process of her grieving, the type of grieving that I want to delve with, that is. For I most definitely would not be able to tell you what happened then. Nor would I not want to conjecture. So, I will keep myself to the topic of the book which is the accounting of the inheritance of this Historic Site.

53. Heirs & Inheritance

Let me walk you through the inheritance process that came about the expanded addition of the acreages that came with the House.

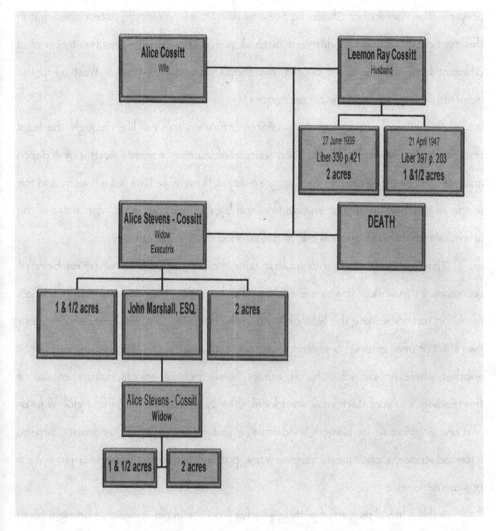

Plate 78 The Acreage Legacy of Mr. Leemon Ray Cossit: Two acre Parcel & One and 1/2 acre Parcel

54.   The Executrix A

The documents show the legal strategic procedures resorted, then applied, that were different from what was first experienced by Alice Stevens with her Mom - Julia Stevens, when her father Chauncey Stevens died. It is interestingly noted here, that in this particular situation, a different method was employed with the assistance of a different legal implement. Of course, the events were starkly East & West as to the elements that surrounded the circumstances.

This example opens windows of opportunities to view life through the legal framework. An array of multi - faceted sources of learning moments worthy of in depth analysis, and passionate brain - storming sessions. Now, since I am not a lawyer, and the scope of this book is not to engage into any legal review, the most I can share is the affirmation that this shows how big, and expanded this Project can be.

There is more room than one can imagine in exploring the areas where each one of you reading this work at this moment is hoped to be inspired to move into action, and get involve in further shining the light of Truth in the contexts touched here or within your own life. For one: getting committed to a cause that make a positive change one way or another, wherever you are - church, school, family, politics, sports, culture, etc. as of this reading. You see, start small, start local, think global effect, and affect globally. For any one aspiring to be lawyers, mediators, investigators, novelists, archivists, artists, informed students, consumers; to name a few, put on the thinking cap, and try to make a positive difference.

Is this a literal picture of getting smarter from the experiences that brought forth pain, an wakening to the harsh realities of life; and somehow coping in whatever way?.

Plate 79-0645 MRS. Leemon Ray Cossitt, Widow:

Alice Stevens - Cossitt, Executrix

1947, October 09 Last Will & Testament: 1954, July 24 Will Probated, File 17379

The following were excerpted from the document:

1   Executrix - directed payment of all just debts, and funeral expenses

2   Granddaughter Connie - the black walnut Hepplewhite table subject to the right of the wife, Alice's lifetime use; then table as gift absolute to Connie.

3   Use of all furniture, and household equipment for the rest of her lifetime then, Equal division between two sons.

4   Grandson Robert Allen of Hamilton, absolute sum of $200.00 cash.

5   Grandson John Leemon of Earlville, absolute $200.00 cash.

6   Rest and remainder of property divided as:

Wife Alice = 60%: Son Alfred = 20%: Son Allen = 20%

7   The Executrix's full power, and authority to continue in operation in whole or in part for 18 months in her discretion if deemed advisable

8   The Executrix have full power, and authority to convert her % in cash as set forth in paragraph six. The Wife have first choice, and selection of any real and personal property.

Page two of WILL:

"Lastly, I hereby appoint Alice S. Cossitt, my wife, Executrix of this, my last Will and Testament, with full power and authority to sell and convey, lease or mortgage real estate, hereby revoking all former wills by me made."

1954, July 07 Will Probated: File No. 17379

1954, July 24 Mr. Leemon Ray Cossit, DOD, testate

1954, July 28 Petition Verified by Alice S. Cossitt

1954, July 29 Letters Testamentary Issued to Alice S. Cossitt

Going back to Alice, the Executrix. She did make a positive change. Fact is, this is the second time she had made that sound judgement that affected this House. Both decisions were recorded so far. That was how I knew. That is why you are reading this.

Remember 1920, August 28, the BUY OUT day.

As the Executrix and heir, the grieving spouse inherited the two land parcels from Mr. Cossitt. This is how MR. Cossitt's legacy came in direct connection with this Historic Site. Yes, through another historic circumstance <u>Entwined in a Knot</u>. A Love Knot. These were the following document trail of Mrs. Alice Stevens - Cossitt as the Chosen and Appointed Executrix of the Estate of L.R. Cossitt. The data were excerpted and presented in the most concise presentation here:

46.A <u>Executor's Deed 1</u>: One & 1/2 acres, Liber 397 p.203 Recorded: 27 December 1947.

1955, June 10 Alice S. Cossitt, Executrix: to John R. Marshall for $1.00

1955, June 23 Acknowledge Date

1955, June 27 Recorded   9:45AM   Liber 510 p. 144

For the parcel conveyed by: Harold J. Evans to Leemon Ray Cossitt dated 21 April 1947

46.B <u>Executor's Deed 2</u>: for the two acres, Liber 330 p.421 Recorded 27 October 1941.

1955, June 10 Alice S. Cossitt, Executrix: to John R. Marshall for $1.00

1955, June 23 Acknowledge Date

1955, June 27 Recorded   9:45AM   Liber 510 p. 147

For the parcel conveyed by: William Trass to Leemon Ray Cossitt dated 27 June 1939

Note: Lemmon Ray Cossitt a.k.a. Lee R. Cossitt

55. John Marshall, Esq.

The document showed the four transactions made the same day. Two were deeds of sale from Alice Cossitt, the Executrix of the Estate of Leemon Ray Cossitt. On the very same day, just a minute thereafter, enough time to affix the signatures, were the other two deeds of sales. Those were from John Marshall, an Attorney. The deeds went back to Alice Cossitt. These were the same land parcels that she had signed over to him for a Dollar, sold back to her for the same Dollar. Quite interesting indeed. Efficient, too. This remind me of the same technique employed by Mr. Gordon F. Burgess, when he bought the land to his name 1946[32], then sold it to himself and his wife[33]. That took care of having the spouse's name be included in the deed. Efficient, quick and legal. This is on the record.[34]

To me, as a lay person, these legal moves are quite different from all the other property transfers we have seen in the Story of this Historic Site, so far. These are fully documented in the recorded Deeds, and are being brought out. The purpose of which is for understanding the lives of the people in the generations past. This is called History.

Bringing these situations to light, and letting any reasonable imaginative mind interpret them to however one may to improve lives, is a possibility for the reader to get occupied with. As to the procedure being acceptably legal, which they are, can therefore be subjected to further analytical dissection, if so desired. I strongly recommend this be done by the specialists in the field of Law, and or under the strict

---

[32] 1946, March 31 Liber 363 pp.56-57 Recorded: 15 April 1946.

[33] 1946, September 19 Liber 375 pp. 131-137 Recorded:

[34] The reader have to compare both documents to appreciate the records.

Plate 80-0647   Atty. John Marshall

supervision of a competent legal adviser, if you are a student. Then a whole new story can be concocted from there. That is another possibility that is encouraged. One very hardy good word of caution: Fact Check!

Make the recorded experiences so presented here a positive learning, and teaching moments, to move Progressive Diversity in Mind, and Spirit, forward. These were the following document trail of Atty. John Marshall. He sold back to Mrs. Alice Stevens - Cossitt the same two parcels she sold him earlier. The transaction wrapped - up the legally accepted procedure used in the liquidation of the mentioned two parcels from Leemon Cossitt 's Estate, and transferred to the new owner: Alice Stevens - Cossitt. These are the two parcels that adjoined the landholdings of Alice Stevens, before she became Mrs. Cossitt. This lawful process was made possible via the authority willed upon her as the Chosen, and Appointed Executrix of the Estate of L.R. Cossitt.

The data were excerpted. The concise format presented below:

47.1   Deed Covenant Against Grantor 1:

Two acres, Liber 510 p. 141 on 1955, June 27 Recorded: 9:46 AM

1955, June 10   From John R. Marshall to Alice S. Cossitt, for $1.00

1955, June 23   Acknowledge Date

Parcel conveyed by William Trass to Leemon Ray Cossitt

For two acres: Liber 330 p.421 on 27 June 1939 Recorded: 27 October 1941.

47.2   Deed Covenant Against Grantor 2:

One & 1/2 acres, Liber 510 p. 138 on 1955, June 27 Recorded: 9:46 AM

1955, June 10 From John R. Marshall to Alice S. Cossitt, for $1.00

1955, June 23   Acknowledge Date

Parcel conveyed by Harold J. Evans to Leemon Ray Cossitt

1 & 1/2 acres: Liber 397 p.203 on 21 April 1947 Recorded: 27 December 1947

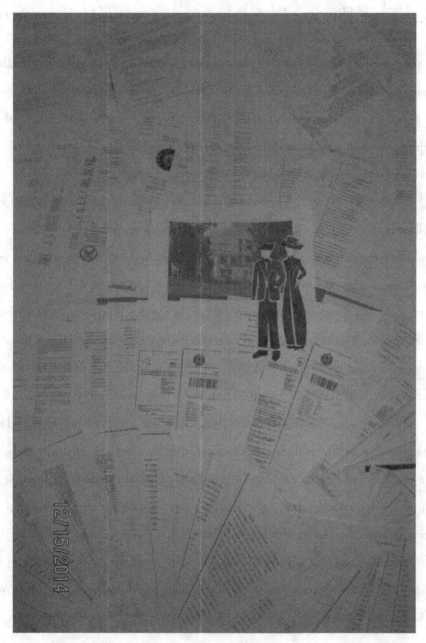

Plate 81- 0649   Looking at the Legacy

XX. The Brown - Stevens - Cossitt Legacy

Somewhere buried within the pages of this compiled documents is the visual that I hope would need no further worded explanation here. A flowchart it is called. From the Four Parcels that came with the House, through the very nervy strategy of an enterprising Woman, with a keen foresight, worthy of respect always - was that one very Historical move made with such audacity. The Buy out.

That is from my vantage point, and from the perspectives that I view these facts, crucial for having this Historic Site Landmarked the story presented from the Deeds. So why was that not mentioned in any narratives out there? As far as data collected, even information covered - up, if not being under constant threat of removal, the trail always lead me to forces doing almost everything to erase the real Story of this Site: House, acreage, and the lives of real people behind the material things we now view. Of course any one can make deductions, and share that to the world, but please ensure that deductions are based on facts, based on documents that are not fabricated.

Thanks to Alice Stevens - Cossitt, the entire place would not only have had half of the issues we are currently facing; there could've have been no structure standing, had it not been for her sound judgement in having chosen the dedicated people, to carry on the legacy after her! Otherwise, no one would have even questioned the veracity of the stories being perpetuated about this Magnificent House. Google it.

Talk about David & Goliath.[35] I am a little voice sounding off the alarm. Why do I have to? Surely keen minds, loads of money, networked machinery of Who's Who standing guard: Government agencies, Historians, Learned People, Specialists and

---

[35] Both the biblical Story & the best selling book of the same title by a very famous author. Check it out.

Experienced Lovers of the Artes, the local Town, could have ensured the safety of this Magnificent Structure, it's real Story, it's true Inheritance. Why did they not? Why are they not rallying behind this effort to restore the Truth? What was so wrong with this Truth? Truth - the foundation and guiding light for Historical Narratives. Accuracy. Veracity. Facts. What happened? What is really going on here? Is there any one out there still standing firm on these Tenets?

The many sound decisions Alice Stevens had made in her life, <u>marrying MR. Leemon Ray Cossitt was one other thing that had a real bright story as well.</u> Unfortunately, that legacy had been under menacing hostile actions. From people that one would not expect to have mean intentions, to those that are blatant in their taking over what is obviously not theirs to take, to those that literally have no regard to the Constitutional Rights to Property, Privacy and Peaceful enjoyment of life under Democratic Freedom. Remember those adjoining land parcels whose Deeds had even worded those Leemon Cossitt parcels to be the monumental boundary indicators?

The parcels had been respected as such - as Leemon Cossitt's, except recently. If that is a Mistake, please, be human enough to leave those parcels be. I feel that from the get go: landmarking application, to the repair, maybe even the roof collapse of the house before it was supposedly repaired by the contractor that took off with the money was, and was choreographed, and had been done by design! Just because Mrs. Alice Stevens would not sell her land to them? Had they expected her to just give it away?

Yes, taking something for nothing. Is that what this attitude of entitlement is about? Then, have taxpayers dollars be set aside for this corrupt plans, legitimize via a non - profit organization. The forever cash cow! At least to some that I had the privilege of first hand experience myself. Hiding behind that IRS designation, a loophole for

Resurreccion Dimaculangan

corruption. These are just basing on the statements literally given to my face about key groups and individuals not going to lift a hand because I am not an Organization. Then every one that are against this Project to be started, and be carried out by a "hyper - pigmented, female in a lilly white neighborhood" was sure to get those "groups boiling mad": "you are not really from here": "we were born here": " Our women groups are for those that were born here": "What do you really know about this History?" These are the Types of welcome remarks showered liberally at me, to name the not so scathing ones here. Yes, from the 501 (c) (3)and some individuals that are within the groups.

So these people gathered enough cohorts to little by little move their way to muddling the understanding on how this Site should be respectfully appreciated. Disrespectful takeover without authentic documentation to own the property in question, and even if their documents specifically say those parcels are not theirs.

So the smear campaign went on. Every agency tasked to protect the Constitutional Rights of Every Citizen under the Bill of Rights had not proactively stopped nor looked at the evidence. One outside independent viewer gave another angle: "Maybe they are looking at another set of evidence?" Then where are those documents that pertain to their ownership? Aren't property documents supposedly recorded to be accepted as legally admitted? I have yet to see that. Race to record. Somebody extrapolated that the first document to be recorded owned the property in question if for instance: one or the same property was sold to two or more people.

Three years had been spent trying to uncover the reasons behind this indecency. What is so hard to understand about MRS. Alice Stevens Cossitt not wanting for the History & Legacy of the Browns to not be divided? Stay Intact, as One, Undivided! She even expanded that. She Added to them. That's what the pattern of making a Positive

Difference One Person at a Time had happened here. Add the Leemon Ray Cossitt Legacy to the Brown. You get Alice in the Middle! Why would that story not Historic enough to be Honored, Respected, and be Landmarked, by themselves?

That is the relationship that had been presented, simmering on the surface, and came spilling hot, on me. This is currently being played, with me inside this very sad circumstance. Is this the History they want to be part of, or would they rather be the people that made sure the acreage legacy of Mr. Cossitt, Mrs. Cossitt, and the adjoining land be based on honest, responsible, kindly land ownership? That meant, we would have accounted for boundaries, that there would be no overlapping, that any information handed to our heirs and assigns would be based on facts, the truthful facts.

Over fifty years! The story to be Historic based on the passage of years had made the cut. We are now running on the next phase of that History. The Wilsons: 1986, today is 2015. In my book, that in itself, is a beautiful add - on story. Another Love Story. Stories need not be perfect, but a story about Love, family, and the frailties of humanity are surely: Stories. Base them on facts. That is the most important factor. Facts. Truth.

Remember love thy neighbors, and Robert Frost on building fences? That was why these lines were documented from a long time ago by the wisdom of the ages. Neighborliness: a two party, two way street. It does take two to tango, too.

XXI.   The WELL

Mrs. Alice S. Cossitt had the water from the well pumped into the House for convenience. The potable water piped into the town, in today's generation, deserved an up close examination in connection as to the Why and How come Mrs. Cossitt had maintained a well for her running water use? She never had her water coming from the Town water connection. I am now made to understand that the water line that had been causing seepage into the basement foundation was a newer and a recent connection. No wonder.

The way that pipe was holed into the stone wall looked like the job done was meant to cause the breach and hasten the collapse of the structure; if I may give my non plumber two cents on how I would describe the situation. That was the reason I had that line shut off. Oh my, in hindsight, it is becoming clearer that the reason the rain water collection container got busted was because the opposition realized I am willing to go that length to literally apply and act on the Conservative Use I had been promulgating. Flushing the sewage system manually, all the way to the second floor. French bath and bird bath style of hygienic maintenance for a girl. WHY not? Wipes, bottled water, Poland Spring, and every other day or two trip for the use of a more up to date a bath implements from someone else's house. All in the name of stopping the water content in the basement where there should not be.

Like all the other aspects of the House that were placed into well scrutinized documentation process since 2011, the Well was again recently just re - subjected to a more intense inspection after a serious once over of the materials used in connecting the branched out lines of analysis with the other data of historic importance. Now, to continue on with the Story that the Deeds are showing: The one real Story that the accepted popular legend swirling around the region got overturned, and intentionally rejected. The one Real Story NOt on record when one Google about this site. The one Story that is not being passed by word of mouth around town; and the Story that neighboring interested areas do not want known; would not want to hear; and not subscribed to.

The one Story that this work is trying to impart to those who wish to understand and filter out amidst the layers of intertwined complexities. What you are seeing is a more organized version of what I had and have to contend with. Imagine, the labour, the sleepless nights, the writing, re - writing, the thought processes invested, and continue to expend immensely just to arrive at the WHY and HOW.

That Town water connection was closed from the Town water main August of 2012. There are two tanks at the basement. The picture shows what and how the basement was. The hired expert on plumbing and HVAC technology gave the information, confirming what was hearsay data that Mrs. Cossitt had her own water system, now factual. The person in charge of the Town water system, the blue prints, maps for this water system confirmed the same.

The one other thing the commissioned Survey would not account was the placement of the well, and why are the adjoining land occupants not keen about it. One of the hear says was that the people backfilled the well. Thats one other attestation of how the people had been trying so hard to cover up the real History behind this Magnificent Structure, and destroy the true land scape. WHY?

On my data collection, and ground searches, this area had been identified. Together with all the artifacts left on the ground, in the House, the House itself, the necessity to have pinpoint precision of the location points are crucial for the accurate transfer to a blueprint. This is one document legitimate Professionals understand all around the world. At the moment of acquisition, year 2011, this is one of the many documents missing from this Site. This is one of the problems aimed to be resolved. The only resolution that can fix this issue is the documentation that stemmed from the recorded DEEDS. Thank goodness there was a record for that. Yet those very same records are the ones under immense threat of Obliteration. Surely, this elaborate Deception is not the working or the Scheming designs of one person? Would it be not fair to believe based on the gathered information that there's got to be an integrated level of Connivance, for the Deeds to be Disregarded as such, in this Serpentine Toxic Charade? One good thing about this situation I found myself in is that I get the privilege of speaking to you all out there in this format. I would not have dreamed it to be this way. I have grown more, and I get the chance of being me, my way of writing, my way of communicating the way I take to this Language.

From the Well, the Spring, the land parcels unaccounted for, the historical bases used in the land marking registration application, and all other socio - economic, community issues besieging this Property, the rationale on WHY the people had been the way they are, continue to boggle me. Thus this work continues, simultaneously, hopefully with the actual improvements, preservation, and conservatory work stages progressing.

If any one can have feed back on how to better understand what happened, what dynamics are being played, and the better ways to bring them in a civilized co - existence to respect the Truth of this Historic site would be appreciated. Blog about this, would you?

Plate 82- 0276 Basement

The Well, H2O Storage Tank at the basement, Pump Connections Visible

XXII. The Fireplace & the Sunrooms

The warmth of Mrs. Cossitt's persona still radiate today. The chimney is very visible on the South side of the added sunrooms. When the hearth is aglow with the fire, and the crackling sounds of kindling sticks from the pine, maple, cedar, oak and sumac, ignite the more robust logs, I am sure, dead sure I am home. It is my hope, my wish, my mission to ensure that responsible people can share that feeling as well. Somehow, that stage of the Project is being hampered by the issue of Land acreage grabbers that this site have the misfortune to be in all around.

The stages of habilitation, structure improvement, and development towards fiscal sustainability that require perimeter definition in areal units have stumped the progress, halted all ground work. The encroachment issues, trespasses, and just plain incivility had gone more remarked and to the point that tell tale signs that can escalate should not be ignored. The Safety agencies prescribed to govern and protect had failed this site, myself. The choice to not subject to any form of harm, those that are just trying to assist me in the project is a no brainer. I had to pause, and take my fight to you, the People at large. The greater members of Humankind.

This is a Story of regular Americans that had lived their dreams to the fullest, in the best way they can and know of. Unto this day, the remnants of their actions, decisions, and choices are still touching our lives in one form or another. Yet their efforts, regardless of having been well documented in the legal acceptable forms of documentations, are being trampled. Is it because they are not of the Last names we are so familiar of? Not the super Royalty nor Hollywood nor of Political recognition? Not the Magnates and heirs and Corporate Titans we are so used seeing being honored

Historically? Not the Intellectual type, and the Nobel Laureates? Well, so are the majority of us. Being honored with a Historical Plaque of recognition need not mean Superhuman traits only!. It does mean that everyone - every individual: For the cause or causes that influence Humanity for the better; that Impact communities, people, in positive ways.

Acts that deserve Respect and Esteem worthy of Immortalization in the pages of History. While the Story is not complete yet, but based on the facts we have here, it would not be a surprise not to notice the wide scope of positive effect the lives of Timothy & Sarah H. Brown had in the Town of Georgetown. Move onto the era of Alice Stevens., and it would be hard not to recognize her inner resolve to hold on to an undivided Brown Legacy. It is no feat for the wimpy person. That is a marvel of Womanhood, I would not mind joining the Sisterhood of. A Stellar Specimen of the Female Specie.

Then come the Stevens - Cossit Legacy. That is a true representation of a Love Story that any one in their right mind would not be ashamed of. View it even from the most practical angle: A merger that is capitalistic resulted to double dividend. How can anyone not like that? Still, no matter how one slice the facts, the Stories bring joy, inspiration, smells and reeks of LOVE, charity, wisdom, civility.

What is it? What is in it, that cause the opposing group to cross the very fine line of deception in an attempt to bring this Story of History to a resounding debacle of miserable mediocrity? Why debase the site this way?

Imagine living off the land, like literally living off the land, only this one is over someone else's land. The feeling of entitlement boggles me. If Mrs. Cossitt wanted for the people to have it, surely she would have given the property to them according to the lawful process. The fact that she did not, means there's gotta be a reason more profound than just not wanting to have the place be trespassed or neglected.

Plate 83- 6225 Hearth

The fireplace located in one of the sunrooms. An extension modification of the South bay of the house.

The Legacy and it's meandering Provenance.

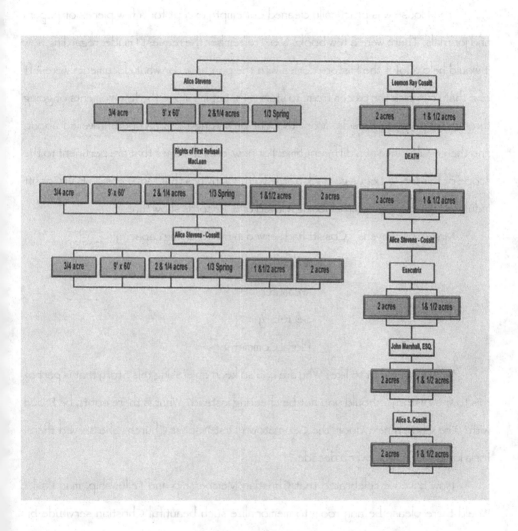

Plate 84 The Search to bestow the Guardianship of a Masterpiece.

XXIII. Alice on Church & Community Relations

The House was practically cleaned out empty except for a few pieces of papers and journals. There were a few books too. I remember the request I made, regarding how it would help a lot if the History comes with the purchase, or what documents were left of it that I can pick the pieces from, to start with. Let me share the few moments of going through what was left inside. More thought provoking facts can be unravelled about, and they would come at a different time. For now, only the ones that are pertinent to the scope of this book. Let us go back a little to the activities that Mrs. Leemon Ray Cossitt indulged in, to heal her pain of losing a loved one. Records show that:

Mrs. Alice Stevens - Cossitt had served in the following capacity:

Church Clerk

Treasurer

Secretary

Floral Committee

What is there not to like? Why are you so keen on erasing this Story that is part of this town's History? Should you not be cheering instead? What is there not to be Proud with? The Church next door: the Georgetown First Baptist Church. She served there, for a long time. A little over a decade.??

How have we celebrated that Christian Membership and Fellowship, may I ask? Would there please be any room to memorialize such beautiful Christian servitude by allowing for the legacy of the House be recognized. The undisturbed use of the 9'x 60' titled piece of land sold back to Timothy Brown by the Trustees of the First Baptist Church should not be erased, I am sure you can agree to that?

One way of honoring that legacy is to allow for the columns to be installed without hostility from the parishioners, that is one.

Second is for you, the 501 (c) (3) Mission to prevail. Improvement of the quality of life. Whose quality of lives? Exclusive to members only? Is taking something that is not ones own, an act of Christ likeness? Is this a way to improve the quality of life who was taken something from? Let us take for example the Parking space where 9' x 60' is supposed to be. Why is the marking of who owns what and what belongs to whom not a step for improving the quality of life? If there would be any emergency, and someone gets hurt, in that contested space, who's Insurance Coverage would assist in the care, and what resources would be used to fix the space and the person hurt?

Surely a few dollars for the use of the space would not bankrupt the Church and its members? It would be the human thing to do. Besides, the liability can be accounted for. This accounting of the liability responsibility for the space being used as parking space can in the long run be beneficial for the people that avail of that parking convenience, ease of worship access, and comfortable peace of mind that just in case an accident do occur, that there would be some funds to assist however small it may be, monetarily. Also, the issue of abuse of use, and the chances of neglect would be eliminated. The bright side would be improvement, visual appeal and the maintenance of the site.

Hear say had it that some elderly person already did get hurt. No assistance was extended. Whether this be factual or not, is this thought somehow not plucking on your heartstrings? Is this something that can be construed for the improvement of the quality of life? Are you being True to your Mission given the designation 501 (c) (3)? How are you able to get away with accountability? Your Fiduciary responsibilities, Trustees? This is not bad mouthing anyone. This is one of the many attempts tried and failed, all done privately and respectfully without any acknowledgement. I am bringing the issues that are challenging the endangerment of this beautiful structure, in a beautiful landscape that is at the very verge of extinction. It should not be. Yet the odds are stacked high up. The people holding the right offices had put on blinders, the failure to recognize the records that are even in their very offices are the lauded widespread culture.

It would be easiest for me just to assume the mousey type of reined in stereotyped Asian girl. That is the expectation? Slavery was supposedly demolished? It is the 21st century in the heart of America, in New York. Women go the Universities. Women are heard. You mean, I have to re - learn to find one's place, and lose one's voice again? When the fight had been Marched on by, and had been progressed by real people that died for this very cause. Rosa Parks, Martin Luther King, The Women Suffragists. I wonder what this experience tell the many young Malala of the world?

This is about doing the right thing because it is the right thing to do. Even when no one is looking. The worst is for one more person not to say anything when there is something to be said about. For this instance, a lot had to be said about the Truth. Not one person's truth, but a Universalistic Truth based on facts. That is the most unfortunate message here: The unfair distortion of the facts. I cannot. I would not be silenced. I need for all to hear this truth. For if this can be threatened to happen here, it may be happening somewhere else. Prevention is before, not after. The Reason, in this particular situation is: To have an Undivided, Unified Estate for the responsible use and appreciation of those that cared enough to ensure the True Legacy of this History be brought forth. I am bringing this very message to you dear readers, to everyone that care to know. Let the chips fall in place.

The Touch of the Master's Hand

The Touch of the Master's Hand
'Twas battered and scarred, and the auctioneer
Thought it scarcely worth his while
To waste much time on the old violin,
But held it up with a smile;
"What am I bidden, good folks," he cried,
"Who'll start the bidding for me?"
"A dollar, a dollar"; then "Two!" "Only two?"
"Two dollars, and who'll make it three?
Three dollars, once; three dollars, twice;
Going for three----" But NO,
From the room, far back, a gray - haired man
Came forward and picked up the bow;
Then, wiping the dust from the old violin,
And tightening the loose strings,
He played a melody pure and sweet
As a caroling angel sings.

Side Notes:
This makes me liken this next chapter about First
Refusal to the story in this poem; and wonder
about the age of Mrs. Cossitt; 1972 to the final
sale in 1986: Was she looking To anoint the
next Steward to this Legacy?

And many a man with life out of tune,
And battered and scarred with sin,
Is auctioned cheap to the thoughtless crowd,
Much like the old violin.
A "mess of pottage," a glass of wine;
A game and he travels on.
He is "going" once, and "going" twice,
He's "going" and almost" gone."
But the Master comes, and the foolish crowd
Never can quite understand
The worth of a soul, and the change that's wrought
By the touch of the Master's hand.

Side Notes:
A poem about an Old Violin
That Resounds like the Story of this House
In more ways crying out loud
A story that needed to be told
To be understood.

The music ceased, and the auctioneer,
With a voice that was quiet and low,
Said: " What am I bid for the old violin,"
And he held it up with the now.
"A thousand dollars, and who'll make it two?
Two thousand! And who'll make it three?
Three thousand, once three thousand, twice,
And going, and gone," said he.
The people cheered, but some of them cried,
"We do not quite understand
What changed its worth." Swift came the reply:
"The touch of the Master's hand."

Side Notes:
This literary masterpiece was penned by:
---Myra Brooks Welch.

This poetry brings out these feelings and emotions that make my mind wander, and wonder whether Alice Stevens, Mrs. Cossitt was then at the point of her life looking for the next Master Keeper to Carry out the Greater Plan of preserving the heritage of this Magnificent Structure Intact, Undivided?   The search was on: 1972 to 1986.

1972

Plate 85-0653 The MacLean Family

56. Rights of First Refusal

The MacLean: Dorothy & Richard

1972, July 11 Liber 664 p. 820 $50.00 Notarized: 11 July 1972 Recorded: 12 July 1972
The following were extracted from the above book of records in it's digested form:

1   The party of the first part to sell, grant and convey to the parties of the second part a right of first refusal in and to the property owned by Alice S. Cossitt, and more particularly described in the following deeds which were duly recorded in the Madison County Clerk's Office: In Liber 510 of Deeds p.138; Liber 510 p. 141; and Liber 262 p. 276.

2   Said right of first refusal may be exercised by the parties of the second part upon receipt by them a written of a written bonafide offer of purchase to the party of the first part. Said written exercise of right of first refusal to be delivered in writing to the party of the first part within twenty (20) days after receipts by the parties of the second part of written notice of a bonafide offer of purchase.

3   The parties of the second part may purchase the said property by an agreement identical to the terms and conditions as are set forth in the bonafide offer from the third party.

4   In the event that the bonafide offer of the third party for any reason whatsoever fails to be consummated, then in such event the right of first refusal shall continue to survive the same.

5   This agreement shall apply to and bind the heirs at law, next of kin, executors and assigns of the respective parties and shall not be changed or modified orally.

Notes: There are not so many information about the people that played the part in this document. The main thing is that there was this interest for this family to take on the responsibility of taking care of the Site. This is apparently clear here. From 1972 to the time Mrs. Cossitt finally turned the property to the Wilsons, fourteen long years interval. I wonder what happened? This is another part of the story that can be told?.

57. Deed of Sale, 1986

1986, December 05 Liber 829 p. 238 Recorded: 1:30 PM : from Mrs. Alice S. Cossitt herself, to the Wilsons. This transaction was very straight forward. The four titles from the Timothy & Sarah H. Brown Estates, with the two other parcels that came legacy of Mr. Leemon Ray Cossitt. Here's the breakdown:

3/4 acre

9' x 60'

2 & 1/4 acres

1/3 undivided rights to a Spring

2 acres

1 & 1/2 acres

We do not have to be Mathematicians to sum this land holdings, do we? Yes? I thought so too. Surely, one would understand that it is more expensive, time consuming, and taxing to the virtue of patience to correct an error made after the fact; than to start a complex project with an expensive initial investment of taking the time to ensure calculated risks with very narrow margin of error that pays off in the end. Do things right. Doing things right, the first time. I believe, that is how the Sages of ancient times say it.

Plate 86-0646   Cossitt to Wilson

58. The Wilson

Mr. James Wilson had a press release: The following were glimpses of reflections gathered from that article penned by MS. Marie Villari, for the Syracuse Herald American Section B - 3.

1   Date: 1989, January 29, Sunday

2   Main title: The Spirit House Lives On

3   Sub - Title: New owner invites the living to a place built for the dead

4   Mr. James Wilson, a native of Troy, Ohio

        Came to Syracuse in 1959, moved to Cazenovia 1980

        Sales Specialist for A. O. Smith, GT- Sylvania, Carrrier, Thrush Inc.

5   James & Valerie bought the Inn, Spring of 1985

        Georgetown Inn boasted of Gourmet Kitchen, Silver & Antique Motif

        Spirit House opened as a B & B, opened for group tours

6   The Couple reached out to the Community, the Town Hall Meeting gleaned the four requests of the local people:

      6.1   No non - Dairy Products

      6.2   Keep the Video Games out

      6.3   Get the porno flicks off the VCR

      6.4   Use local Help

Notes: From what documents I had the privilege of perusing over, the Wilsons had been really good about the requests. The Inn turned gourmet Restaurant, provided employment for the local workers. The kindness; the conscientious penchant to quality service; the wholesome work environment; were evident in the records reviewed.

Plate 87-0625   James & Valerie

59.   James & Valerie

James AB Business Admin.

Miami University, Oxford, Ohio

Business Specialist, Sales

Valerie was a long time Educator

Social Sciences, Civics, Law

Fayetteville - Manlius High School

1989, October 02   Liber 895 p.316 for $1.00 Recorded: 02 Oct. 1089 at 4:15 PM

The Wilsons quitclaimed the property to the Kartorie Family. As far as the descriptions, nothing had changed. From the purchase date to the time they had turned over the responsibility for the Site: three years transpired. What happened?

WHY?

So many hear says, so many bits of anecdotes contradictory to one another. My take on it given the facts and the experiences I had been subjected to; the following questions. Food to feed the brain and bring it to mull. They keep coming over and over like the froth on the waves that get thrashed over the edge of rocky shores at high tide.

1   What is the culture that permeate this Town?

2   Is it the kind that when a hand reaches out to assist, the arm and the entire body gets thrown into the pit instead?

3   Is this the culture that Mrs. Alice Cossit had been trying to get away from?

4   Or should I word this as: This is the reason as to the why she had not placed this property to such a type of corporation to handle this Trust with? Because the people she thought she had entrusted this with, will divvy it up; take the loot; torn to the tiniest of bits and pieces; blown by the wind, and then gone. That is, as if nothing was really ever here to begin with?

Plate 88-0651 Wilson - Kartorie Family

XXIV. Wilson - Kartorie: A Family Affair United to a Promise

The records showed that MR. James Wilson quit - claimed the Property to the Kartorie Family. I remembered the local people telling me that "the woman" Promised that she would never sell the Property until she dies of natural causes. She feared an untimely death if she ever does otherwise, it was told as if this was supposed to be a curse of some sort. I have not come across any Scientific rationale or tangible documents accepted beyond question on this, and therefore I am resting this piece of hearsay to rest.

It is factually documented that from time the James & Valerie Wilson took on the responsibilities, the baton was then passed to the Helen & Valentine Kartorie Family. This is the family where Mrs. Valerie Wilson came from. The property was passed to her via the Executrix route when all the primary willed heirs met their creator before her. The imposed responsibility now laid back on her shoulders for sound judgement on choosing who to pass this gigantic duty to move the legacy forward, positively. The years went by. I was informed that this was offered to the Historical Society. Then the "for sale" sign, that stood there - for years. The rest, is easy for you to fill. As the facts are recent, they can be to google out quickly. I just want to request caution in coming to narratives that impugn reputation regarding the purchase. That will be on the next page, my page.

What is remarkably noble in this Family Affair was for them to hold onto the Promise that cost Money, without any return. The taxes had to be paid, the House and its estate had not been generating any revenue. Everyone who had been there had taken something out of it. The grounds. The House. Be it about memories which I hope would be positive, and not some life changing traumatic ones that one need to oxidize down the road, a picture, pictures - an abundance of them. Yes, a plant, a stone, a corner here, a corner there. Even perhaps said something that had been stretched beyond the framework of the Truth. Not one from any one of those members of the public had given something back except the carbon footprints left nonchalant.

These were visible in mounds of pet liters, fecal matter, clam shells by the tonnage, and the practically free use of the site, without any permission from the owners. If this is the idea of Respect in the Most advance of Civilization, I wonder what it would be back in the Era of the Flintstones. Hanna Barbera seemed to have more, in Privacy, Honor, Civility, and Decency. Have anyone ever thought about renting the place if anyone wanted to use it for any outdoor functions from walking around, ogling whatever, barbecuing, using it as a dumpsite, people pay a fee to bring trash at the landfill, you know. They are priced by the bulk, and tonnage.

Even Government funded Parks, together with Government run recreational facilities, are charging Entrance Fees. There are schedules, restrictions. There is such a thing as regulated use. Accountability, Responsibility presented in fees accordingly charged. Such prescribed decorum, type of use and functional purpose acceptable in a civilized society.

In this instance: This is a farming community. Why would the same values not be applicable? You and I have made purchases from a farmer's stand by the side of the road, without the farmer there. I believe it is called Honor System. A locked box with a slit for the money, would be there. That would be for the more sophisticated ones, but surely, one have seen the farm stands where there would be an actual glass jar for cash right there in the open, to have some change if the need presented itself.

On these occasions, one feels wonderfully honorable leaving more money than taking the rest of the few cents back for change. Do you not feel Superiorly Civilized, like a real human being, just reading this scenario that you may have been in, yourself? Honesty, Integrity, Truth. These are the Basics of Existence. The Human Existence. Last time I check, and continue to do so, even after this writing, I have not come face to face to any that would change that observation. Do help me change this, and Thank you.

That, or should we gather round and not let this "thoughtless crowd" type of mindset be the catalytic vehicle of hastening the meltdown of this Community just because a few in town had been trying to auction the Estate Cheap? That even though a few tried to literally and physically tried their Master's Hand be guided to touch this Site into something more than a dumping ground and free for all irresponsible play area, "but the Master comes, and the foolish crowd still cannot quite understand" that it is for the good of humankind for which the locals are a part, that these people who had invested efforts, energy, resources, now includes me meant well, not just for my own interests, but for the overall and in the long run?

> And many a man with life out of tune,
> And battered and scarred with sin,
> Is auctioned cheap to the thoughtless crowd,
> Much like the old violin.,...
> But the Master comes, and the foolish crowd
> Never can quite understand

Let this six line passage not be the official mantra anymore. Instead, take the "Beatles" line on: "Let it be, let it be, Acting on words of wisdom, because the Light is still in front of us, Let it be". Or Bette Midler with this: Because "YOU ARE the WINGS BENEATH This [PROJECT'S] WINGS". A far better cry than Silverstein's "The giving tree"!?.

60. Death 5

The Matriarch that kept the Promise have given up the ghost. This is the fifth permanent end in the chain of ownership. Once too often, we revisit that fork. We arrived at another one of those crossroads in the journey of this House.

Let us therefore, take another look at the circumstances surrounding this event. This time, it is a little too close to home, as it is very much within the modern era. You and I, are either born already, or in school, or doing some other things important only to each of us alone. One thing for sure, if you are reading this book, it would have meant, you are of the maturity crucial to knowing or understanding. That you can almost touch it, or play any of the characters in this story. Who knew?

That you would one day read about this place in this type of format.

That all the plans conceived by this beautiful woman would not all be realized,

That the unrealized can come to fruition, no matter where the dreamer was

That for every life that ended in finality, the dream lives on to new beginnings

That equally ambitious individuals would step up the plate no matter what

That to try & carry the torch is the challenge of a lifetime, embodied in the House

That these goals are reified in words, in deeds, in action - visual & performance

That after Death comes calling, lives lost connect more lives, fuller and richer

That some nobody like me, would dare celebrate the positive in it, about it, with it

That through this permanent good - byes, an edifice etched with good deeds can

take the shape of print & cyber form

That somehow, a tribute readable, touchable, portable, can be made

That commemorate the good deeds of the dead, found in deeds?

61. The Will 2

Helen Kartorie's Estate in direct correlation with the Brown - Stevens - Cossitt Legacy.

The people that can truly say that their lives literally crossed paths with the characters of the saga of this Historic Site, are the Wilson and the Kartorie Family. This is true in the sense that the era is something can still relate to. Here is the visual of that webbed interconnectivity. It is very unfortunate that there was a huge disconnect with the local individuals. Thirty something years, and we are still not moving forward. Did I inherited the angst of whatever it is that ails this Town?

1864, 1872 & 1871, 1884	The Brown
1898	The Stevens
1920	The Alice Stevens Buy out Move
1955	The Stevens - Cossitt Legacy
1986	Alice Stevens - Cossitt to the Wilson
1989	Wilson to Kartorie

Helen Kartorie survived her Husband Valentine Kartorie. Valerie Wilson survived Willis Kartorie, her brother, the Executor of the Helen Kartorie Estate. Thus Valerie Wilson stepped onto the plate to take on the responsibility of choosing who would be the successor in the responsibilities that come in the Ownership Role for this Magnificent Home. It was no easy feat. The years rolled by. Do people even realized that this responsibility left on her shoulders was like an albatross, especially when there was no gratitude lost from the local people? At least from those that I had the awakening moments of recognizing there's more than meets the eyes. A very Sad Notion.

62.   The Executrix V

Sound Judgement, Responsible Choices, Solid Decisions

Key			
M	1864	Timothy Brown from Samuel Clark	H
O	1871	Sarah H. Brown from Zinah J. Moseley et al.	I
M	1872	Timothy Brown from Elnathan Ellis	S
E	1884	Sarah H. Brown from Hiram Atwood et al.	T
N	1920	Alice Stevens from Bertha, Frances, Julia & Alice	O
T	1939	June 27 Leemon Ray Cossitt from William Trass	R
S	1947	April 21 Leemon Ray Cossitt from Harold J. Evans	Y
IN	1986	Alice S. Cossitt to the James & Valerie Wilson	
	1989	James & Valerie Wilson to Valentine & Helen Kartorie	
	2011	Executrix Valerie Wilson to Resurreccion Dimaculangan	

Waiting all these long years for the Magic. Behold Steaming under the surface, reflective of it's present gutted state is Pain. Oh, if the House possess literal vocal cords! The more than 30 years of stagnation, and a story of cover up in Historic Proportions. Let this farce not continue.

Allow me to pay tribute to the person assigned the most important task of finding someone to have the heart, the head, the means, one way or another, and the passion to dedicate a lifetime to this responsibility. This is without question a formidable quest. For her to achieve that, is worthy of recording the effort in granite documentation. Since this is not an immediate possibility as of this writing, let it be recorded here: This is to acknowledge in the Solace of Gratitude, what transpired. 2011, the year that was.

Past, Present, & Moving forward.

XXV.   Deed of Sale 2011

The Magnificent House & Additions

The Detached 2 car - Garage with separate lift doors

The Mansard Roofed - Barn with Glass lift door

Plate 89 Charted Conveyed Acreages

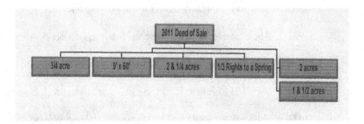

Step 1   Inquiries:

Why is a Magnificently Beautiful House, Historically Landmarked for Sale? What are the challenges? How is the neighborhood? Who are the Key Pillars of the Community? What is the Demographic Make - up? What is the inter-societal Culture that permeate the core of the Town?

Step 2   Procurement

The cash transaction was the form chosen to put the Project in the Fast Track Mode. The need for immediate, and urgent action to ensure that the House does not fall into Oblivion was the reason for this. The following were the actual initial steps undertaken to adhere to the notion of the Project, that is in the "Spirit of Making a Positive Difference, One Person at a Time."

Step 3

The six parcels together with the Structure were accessioned upon the signing of the Sales Transaction in the Process of Closing. That should be a no brainer. That was when the inconsistencies of the Documentations were finally brought to the surface.

It was then fully realized that there was this cauldron of boiling hot lava ready to be spewed out all these years. That was not disclosed to me while attending all the meetings of all the Key Agencies within the Town, preceding the purchase, and during the time of getting to know, inquiry, and scouting stages embarked upon. Then a little after the purchase, there was the dance of wait and see, which I will call the honeymoon stage, if there was one.

Step 4   Inquiries 2:

Fact Finding Efforts to diagnostically pinpoint where the issue started as to the WHY, HOW, and WHO to Go to, what type of antidote to be applied to fix the Problem the civilized way.

Step 5 Review of the Nomination Application Forms[36]

Revealed the most inconsistent, the most biased, the most one track context of setting a site for Historic Registration using narratives of persons with only one subject in mind. Not one read the titles and the deeds. This is one of the many reasons why the Project is in a standstill. Defining the Area, Marking the Periphery for Liability reasons and for Documenting History based on Facts. Facts recorded in legally accepted proofs of Documentation.

The work is not over once the last page is turned over. It is just the beginning. The journey is long and tedious. This is not about liking the actual people. This is about Respecting the Cause that is being Waged. The cause of History to be based on facts, this story, this History in particular. Accurate, Authentic Documentation of the Real Story. Land Recordings are based on Math, and with today's techno gadgets, we should be able to Scientifically retrace what the documents say they are.

Step 6   Rectification Process to Start the Healing towards Unification

The sixty - five thousand dollar question: Wherein answers to be understood need not be verbalized, but put in action. Acts that make a positive difference for every one concerned; for the whole of human kind.

---

[36] www.NYPARKS.gov

$65,000.00?

The Touch of the Master's Hand: Drawing the Parallels

'Twas battered and scarred, and the auctioneer - Thought it scarcely worth his while
To waste much time on the old violin, But held it up with a smile;
"What am I bidden, good folks," he cried, "Who'll start the bidding for me?"
"A dollar, a dollar"; then "Two!" "Only two?" "Two dollars, and who'll make it three?
Three dollars, once; three dollars, twice; Going for three----"
                    But NO,
From the room, far back, a gray - haired man, Came forward and picked up the bow;
Then, wiping the dust from the old violin, And tightening the loose strings,
He played a melody pure and sweet, As a caroling angel sings.

Note:

Let me take these words often used as a way to lift souls, spirits and the physical being of people; and use them instead to animate this Magnificent Structure. In every way this House is like this Old Violin. Battered, scarred and given up for junk except that for some fortuitous circumstances, these efforts to erase its real story had not been quite fully realized. I may not have been the gray haired Master of a Man in the literal sense, but that is just the point, the Master in each one of us come in different forms. There is not one exact way. At this point, I am trying to make Music at least figuratively for now; a beautiful one. Stage One of that is: Habilitation of the site from the grounds up. That includes accounting of the six deeded parcels that came with the House.

The music ceased, and the auctioneer, With a voice that was quiet and low,
Said: " What am I bid for the old violin?" And he held it up with the bow.
"A thousand dollars, and who'll make it two? Two thousand! And who'll make it three?
Three thousand, once three thousand, twice, And going, and gone," said he.
The people cheered, but some of them cried,
"We do not quite understand; What changed its worth." Swift came the reply:
            "The touch of the Master's hand."

Note:

Here I am calling out to the public in this format to make you understand that what I do now, is tantamount to the bid. The pricelessness of this Project depend on the actions I take on today. I hear the cynicism, the skepticism, the antagonistic stances. Unfortunately, I steeped up to the plate evidenced in the procurement of the site. I have tried to get your voices through the tax exemption. Nobody cheered, no one cried. This noble effort to connect to you was returned with derision. Did I misread the reception?

And many a man with life out of tune, And battered and scarred with sin,
Is auctioned cheap to the thoughtless crowd, Much like the old violin.
A "mess of pottage," "a glass of wine"; A game, and he travels on.
He is "going" once, and "going" twice, He's "going" and almost" gone."
But the Master comes, and the foolish crowd Never can quite understand
The worth of a soul, and the change that's wrought By the touch of the Master's hand.

---Myra Brooks Welch.

Note:

You forget, this Beautiful House is in danger of receiving the same fate as the Muller Mansion that you are so proud to talk about. Yet, not a scrap of it's beauty remained today. A myth. Is this what you want? *"Auctioned cheap to the thoughtless crowd"?* You trample this place all these years: trespassers, free users, encroachers, all for personal vested gain and interests; without thoughts for the upkeep of the place. Everyone out to get a slice off it, one way or another. That is not what Alice Stevens had in mind in 1920 as I see it today. That is not Mrs. Alice Stevens - Cossit's intent for this site to be, as I feel my way through the pages of the deeds. That is not the story oozing out of all the collective data available.

It is about the unified whole, intact, the way it is as the documents say. It is about responsible use, accountability of actions and choices to ensure the longer lasting presence of this Structure as a reminder of the lives lived, personal achievements, hardships, economic, cultural mileposts moved in successive progression. What is there not to like? You have not even shelled out a dollar. You have taken more and continue to do so. You have the gall to even erase the truth. *"the foolish crowd Never can quite understand, The worth of a soul, and the change that's wrought"!*

We can only fail ourselves when we stop recognizing what is right from wrong. What is good from bad. We are expected to have learned these from our childhood. What happened? Surely, it would not be too late to take pause, and retrace our steps to opening our minds to what really is happening here?

Recognize. Rectify. Even Repatriate To Reap, the Results of Realizing that Records do Recite Realities that Restore Relationships.

63.   Rexie

A page to talk about myself would not be sufficient, and it is beyond the scope of this book. This is not about me, this is about the Project. The Journey of that Project, as it traverses that winding, lonely road. The House cannot speak for itself. If that was so, it would have told the story long ago. Tragic. For a long while now, but let it not be a sad one forever. Let us give this Story, a Love Story from the people, a Happy ending. Let the end of that unfortunate story be NOW, so a new sequel in good spirits can be ushered in, and move on positively forward cheerfully. If nothing else, let it be a home that can be open to receive guests.

Responsible guests, and visitors that understand that upkeep costs aplenty, and would be generous. Since when did anyone visited a home and never brought anything, even just on the first visit? Especially the first visit? What about when you do not know the person and you want to have a positive impression? Any takers on the notion of just plain cultural exchange and understanding?   How about being a friendly neighbor? Remember how the new student need to be welcomed? How about that type of outreach? It is not always what one can get out of the new kid in town, but about how we can sustain one another for the long haul. A Synergistic coexistence is something that is invested on with love, charity, kindness, empathy - my brothers' keeper.

The focus should be on the fate of what this Site would be. The Deed of Property ownership is intact. What are not, are the attitudes of the people that have selfish vested interests that do not include the perpetuity of the presence of this structure for the long haul. By all records and data gathered at this point, the House should have been self - sufficient all these years. The Maintenance, [through the actions of a Certified Competent Survey of the actual Titled Land Estate that came with the House], and even Improvements, could have been funded just from the income that should have been generated from the use of the land.

The Thank you / s from the pictures taken, do we have to ask for it? Really?

The LAW and The Values of SOCIETY INTERWOVEN with the BEST INTERESTS of this SITE.

Once you knew this was now Private Property, which it had always been even before 2011 and to today; and pending the Rehabilitation Stages, that can pave the way for a more civilized, responsible use of the Site, How did the community supported the progress of this Historically landmarked Site? Did any one? What ways?

Remember Elizabeth Barret Browning (1806-1861), when she penned this? Sonnet 43:

How do I love thee, Let me count the ways
I love you to the depth and breadth and height
My soul can reach, when feeling out of sight
For the ends of being and ideal grace.
I love thee to the level of everyday's
Most quiet need, by sun and candle light
I love thee freely, as men strive for right

I love thee purely, as they turn from praise
I love thee with the passion put to use
In my old griefs, and with my childhood's faith
I love thee with the love I seemed to lose
With my lost saints, I love thee with the breath,
Smiles, tears, of all my life, and if God choose,
I shall but love thee better after death.

Well? Let met me count the ways. Particularly this Literal site, needed tangible, measurable ways.

The issue of landholdings, and the legacies of the owners that dutifully went through the legal process of procuring each parcel, why take possession of them unlawfully? Where is decency? Is this the type of Historical facts that this Site should be narrating another hundred years from now? Well, that is what you should hope not. Please think about it, you were here yesterday. You'll be here today, and tomorrow, maybe. It is you writing your story, the kind of story that the future generation would retrace, and read about. It is up to you. Right now, the entire estate and the History is intact. That is until you, threatened to undermine the recorded documents of this beautiful marvel of History, in its roots today. Yes, in the era where nothing cannot be uncovered nor be left unexplained any more. Supposedly?. This ball is in your hands.

Here are the ways: Via the Authentic, Historical Legacy accounting of Acreages Inventory. Immortalize the ways this Town and the People had benefitted from all the functions of the potable water source, the plank road, the OVRR, the cemetery, the parking space, the unaccounted proceeds past and present, that would usher in the responsible, accountable future. Rally behind the Cause of historical Integrity, accuracy and truth!

So many lawyers consulted, all professed specialists. There was just one answer: cut the site the way the adjoined property owners wanted it, without even looking at the documents. I have literally took upon myself to metaphorically hit the books, and now am looking at the law to guide me in all my actions and decisions here. This is also to share to the reader right away the laws regulating the actions of every person, citizen or not without going out of the way to check them while reading this work. This does not mean discouragement to fact check; on the contrary, as growth in understanding is achieved by search and research. These are some of the tons of documents I have taken into account and placed considerations with, as I pored over the facts of this Site for better in depth comprehension. I am no lawyer, nor I am not trying to be. I am a person with civic responsibilities to my government, conscientious beliefs guided by my faith in God, and human need to account for my contributions to the betterment of oneself, my family, my peers, the community, the society at large. Here are a few of them, and I encourage for all of us to cross reference again; brain storm with proficient and skilled law specialists; search for the unbiased understanding of what we have in front so we may all deliver justice to the efforts of those that were ahead of us in the journey of traversing life.

"GOL Title 3 Certain Prohibited Contracts and Provisions of Contracts:
General Obligations Law

Section 5-331. Certain covenants and restrictions in conveyances and other agreements affecting real property void against public policy

Any promise, covenant or restriction in a contract, mortgage, lease, deed or conveyance or in any other agreement affecting real property, heretofore or hereafter made or entered into, which limits, restrains, prohibits or otherwise provides against the sale, grant, gift, transfer, assignment, conveyance, ownership, lease, rental, use or occupancy of real property to or by any person because of race, creed, color, national origin, or ancestry, is hereby declared to be void as against public policy, wholly unenforceable, and shall not constitute a defense in any action, suit, or proceeding. No such promise, covenant or restriction shall be listed as a valid provision affecting such property in public notices concerning such property. The invalidity of any such promise, covenant or restriction in any such instrument or agreement shall be listed as a validity of any other provision therein, but no reverter shall occur, no possessory reason of the disregard of such promise, covenant or restriction. <u>This section shall not apply to conveyances or devices to religious associations or corporations for religious purposes, but such promise, covenant or restriction shall cease to be enforceable and shall otherwise become subject to the provisions of this section when the real property affected shall cease to be used for such purpose.</u>

Add, L 1963, ch 576, § 1, with substance transferred from Real P § § 259-b; amd, L 1964, ch 196, § 2, eff Sept 27, 1964."

This is bringing the issue of the parking space used by this church. There were many communicative efforts to openly discuss this elephant in the room. To clarify the use, the improvements, and account for responsibilities necessary in the documentation of the Project that had been ignored adversarially. I wonder why?

Surely, at this point, it should not be an argument as to the responsible use of parking spaces? How many times have any one here paid for the parking space use? This is not about nickeling and diming. This Project is very much out in the open. This is to move this Site forward in relation with the present. Why oppose? Especially when the effort is to improve, account for and ensure the safety and insurability? Top that with neighborliness, and common usage for the improvement of quality of life? What is there not to like? Can't afford parking space donations?

Now, going back to the efforts of placing cornerstones to mark the acreage legacy of this Historic site that were rebuffed with both covert and overt hostility is besides me. How does one rationalize these negative adversarial actions from a religious group that is IRS designated 501 (c) (3) which meant that the mission is for the improvement of the quality of life, yet keep their actions on the opposite course? What about the Trustees? Trusteeship and it's fiduciary responsibilities? Surely, we should be able to understand that keeping tract of the truth of History is part & parcel of keeping up with the mission of improving the quality of lives? That meant moving culture, society and community positively forward? That means not forgetting the past? That means telling the story that is based on the facts? That if there are differences, and there would always be, these can be aired in a civilized manner called discourse?

Here is to my beloved neighbor, a key family in the town that had ripped the containment barriers from the northeastern end of the tree line. If they are really so adversed about the ugliness of these rehabilitation containment barriers, why have they not wrote the check to fund this Project? To spread the unfounded notion that they even own the site without the "conveyance document to prove ownership" is appalling. To have law enforcers side with them is beyond me. Is this really what New York in the suburbs is about? The property law articles and sections chosen to represent an array of them that pertain to the situational complexities detailed here are nothing but gists in a peanut shell.

The in depth, and more explorative viewpoints can be taken cared of by the most proficient law professional that I hope I get a chance to collaborate with. One that would feel the real story and the goals of this project and again as a passion to adroitly protect the real Truth. What had been presented here, are just the basic laws that any law abiding citizen or person can gear oneself to be informed, so as not be given the ran around; and not meant to step over any one. It would just like being the educated consumer, of any aspect of life, be it politics, food / clothes shopping, choosing a plumber or a manicurist, etc. Just to inform and be informed. If by any chance you readers had been educated in the most expensive tuition of real life, do please share us greenhorns, so we may not trample the same hot coals as badly. Thank you, in advance.

On one hand, this is to record the most disturbing of all: for law enforcers to say that they do not know, would not know whether a person own the title or the document of conveyance for this property when the file had been offered to them and my neighbors had not, is truly incomprehensible. Coming from the agency that enforce the law, truly, we can do better than that? Should I view this reaction as the scale already tipped differently, because of bias, and prejudice? I trimmed the vegetation within the property for grooming maintenance. I was told by some person that since the police car hides behind this evergreen bush, that I cannot, and should not trim it. Also, the reports of the visits? There's a lot to say about that, too. Am I safe?

RPAPL Article 8 Waste and Other Actions and Rights of Action for Injury to Real property § *841. Action for nuisance*

An action for a nuisance may be maintained in any case where such action might have been maintained under the laws in force immediately before the taking effect of article seventh of title <u>one of chapter fourteenth of the code of civil procedure as added thereto by chapter 178 of the laws of 1880</u>. A person by whom the nuisance has been erected and a person to whom the real property has been transferred may be joined by defendants in such action. A final judgment in favor of the plaintiff may award him damages or direct the removal of the nuisance or both. This section does not affect an action wherein the complaint demands judgement for a sum of money only.

Add, L 1962, ch 142, eff Sept 1, 1963; with substance transferred from Real P Law § 529.

Note: 2014, July 04 The farmer ripped the barrier enclosure used for rehabilitation purposes, as part of the Conservation & Preservation Stages of the Project Spirit House, with his huge tractor: the thunder of head on hit left the corner smashed. The police said it is "a civil action on my end". How was so? If the farmer had an issue about it, he should have filed a suit-civil. Now that he had destroyed my property, within my deeded property, is that still civil?

The farmer threatened there and then to remove them. The law enforcer did not do anything about it to stop. A few days after, that entire barrier enclosure on the East line around the trees [parcel of Sarah H. where L.R.Cossit's 1939 parcel would have connected to] were then individually removed as he cannot do it without harm to his farm equipment. One has to have help to take them down, [the way the barrier were designed to withstand adverse weathering conditions] and lifted them all off to the front of the yard by the Highway 26 for every one to see, a few days of their Town parade. This is one of the many reasons this Site had not been able to move forward, all these years.

RPAPL § 843. Fences and structures, when private nuisance

Whenever the owner or lessees of land shall erect or shall have erected thereon any fence or structure in the nature of a fence which shall exceed ten feet in height, to exclude the owner or occupant of a structure on adjoining land from the enjoyment of light, or air, <u>the owner or occupant who shall thereby be deprived of light or air shall be entitled to maintain an action in the supreme court to have such a fence or structure adjudged a private nuisance.</u> If it shall be so adjudged its continued maintenance may be enjoined. This <u>section shall not preclude the owner or lessee of land from improving the same by the erection of any structure thereon in good faith.</u>

Add, L 1962, ch 142, eff sept 1, 1963; with substance transferred from Real P Law § 3.

Note: When do civil acts cross over and become a crime? The rehabilitation barriers were made of white plastic barrels, sliced in half meant to contain the debris within the tree lined part of this Site acreages, according to the title, and within the flagged pins of the incompetent survey even. Take heed, not one property owner excepting that of the Wm. P. Hare / ROSS' Lot was more recently surveyed; and the commissioned survey for this site never dovetailed with that, as the deed descriptions say.

Plate 90   Containment Barrier for Rehabilitation Purposes

GOL Title 7 Requirements of writing, execution or acknowledgement for effectiveness or enforceability

Note: To minimally address the issue written in the article on the Newspaper the 5th of November 2011, expressing the idea that a rug had been pulled off under these group who had been trying to procure the property for over two years: here is the lawful reason this land purchase should not be encased in a cloud of inappropriate malice by the naysayers.

Section 5 - 701   Agreements required to be In writing

a. <u>Every agreement, promise or undertaking is void, unless it or some note or memorandum thereof be in writing</u>, subscribed by the party to be charged therewith, or by his lawful agent, if such agreement, promise or undertaking; (1 to 10)

Now, on the "lawful yet angling on moral turpitude equation": there should not be any question about it as well, on my end of it. That was the first question I asked the representatives, legal and real estate. I still am, researching every data to ensure everybody gets the benefit of the doubt. That is the reason this compilation of data is on this format, mind you.

What is questionable is to put a website as if this House had already been owned. Check this yourself on - line. Add the continuous propaganda against my efforts, word of mouth, in blogs and social media. That includes collecting donations for the House without any expressed permission from the owner. This one is in a "you tube" format legitimized with the picture stitched together in art form by one of the local university professors. To those that had been supporting these indecent and unethical acts; how about trying to check the criminality behind the actions? I believe it is worded as fraud, and taking something that is not one's own is stealing; saying something that is not true, much more factually incorrect is misrepresentation, borders fraud, forgery, deceit.

Another, what do you call boasting and bringing friends over to show off this House they pretend to be theirs? How many times had I been disrespected to put it very delicately here?! These people range from youngsters, teens, to adults, at all hours. What is unnerving is the fact that if this is the way adults transfer the twisted information about this site to their younger generation, can any one reading this imagine what that mean for the real History of this Magnificent House, and the acreage legacy of the people that literally walked this town, now buried deep in the grounds, and their real contributions with them? Is this really what the field of History is about now? Is this the field of Museology about as seen today? Is this Education? Is this the moral obligation of telling the Truth? Is this our Society's moral fibre in the 21st Century?

Section 5- 703 Conveyances and contracts concerning real property to be in writing

I   An estate or interest in real property, other than a lease for a term not exceeding one year, or any trust or power, over or concerning real property, or in any manner relating thereto, cannot be created, granted, assigned, surrendered or declared, unless by act or operation of law, or by a deed or conveyance in writing, subscribed by the person creating, granting, assigning, surrendering or declaring the same, or by his lawful agent, thereunto authorized by writing. But this subdivision does not affect the power of a testator in the disposition of his real property by will; nor prevent any trust from arising or being extinguished by implication or operation of law, nor declaration of trust from being proved by a writing subscribed by the person declaring the same. (2-4)

Note: I recall one of the local Town Councilors asking me to sign an agreement with them as advised by the Fayetteville Historical Society that the House can be made available for use. When I informed them that I can say for sure that there were cases that at least once a year, private landmarked sites had been made open to the public. They doubted the idea or should I say the idea of having a Historically Landmarked Private House will be opened to the public at least once a year, did not sit right with them. This person insisted I am wrong, and thus I responded that the particular Historical Society he had friends with and I go a long way, unfortunately not in the best experience on my end. There's an entire e-mail about that circumstance: 2010-2011 time range. To me, This prove that these people are not playing fair regarding the situation of this Magnificent House. I am inclined to believe that they have no intention of anyone succeeding in this endeavor. ? Do correct me if I am wrong, here please.

REVOLUTIONARY EVOLUTION of PROGRESSION in SUCCESS and SUCCESSION.

Plate 91 Rehabilitation, Documentation, Interaction, from an Organized Chaos, the Green Way

64. Pepp E. Ronni

There are Silent deeds not deeded, and overshadowed behind the Project. Be it physical resources, time, effort, energy, the unseen traits of authentic kindness, and understanding on why things are done the way they are, and what make them important. These are the resources that any body in their right frame of mind would not want to go to waste. Tie that with the financial resources invested all these three years, going four. Add the almost two hundred years, 167 to be exact. These were years of waiting for this day to come just to be rescued scientifically. Give this Home a rest into Conservation, Preservation Mode. Yes, it is still standing, but needing urgent resuscitation Now. Act before it is too late. The fine line of no return: No to do over, it is time consuming. No second chances, in this case, as it would be really costly. No to "in hindsight."

This is one of the very first thing the public can do: To not waste the noble deeds bestowed towards the Site. Out of the inherent beautiful heart this Pepp E. Roni was blessed with, even if a not so willing benefactor for the cause; yet, had been so generous. The person is human, and gets affected by the hostilities of the actions that surrounded the area. Surely, civilized society can agree to be grateful, somehow?

It is my belief that this Town would not have another chance for people like us that had been so understanding, so kind, and so considerate and respectful of everyone's position and points of views about this beautiful Site. I do hereby sound the alarm for a call to action for a positive interaction, to allow for the acreages be accounted for, without antagonism, dissidence, resistance, nor aggression. If any one had chanced about this book, please do read and try to see the very positive views I had painstaking try to bring to you. Here's To that which is productive and positive.

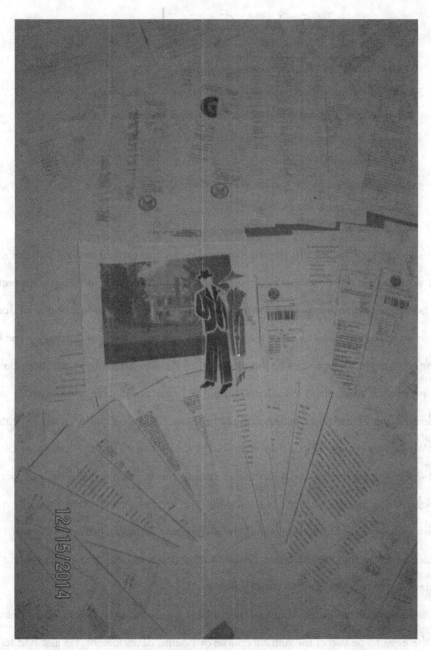

Plate 92-0654   rexie & albert

65. In A Capsule: FYI

1 Deed of conveyance - presumption of ownership

2 Taking something not one's own is stealing; Stealing is a Crime, punishable by law

   Individuals that facilitated such commission of a crime are called Accomplices.

   Individuals that committed the act of stealing are called Thieves.

3 Misrepresentation

4 Fabrication of Government Records + Fraud + Forgery

5 Malfeasance; Fiduciary Responsibilities

6 Inconsistent Documentation - Repatriation, Reparation

Correct errors, rectify the inconsistencies, fix the broken hearts, put the salve that would settle the desecration of lives that lived before us; that we may appreciate the beauty of simple things transformed out of love, and that passion can bring forth. There are different ways to make them right in a rational manner according to the law. Bringing these inconsistencies to the attention of the Departments in question; making the information available in story format that the larger population may hopefully glean understanding of the facts better, not just hearsay. Lastly, via civil & criminal litigation; but Why go there and help clog the judicial system when civility can take care of the facts? These statements come to mind in finding the balance: Lawful yet not morally upright; Morally just and Right but unlawful. The knights in the round table, they sat down, and faced off like human beings then. Why can't we be so, in the 21st Century? Is it because finding that middle ground meant "Without sacrificing, and compromising the obliteration of the Truth of this Historical Story"?

Remember the goose that laid the Golden Eggs? How the farmer could not wait for the eggs to be laid in the natural course of oocyte development. He just had to cut the goose wide open. Relevance? The state of affairs of this Historic site. The only thing different here was that the egg continued to support the day to day lifestyle of the people but without the acknowledgement of where these things really began? Yes without acknowledging that there was even a goose. The eggs were taken for the continuing value, the goose was obliterated. The Problem with covering the issue of the goose? The Truth always come out. Only with this one, the truth had been buried deep and currently is having a hard time coming out of all the muck and debris.

This is the story of the one - third undivided rights to a Spring. The piped water system that came out of the Spring. People in the 1800's acknowledged the importance of water as a cleansing resource, a hydration substance that need to be protected. The people also understood the commercial value of it, then and especially today. We bottle them, purify, distill, treat the source as" the make it or break it" base for the connoisseur mixes. The Cooperative that today it had evolved into, refused to admit the existence of this truth by recognizing the real owners of the divided parts that became of that property.

My goal for history to be factually true is to express gratitude to those that had owned the parts of this whole. Having revenues unaccounted for: The least that civilized human beings that profess to be Guardians & Trustees of the interests of the people, is to adhere to the lawful, and legally admitted notion that title holders meant rightful ownership, unless there is some document that says there was otherwise. Where is that document that contradict the deeded ownership of the House to all these inheritance? Is this another "let's use the spaces devoid of fees and responsibilities; then mow the lawn to let the appearance of ownership be the prevailing practice", preventing the titled owners to make improvements that would support the Historical Story of this Site?

AfterWords

While all the things brought out to light, if, for the benefit of basing History on Facts are of great import to anyone other than me; at the end of the day it is our goal to achieve positive results that would improve the quality of life of the people that we would have been privileged to cross paths with, along the way. Having the chance and the very dismal fleeting moment of capturing an opportunity to gather bonafide facts, in the laborious effort to try to do what is right, the choice to present the truth of the facts is the higher and only alternative. Many more horizons were opened, many doors slammed shut as well, and would be - moving forward, if my instincts serve me right. Yet, it is the trick the circumstances have brought upon me when I fell in love with this home, my Home now; that I have to take ownership of those circumstances and the decisions I am faced with. If for any reason, long dormant wounds were brought back to life; after the scab had somehow seemingly developed, were found to be still not quite dry yet, Pardon me.

The efforts to retrace the true story based on recorded data are due to the deep seated conviction that to move forward is to set things right. Join me in doing what is right for this magnificent structure, that is very factually a labor of love. This is in the hope of enabling to pave the way to correct the erroneous actions and habits of the past. The facts are stacked up high. If the way to have the past be found to be in oversight is via due process, then so be it. There are no shabby feats of consequence either, mind you. These are especially true when the environment do not merit the cognition of the blunders. For there would not be any rectifying if there were no cognizance of errors, correct? Yes, and that make the efforts of trying, the most difficult. Because, the mistakes are being legitimately buried, ignored, promoted. That process of recognition versus denial is just too overwhelmingly taxing to any one's patience. Even the patience of the Saints, I found out. Let these not be deterrents in the focus towards the goal of Positivity, I coax myself. This Project, the cause and me, as a person and a conscientious citizen can surely benefit from a transfusion of efficient professional collaborations that which are prescribed within the laws. The support to achieve that should be self - evident from the agencies designed to do so.

And then this question: Do we have to go to these great lengths when we can all just sit down civilly and humanly admit to the truth, so we may express gratitude to those who had brought us all together in this type of circumstances? These things can be taken cared off without wasting the years go by, and ruining the chances of a more peaceful, productive co - existence. We can go over the Land Acreage accounting again: Timothy Brown: 3/4 acre, and 9' x 60'. Sarah H. Brown: 2 & 1/4 acres, and 1/3 undivided right to a Spring. Alice Stevens: ensured that the Timothy & Sarah H. Brown Legacy remain intact, undivided, the major link to the Leemon Ray Cossitt legacy: 2 acres, and 1 & 1/2 acres.

The over all total: less than 7 acres: What happened to them? Why is this magnificent Structure like the pauper, with these much inheritance and interesting legacy? It may not had been Vanderbuilt or of Downton Abbey calibre, but my, oh my... Is obliterating the truth, the factual truth better than fabricating and weaving a myth beyond the values this community was really brought up with? Is the made up story more sustainable, more important than acknowledging that these inheritances most of you so deny even today as beautiful as the legacy of the Spring bubbling forth from the ground that sustain you economically be left out from the pages of History?

The story of Oliver Twist never stop to make dry eyes get flooded with tears. The House is the non - living equivalent of Oliver Twist. It is Oliver Twist. Remember the part of tracing if he was the missing heir, so he can claim his true inheritance. The same was the will of the Englishman James Smithson, whose name was how Smithsonian Institution came about. Why can we not do the same for this House? The documents are still intact, why break the legacy and obliterate the true story? Why? Why?

Epilogue

Chronological Order of Key Events:

1864, 1871, 1872, 1884 Timothy & Sarah H. Brown

1895 John Currier

1897 Floyd Currier

1898 Chauncey G. Stevens

1920 Alice C. Stevens

1939, 1947 Leemon Ray Cossitt

1986 James & Valerie Wilson

1989 Valentine & Helen Kartorie

2011 Resurreccion Dimaculangan

A look back: The House had been for sale for about 3 years before I came along. By the time the purchase was concluded, a press release not from yours truly was printed the following day of the 04 November 2011 maligning the act to appear as had been " pulled the rug under the Group" that already had the Website about the House, collecting money. This is serious malice. For what reason, I still have not fathomed. Because the purpose of the deed was to make a positive difference; an invitation was sent to the other groups, and people interested about the preservation of the House; for a gathering at the Oneida Room of the Mansion House. The self identified main ambassador / spokesperson of that group was venomous. Maleficent, and very disagreeable. I tried to dampen such attitude, the person left harried. Looking back, I feel it is part of a grand scheme to smear campaign against me. Nothing came out of it but just that, a social gathering, no collaborative effort of any sort. At least I tried. A few weeks after that, in the middle of winter that following year, I felt like I was being roped to sign an easement with one of NYS' supposedly more preeminent private preservation group, for something that I am not clear nor would they have the inkling to clarify with, to make it crystal. That they would not be straight up front with me on what it was exactly they were asking me an easement for, was troubling.

This huge covert yet overt treatment to undermine led me to stop communicating with them, and focused on the many tasks ahead. I was the least favorite person to put it nicely here; all web hack forms were doled out to me aplenty. Not to mention the physical visitors that go running or hiding when they see me in all my raggedy Ann farm outfit. A joke? No. Petty, on the surface - yes. With all the jabbing received from all sides of those that love or value this Site, literal, physical, web, and otherwise, the mission still holds: to make a Positive Difference.

I am bringing these experiences out in the open as I feel that containment of the issues within the bounds of the local area was the best way to come to a resolution, then. Unfortunately, this would be the fourth year, and the cause received nothing but pain, without forward action. Adverse reactions detrimental to the Structure that is being Conserved, and to every one involved. These being the reasons, I had to involve the rest of Humanity at large, that this authentic story about this site may gain the traction it so deserves. It is also in the hopes that actions of those deviating from the laws, ethics and moral responsibilities be on check, and be redirected back on track.

People keep themselves wondering what would I do with the House. Some would even go to lengths to blatantly ask as: "What is the interest of your kind about this place?" Let me ask us all: What does a member of the Homo sapiens does with a House?

Even the birds build their houses called nests. Ants, their anthills. All right, let me say it here again. I invested the money to realize the following:

1   Roof over my head, as an owner

I am practically, literally homeless without it. The site, now became my permanent address which previously I did not have. With the structure, I am now home. If by all humane standards, may not be the best nor comfortably ideal for now: but we can all agree that it is good enough for a start up.

2   Sustainability

For the site, that can be expected to radiate back to me, to you, and the community. Far beyond how the Cooperative have managed the issue of the Spring by covering up the real owners! In my case; A career is needed. A source of revenue is crucial. Nourishment, clothing, shelter, debts, to pay and other socio - economic responsibilities have to be attended to. Taxes have to be paid. In this case, it came with real history being covered up and threatened to be effaced. What does one do with a piece of land in a farming community? Food can be grown. How so? You have animals , plants, flowers, water organisms. Farm resources, grown and harvested can be turn into revenues. Farm endeavors can be very lucrative, too, look at Monsanto. This Project may not be that gigantic, but hey, everything started small. Things, businesses, even life EVOLVE.

Faced with the knowledge that a Landmarked History whose real story intentionally switched over with a popularized myth stamped legit; What would a competent Registrar do? What about a Reputable, Respectable Historian? One that has a Masters Degree in Museum Studies? What about Me, at your service? Since you and many others are curious to look at this place, you can come and shape up to be the responsible, mature human beings, smart enough to pay your dues. Would you have me and many others come to your house or wander around your yard without the responsibility of respectful human civility?

Even government - run public parks, charge admission. Do I have to ask or would you rather be on the side of individuals, whose lifestyles are studded with noble acts of kindnesses? These can be measurably expressed either by making a donation, a gift, a thank you in useful valuations of your volition versus trespassing, sneaking when the owner is not home, or stealth utilization to get away without being accountable? What values do people of this community promote? Are these the same attitudinal legacy that are passed to the young ones? Is this the model behavioral decorum you want to be known for by effacing your own History that I have so respectfully embraced and given voice to, advocated for, taken on upon me to invest my university learning, in deference to the dictates of my Professional Responsibilities. You are all witnesses that there is no fear in me for hard conscientious work on the literal ground. You have seen the fiery spirit of personal passion, attested by years of trying to make every one understand: History should have factual Integrity! This one already does. Why go out of your way to break the laws to change, even expunge the authentic legacy?

Should I not be respected by taking the cause, and putting values, 5 digit values and counting? Is there anyone that recognize the noble acts of consideration to honor the legacy of the ancestors, who made this beautiful place a site of making a positive difference to the community, to the adjoining towns, to the region, the state, the world?!

Really, for me to itemize here what one does with Historic sites privately owned, and even those that are recipients of tax dollars seemed churlish, but I guess, even regulations, guidelines or laws had to be specifically written because there are needs for them to be delineated, huh.

3   The Plan. The Plan? Hmm, for those that are still asking.

This is the easy one. Unfortunate because again, why this had to be individually explained here? For those who understand financial matters, a budget designed for one person cannot be used for 20 people without busting the mission, the goal, the purpose. So is the reverse of that. If the overarching goal is for sustainability, that means the investments had to generate a return = ROI. Even Farmers, honest or not, operate on this premise. First, one has to know what one owns. Identify the resources, what issues are addressed, need to be addressed, etc. SWOT.[37] If you are still wondering what the plan is. May I ask: Did you really read everything I have written here? Well, thank you. So, why are you still asking? Okay, Okay. For the sake of repetition for better comprehension. Here is another way to say the same things over. ^o^

$65,000.00 is a capitalistic investment, mind you. For that much acreage, surely that is a great possibility? Then lay off the dog poop. Organic did not mean, E. Coli contaminated. If the grand scheme of making a Positive Difference One Person at a Time be allowed to flourish in it's natural course, then Sustainability can be achieved. Economically self - sustaining ventures create waves that radiate to the community. Let this Project be the vehicle to bring that without the hitch of rancor, controversy, gossip etc. Let is be straight forward neighborly conversations by calling on me next door in person, and share ideas, ideals, information, freely - like civilized, educated human beings. We can all start by acknowledging the truth, and letting the facts be aired. Defining the periphery clears the spatial acreage for full blast habilitation, movements and improvements, to name a few of what can be achieved.

4   What you can do?

---

[37] strengths, weaknesses, opportunities, threats

The least each one of us can do is to allow for the Truth to be heard, louder and clearer as people seem to be inclined to hear more, understand better and listen attentively to the fad of mysticism, legends and fables and had come to regard such as facts over the complex specifics found in recorded legal documents. This is scary for me to see that the experience, the next generation are being taught had been this way. Passing the bonafide information, comprehending authentic data, weighing them for their weight in gold, still do matter.

For my investments, and for the upkeep of the property that would lead to improvements, for experiments, testings, taxation, materials, assistants, insurances, among the many things this site need, and my personal expenditures: please feel free to not be ashamed to pay your way or donate your way to the right door, to the right gate be it taking pictures, postings, enjoying works in progress, and inspecting the different stages, or mere interacting with me. Your taxable contributions and gifts are expected and greatly appreciated. Make sure I personally thank you in recognition of your support, appreciation or camaraderie for the cause of this Project: Preservation and conservation towards self - sustainability for the House, and the site.

Remember, I am not ready to receive visitors and guests, so when you brave coming, that is with the knowledge of this disclaimer that you do these actions on your risks. Yes, I would make sure that nothing untoward harm any one, but accidents do happen, and situations do occur. Let us all be responsible and accountable of our actions. Take heed, despite all these, it is still a private home. Thank you.

5   What's in it for you?

A) First, you'll be able to not have a "cheap roadside show" for a "curiosity" within your midst anymore, but a destination worthy of economic pride. That, without a doubt will open and move every one, to take on a vocation that you have dreamed and so deserve. Look at the English towns, or any bustling historic towns. Think of the art shoppes, novelty items, special skills shown you have stopped in your travels. I know of a town in Italy where the entire vocation is to make the violin. From tree planting, growth & care, harvesting, lumber and timber procedures, to the actual luthier work shoppes scattered around the area had been designed to a Science.

This town does not have to offer one of the same. Innovative, creative views are key concepts. Surely, each of the folks in Town have skills and talents to share and be admired in an economically sustaining appreciation! For example: The Winter Lodge, the Inn, The Corner Store, The Farmers, the Amish, to name a few. From all types of Arts, artisanship in crocheting, embroidery, knittings, special foodie recipes, beautification, and physical well being that any house wife, senior and elderly man or woman, teens, young people have something to offer. Get paid for it. Why NOT? One does not have to go anywhere, anymore. The web is in every one's fingertips. Also, people do travel.

What is the point of looking at a "road side show" if travelers can spend, interact with and admire what the Town have to offer as a Destination? What products can we all provide as a commodity? Collectively we can move forward by Individually, tapping each person's talents and skills. Support one another, instead of just seeing what can be taken at the moment, and grabbing that. There is more to life than material things that can be pilfered, just because one thought the other can be bullied, or is of the weaker person. This town have great values, back then and probably still. We can review them and see the good in them that can be useful in the fair delivery of the truth. What you do in those areas, lend to the overall results of what I do.

I have answered the calling to take the job of the literal heaviest responsibilities and metaphorical strongest accountabilities, that some of you had been trying to get stalled. The conversation and support towards inclusive diversity of mindset has to start within you. When You do, you can assist stopping these land grabbing efforts to also back off this Project, and let me create that ambiance so long coming with this Site, in the True Historic Legacy explicitly deeded and worded within the pages of ownerships' records of the dead legally passed on to me the one still alive. We owe them that. Not to desecrate, but consecrate the Truth. Then we can all lean back, and observe the collective results from individual efforts, that are lawful, fair and beautiful.

B) The Property Value will rise, the living standards will improve immensely. I have heard that people are not happy paying taxes; but does every one in Town wants to peddle asking for alms and subsist off government subsidies for a lifetime, in cyclical generations? Surely, there are more ways to remove that stigma of poverty, and one that has all the signs of honesty, integrity, truth, self - reliance, law abiding, dutiful citizenship in practical application trumps winded words exhibited by just being led blindly to the mire of impoverished, depressive state of one's Spirits.

C) Dignity. This Magnificent House is the "story of Oliver Twist", and the saying that "It takes a community to raise a child". Productive, children that would be the Honest Leaders of the next generations, after you and I. The House is tantamount to Oliver Twist. You are the people that would help ensure Oliver gets his true inheritance delivered intact, and find his place back to the world of the living, honest, civilized, accountable. In this particular situation, the House needs to reign on it's fully deeded

Inheritance; be served and cared with the proceeds from the property and not to be shabbily deprived of what truly came in it's PROVENANCE.

These things do not happen in a magic wand second. These take work, plenty of them. Total cooperation, reaching - out and out - reaching with trust, and transparency. Empathy to lift those that are stumbling versus treading and crushing those that are seemingly weaker than you. We are our brother's keeper. Just as the House is not the only thing worthy of celebration, but the people today should be able to share the truth of the lives lived before us, all.

To name a few Other Leading Personalities of the 19th Century Georgetown, NY:

Elnathan Ellis & Mary, then Diana: Wives   Zinah H. Moseley   The Whitmore Familly

B.T. Miner & Edson Miner

YOU CAN ALL ADD YOUR NAME AND OR FAMILY HERE;

On what contexts and which side of History -

IT IS YOUR CALL.

Bibliography

Abstract of Title.11/4/2011.9:36:04 AM .Receipt # 20011165877File No.18858M.69pages

Georgetown Horse & Wagon Days 1803 - 1905

Department of taxation: www.IRS.NY

Dispatch

www.lexisnexis

www.madisoncountyny

Names & Sketches of the Pioneer Settlers of Madison County, NY. p.36 by William H.
        Tuttle.Edited by Isabel Tracy.1984. Print.

1966 Trustees' Report submitted by Ronald Davies, Secretary

1968 Trustees' Report submitted by Ronald Davies, Chairman: Page 6

Business & Property Law. Robert Stone. The Foundation Press.Chicago.1941.Ch.3.p.104
        paragraph 2.a.

Madison County Leader and Observer Morrisville, NY Thursday Morning April 4, 1912. Twenty
        -Seventh Year No. 43

Madison County Leader and Observer Morrisville, NY Thursday Morning May 16, 1912.
        Twenty -Seventh Year No. 49

13 Madison County Leader and Observer Morrisville, NY Thursday Morning April 4, 1912
        .Twenty- Seventh Year No. 43

Syracuse Daily Journal Last Edition Vol.LIII.- No.184 Wednesday Aug. 4, 1897. Binghamton
        Interested: Business Men Look with Favor on the Proposed Otselic Valley Railroad.

1906, October 04 Madison County Leader and Observer.Georgetown Trolley Road

Liber AN pp.474-475 Recorded: 10 Aug. 1836, 3:00 PM

1836, July 25 Zinah J. Moseley & Mary to Edward Ellis

Liber AO pp.422-423 Recorded: 06 Feb. 1837, 3:00 PM

1836, December 23 Elnathan & Mary M. to William P. Hare

Liber AS pp.314-315 Recorded: 09 Jan. 1839, 10:00 AM

1837, May 25 Epaphroditus Whitmore & Susannah to Russell Whitmore

Liber AU pp.418-419 Recorded: 17 Oct. 1839, 12 NOON

1839, January 12 Epaphroditus Whitmore, John Brown & Emily, Samuel W. Barnett & Eleanor
        to Elnathan Ellis

Liber AU pp.419-420 Recorded: 17 Oct. 1839, 12 NOON
1839, July 18 Lewis G. Morris to Elnathan Ellis

Liber 1 pp.125-126 R.Incorporations Recorded: 03 Feb. 1840
1840, January 21 Inspectors of Election, First Baptist Church

Liber: Recorded: 19 Sept. 1854, 10:00 AM
1840, March 24 Elnathan Ellis & Mary to John Brown, Zinah J. Moseley & Samuel Ballard,
    Trustees of First Baptist Church

Liber AZ p.475 Recorded: 11 May 1843, 2:00 PM
1843, May 09 Elnathan Ellis & Mary M. Ellis

Liber BH pp.471-472 Recorded: 01 May 1847, 5:00 PM
1847, April 29 Isaac V. Purdy & Rebecca to Timothy Brown, VT.

Liber BO p.305 Recorded: 21 August 1850, 3:00 PM
1848, March 22 Timothy & Sarah H. Brown to Obadiah Caniff

Liber BO pp. 305-306 Recorded: 31 August 1850, 3:00 PM
1850, February 12 James H. Curtis to Obadiah Caniff

Liber BO p.515 Recorded: 11 Nov. 1850, 5:00 PM
1850, September 10 Epaphroditus Whitmore to Zinah J. Moseley & William W.Hare

Liber BO p.516 Recorded: 11 Nov. 1850, 5:00 PM
1850, September 26 Ebinezer Moseley to Zinah J. Moseley & William W. Hare

Liber BO pp.516-517 Recorded: 11 Nov. 1850, 5:00 PM
1850, September 26 Ebinezer Moseley to Alvin Moseley

Liber CN pp.396-397 Recorded: 30 April 1859, 2:00 PM
1850, December 09 Timothy Brown & Sarah to Jonathan Robie

Liber BR pp.107-108 Recorded: 10 Nov. 1851, 10:00 AM
1851, October 21 Timothy Brown & Sarah to Wheeler Dryer & John Dryer

Liber BX p. 181 Recorded: 22 Feb. 1854, 2:00 PM
1852, April 01 Robert Ray Jr. & Mary to Pierce C. Nichols

Liber BX pp.181-182 Recorded: 22 Feb. 1854, 12 NOON
1853, December 28 Timothy G. Brown & Malvina to Philinda Nichols

Liber CN pp. 199-200 Recorded: 04 May 1858 1:30 PM
1855, October 03 Timothy Brown to Harry Robie

1859 Gillette Map of Georgetown, NY
The 1859 Gillette Map Adaptation

Liber 99 p.126 Recorded: 11 May 1863, 3:00 PM
1863, May 01 William Way & Adeline M. To Zinah J. Moseley

Liber 102, p.434 Recorded: 17 Dec. 1864, 3:00 PM.
1864, November 21 Samuel Clark to Timothy Brown

Liber 2 p. 144 Recorded: 21 July 1865 R. Incorporations
1865, July 05 Directors of Georgetown & Otselic Plank Road Co.

Liber 111 p. 82 Recorded: 10 April 1867, 2:00 PM
1867, April 01 Isaac Fletcher to William Thompson

Liber 111 p. 83 Recorded: 10 April 1867, 2:00 PM
1867, April 01 Isaac Fletcher & Mercy to William Thompson

Liber 123 p. 347 Recorded: 30 March 1871, 11:00 AM
1871, March 22 Zinah J. Moseley, Milton D. Allen & Mary, Isaac Fletcher & Mercy to Sarah H. Brown

Liber 126 pp. 70-71 Recorded: 21 May 1872, 10:00 AM
1872, April 15 Elnathan Ellis & Diana to Timothy Brown

Liber 127 p. 516 Recorded: 06 Dec. 1872, 11:00 AM
1872, September 23 Timothy Brown & Sarah H. To Nathan Pritchard

Liber 127 p. 519 Recorded: 28 Dec. 1872, 2:00 PM
1872, November 01 Orlando Dutton & Martha to Timothy Brown

Liber 127 p. 520 Recorded: 28 dec. 1872, 12 Noon
1872, November 01 Timothy Brown & Sarah. H. To Orlando Dutton

Liber 133 p. 430 Recorded: 25 May 1874, 4:00 PM
1873, November 01 Timothy Brown & Sarah H. To J. Henry Stanbro

Liber 133 p. 365 Recorded: 28 April 1874, 2:00 PM
1874, March 19 Timothy Brown & Sarah H. To Horace Hawks

Liber 135 p.26 Recorded: 17 Aug. 1874, 2:00 PM
1874, August 01 Timothy Brown & Sarah H. To Mary J. Johnson

Liber 133 p. 535 Recorded: 13 July 1874, 10:00 AM
1874, July 10 Timothy Brown & Sarah H. To Milton D. Allen

Liber 138 p. 516 Recorded: 11 Aug. 1876, 4:00 PM
1874, November 14 Timothy Brown & Sarah H. To Edwin Joaquin

Liber 71 p. 222 Mortgage Recorded: 18 May 1875, 1:00 PM
1874, November 20 J. Henry Stanbro & Lenura L. To John W. Chapin

1875 Atlas: Map of Georgetown, NY

Liber 135 p. 360 Recorded: 23 Jan. 1875, 2:00 PM
1875, January 19 Epaphroditus Whitmore & Susan to Russell Whitmore

Liber 139 p. 263 Recorded: 09 Feb. 1877, 12 Noon
1877, February 08 Timothy Brown & Sarah H. To Jane Saunders

Liber 139 p. 364 Recorded: 14 March 1877, 1:00 PM
1877, March 09 Otis H. Whitmore to Charles W. Smith, F.E. Franklin, Joseph Neal, W.D.
Utter, O.M. Dutton, Benjamin Franklin: Trustees of the First Baptist Church

Liber 7 pp. 374-376 A & A Recorded: 21 Jan. 1879, 2 PM
1877, October 23 Job Mack to Sarah H. Brown & Timothy Brown

Liber 123 p. 529 Recorded: 21 Jan. 1879, 2:00 PM
1877, October 23 Sarah H. Brown & Timothy Brown to Orville Mack, Chauncey Partridge,
     Charles H. Smith, Henry Wadsworth & Lucian Chapin.

Liber 151 p. 12 Recorded: 16 May 1881, 1:30 PM
1881, May 09 C.H. Thompson Whitmore to Frank E. Whitmore

Liber 151 p. 13 Recorded: 16 May 1881, 1:30 PM
1881, May 14 Russell Whitmore & Jane M. To Frank & Carrie H.T. Whitmore

Liber B p. 262 Misc. Recorded: 23 Feb. 1882, 3:00 PM
1882, February 16 Brown Hall Meeting for Hillside Cemetery Formation

Liber 157 p. 56 Recorded: 07 May 1883, 11:00 AM
1882, August 15 Orville Mack, Chauncey Partridge, Charles W. Smith, Harry Wadsworth, Lucian
Chapin to the Board of Trustees of the First Baptist Church & Society.

Liber 157 p. 57 Recorded: 07 May 1883, 11:00 AM
1882, August 15 Timothy Brown & Sarah H. To Trustees of Baptist Society

Liber 161 p. 20 Recorded: 05 Aug. 1884, 11:00 AM
1882, August 15 Trustees of the First Baptist Society of Georgetown to Timothy Brown

Liber 156 pp. 329-331 Recorded: 07 May 1883, 11:00 AM
1883, May 05 Palmer Hopkins & Hervy W. Mann, Executors of Isaac Fletcher's Will to Jabez C.
     Tillotson

Liber 190 p. 262 Recorded: 14 April 1896, 9:30 AM
1884, January 28 Sarah H. Brown & Timothy Brown to Reuben Mawson

Liber 215 p. 389 Recorded: 05 May 1905, 8:00 AM
1884, May 06 Sarah E. Brown & Charles D. Brown to Albert P. Tillinghast

Liber 215 pp. 389 Recorded: 05 May 1905, 8:00 AM
1884, May 06 Sarah E. Brown, widow of Alfred A. Brown

Liber 168 pp. 511-512 Recorded: 16 Sept. 1887, 4:00 PM
1884, September 12 Albert Stevens' Will Drawn. Probated: 12 Sept. 1887

Liber 162 pp. 140-141 Recorded: 14 May 1885, 9:00 AM
1884 December 16 Hiram N. Atwood & Sarah, George Curtiss & Mary A. To Sarah H. Brown.

Liber 165 p. 155 Recorded: 14 May 1885, 9:00 AM
1885, May 05 Timothy Brown to Sarah H. Brown

Liber 168 pp. 178-179 Recorded: 05 May 1885, 9:00 AM
1887, May 03 Louisa M. Hillard to Levi Stevens

Liber 171 p.119 Recorded: Notarized: 19 April 1888
1888, April 19 John H. Chapin & Betsy to Otis H. Whitmore

Liber 187 pp. 166-168 Recorded: 26 March 1894, 2:00 PM
1893, March 13 Will: Sarah H. Brown to Cora V. Marvin

Liber 187 pp. 364-365 Recorded: 17 May 1894, 2:00 PM
1894, April 10 Cora V. Marvin & Laverne Marvin to Sarah H. Brown

Liber 188 p. 159 Recorded: 26 June 1895, 9:00 AM
1895, June 01 Sarah H. Brown to John Currier & Arvilla

Liber 205 p. 22 Recorded: 31 Dec. 1900, 11:00 AM
1895, October 19 Milton D. Allen & Mary S. To Lurinda A. Hare

Liber 192 p.267 Recorded: 08 Dec. 1897, 1:20 PM
1897 December 06 John H. Currier & Arvilla L. To Floyd Currier

Liber 199 p. 490-491 Recorded: 05 Dec. 1898, 3:00 PM
1898, October 31 Floyd Currier & Lilian E. To Chauncey G. Stevens

Liber 222 p. 79 Recorded: 11 May 1907, 11 AM
1906, September 18 Julia V. Stevens, Widow to Grove S. Thompson

Liber 222 pp.79-80 Recorded: 11 May 1907, 11:00 AM
1906, September 18 Elwin H. Stevens & Alice C. Stevens under 21 yrs.; Julia Stevens,
        Guardian to Grove S. Thompson

Liber 1906-15 Recorded: 19 Nov. 1906, Instrument 1906-00000015 Seq. 1-3
1906, October 08 Certificate of Incorporation, Otselic Valley Railroad Norwich, Chenango
        County Records

Liber 240 p. 74 Recorded: 20 Dec. 1913, 11:00 AM
1913, September 06 Marietta Burroughs to Minnie E. Briggs

Liber 240 p. 73 Recorded: 20 Dec. 1913, 10:30 AM
1913, December 19 Luella H. Perry to Enice F. Lamb

Liber240 p. 74 Recorded: 20 Dec. 1913, 10:30 AM
1913, December 19 Enice F. Lamb & Addie E. To Benjamin E. Ross & Effie U.

Liber 251 pp.564-565 Recorded: 28 June 1917, 4:25 PM
1914, November 14 Mary J. Ostrom Wolcott: Will

Liber 250 p. 384 Recorded: 30 Oct. 1917, 9:00 AM
1917, October 26 Elwin H. Stevens & Bertha M.; Julia V. Stevens & Alice C. Stevens to
        William Trass.

Liber 252 pp. 190-191 Recorded: 30 Oct. 1917, 9:00 AM
1917, January 17 Noel E. Jackson & Bessie E to Ella M. Trass

Liber 262 p.276 Recorded: 01 Oct. 1920, 9:00 AM
1920, August 28 Bertha Stevens, Individual, Special Guardian to Frances Stevens, Infant; Alice
        Stevens & Julia Stevens to Alice Stevens.

Liber 262 p.192 Recorded: 31 Aug. 1920, 9:00 AM
1920, August 28 Bertha Stevens, Individual, Special Guardian to Frances Stevens, Infant; Julia
    Stevens & Alice Stevens, heirs at law & next of kin of Chauncey G. Stevens to B. Treat
    Miner & Edson R. Miner.

Liber 268 p.145 Recorded: 05 March 1923, 10:00 AM
1921, August 19 B. Treat Miner, unmarried & Edson R. Miner & Luella to Alfred Moore.

Liber 268 p.146 Recorded: 05 March 1923, 10:00 AM
1921, August 19 Alfred Moore & Harriet to B. Treat Miner & Edson R. Miner

Liber 259 p.327 Recorded: 05 March 1923, 10:00 AM
1921, August 19 Frank Woodman & Lottie A; Clarence A. Parker, unmarried, to B. Treat Miner
    & Edson R. Miner.

Liber 269 p.299 Recorded: 19 Jan. 1924, 9:00 AM
1923, November 23 Henrietta J. Curran to J. George Norris

Liber 269 p.315 Recorded: 29 Jan. 1924, 1:00 PM
1924, January 14 George Stevens to Colenus M. Marvin & Blanche

Liber 269 p.330 Recorded: 04 Feb. 1924, 2:00 PM
1924, January 23 Floyd Currier & Lilian E. to Edson R. Miner & Luella

Liber 269 p.427 Recorded: 20 March 1924, 3:00 PM
1924, March 15 Benjamin E. Ross & Effie U. To J. Fred Currier

Liber 66 p.458 Recorded: 03 April 1924, 3:00 PM
1924, April 03 Probated: Will of Mary J. Currier; Drawn: 18 May 1891

Liber 273 p.469 Recorded: 16 Feb. 1925, 2:30 PM
1924, November 07 LLoyd D. Upham & Maud J. To Edson R. Miner & Luella

Liber 278 p.27 Recorded: 27 Aug. 1925, 3:00 PM
1925, July 31 Probated, George D. Stevens' Will, Drawn: 12 Feb. 1916

Liber 330 p. 421 Recorded: 27 Oct. 1941, 10:30 AM
1939, June 27 William Trass to Lee R. Cossitt, Hamilton

Liber 339 pp.19-23 Recorded: 25 May 1944, 10:00 AM
1944, April 26 Edson R. Miner & Luella to Harold J. Evans

Liber 363 pp.56-63 Recorded: 15 April 1946, 11:00 AM
1946, March 31 Maud J. Upham to Gordon F. Burgess

Liber 375 pp. 131-137 Recorded:
1946, September 19 Gordon F. Burgess to Gordon F. Burgess & Theresa B.

Liber 395 pp. 239-241 Recorded: 15 Nov. 1947, 9 :00 AM
1947, March 30 Gordon F. Burgess & Theresa B. To Harold J. Evans

Liber 395 pp. 253-255 Recorded: 17 Nov. 1947, 10:30 AM
1947, April 21 Harold J. Evans to Charles C. Wagner & Harriet S.

Liber 397 pp. 203-205 Recorded: 27 Dec. 1947, 11:30 AM
1947, April 21 Harold J. Evans to Leemon R. Cossitt, Georgetown

Liber 341 p. 253 Recorded: 26 Jan. 1949, 11 AM
1948, December 31 Harold J. Evans to Leon Chapin & Ruth

Liber 426 pp. 391-394 Recorded: 09 Aug. 1949, 11:20 AM
1949, March 10 Harold J. Evans to Leon E. Chapin & Ruth

Liber 510 pp. 138-140 Recorded: 27 June 1955, 9:46 AM
1955, June 10 John R. Marshall to Alice S. Cossitt

Liber 510 pp. 141-143 Recorded: 27 June 1955, 9:46 AM
1955, June 10 John R. Marshall to Alice S. Cossitt

Liber 510 pp. 144-146 Recorded: 27 June 1955, 9:45 AM
1955, June 10 Alice S.Cossitt, Executrix of L.R. Cossitt to John R. Marshall.

Resurreccion Dimaculangan

Liber 510 pp. 147-149 Recorded: 27 June 1955, 9:45 AM
1955, June 10 Alice S.Cossitt, Executrix of L.R. Cossitt to John R. Marshall.

Liber 539 pp.353-355 Recorded: 11 June 1957, 3:10 PM
1957, May 14 Charles C. Wagner & Harriet to Leon Chapin & Ruth

Liber 551 pp.14-17 Recorded: June 1958, 2 PM
1958, May 16 Leon Chapin & Ruth to Gerald A. Coye & Patricia

Liber 568 pp. 172-175 Recorded: 22 Oct. 1959, 10 AM
1959, October 19 Harold J. Evans to Archie E. Coye & Ona H.

Liber 602 pp. 84-86 Recorded: 26 Oct. 1962, 1:30 PM
1962, October 15 Harold J. Evans to Grace Weare Chapin

Liber 610 pp. 519-521 Recorded: 02 March 1964, 3 PM
1963, December 16 Grace Weare Chapin to Melvin G. & Adaline E. Briggs.

Liber 664 pp. 820-821 Recorded: 12 July 1972, 9:30 AM
1972, July 11 Alice S. Cossitt to Richard & Dorothy MacLean

Liber 697 pp. 741-746 Recorded: 21 March 1977,
1977, March 21 Leon E. & Ruth Chapin to Charles D. & Sarah Elaine Chapin

Liber 421 pp. 28-33 Recorded: 21 March 1977,
1977, March 21 Charles D. Chapin & Sarah Elaine Mortgaged to Leon E. & Ruth C. Chapin.

Liber 829 p. 238 Recorded: 18 Dec. 1986, 1:30 PM
1986, December 05 Alice S. Cossitt to James & Valerie WIlson

Liber 895 p. 316 Recorded: 02 Ot. 1989 4:15 PM
1989, October 02 James & Valerie Wilson Quitclaimed to Valentine & Helen Kartorie

Liber 0914 p. 097 Recorded: 1990, August 07 Image 2 of 6
1990, Under heading Parcel One, Second Paragraph:

Liber 2011 - 6312 Recorded: 04 Nov. 2011 9:36:04 AM

2011, November 03 Valerie K. Wilson, Executrix to the Estate of Helen Kartorie To
Resurreccion Dimaculangan

A Guide for Local Historians [Mills on the Tsatsawassa: Teechniques for Documenting

Early 19th Century Water-powered Industry in Rural NY- A Case Study-] by Philip L.
Lord, Jr.; Martha A.Costello, Illustrator The State Education Department, NY State
Museum

NY State Archives Website: www.NY Archives.gov

1875, D.G. Beers. Ublished by Pomeroy, Whitman & Co. Philadelphia

1882, April 27 & 28 a Grand Concert entitled "The Cantata of Esther, the Beautiful Queen."

1917, November 24th "Grand Pageant of American History, given by the Georgetown
Auxiliary of the Red Cross, Town Hall, Georgetown, NY

1906, October 25 DeRuyter Gleaner News of DeRuyter

1906, November 15 DeRuyter Gleaner South Otselic News Happenings of the Past
week at the Burgh

1907, January 10 Madison County Leader and Observer Georgetown: Edward Givens
and MS. Ada Andrews Nursing Injuries from Accidents

1907, January 17 Thursday. The Cincinnatus Times Vol.09 Number 33 Cincinnatus,
Cortland County, NY. L.D. Blanchard, Editor The Otselic Valley Railroad

1907, January 24 Madison County Leader and Observer Morrisville NY Georgetown
Station: Work on New Railroad to be Resumed Feb. 1st - Apparent lack of Funds

1909, January 28, Madison County Leader and Observer, Morrisville NY Georgetown: Who owns the O.V.R.R. Rails?

1911, July 20. Thursday DeRuyter Gleaner Vol. 33 No. 45.$1.50/ yr. Local Views of Interest to the Summer Visitor.

1911, September 28. Thursday DeRuyter Gleaner Page 7. County Tax Sale Georgetown.

1912, April 04. Thursday Morning Madison County Leader and Observer Morrisville, NY Twenty - Seventh Year No. 43.

1912, May 16. Thursday Morning. Madison County Leader and Observer Morrisville, NY. Twenty - Seventh Year No. 49 May 15.

1912, May 28. Thursday Morning Madison County Leader and Observer Morrisville, NY. Thursday Morning May 28, 1912 Twenty - Seventh Year No. 50 GEORGETOWNOTSELIC RAILROAD.

1909, January 28, Madison County Leader and Observer, Morrisville NY Georgetown: January 27. Madison County Leader and Observer Morrisville, NY. Thursday Morning April 4, 1912 Twenty - Seventh Year No. 43 Georgetown

Madison County Leader and Observer Morrisville, NY. Thursday Morning. May 16, 1912. Twenty - Seventh Year No. 49 May 15

1946, October 11 Friday. The Cortland Democrat, Cortland, NY. Page Four. Cincinnatus. 40 Years Ago.

MS. Marie Villari, for the Syracuse Herald American Section B - 3. Date: 1989, January 29, Sunday Main title: The Spirit House Lives On.

Endnotes

1   Department of taxation. www.IRS.NY.

2   Madison County Courier Article

3   Anodized metal picks shaped as cork screws 12' long, used as ground penetrating restraints.

4   see RPAPL 843, fences & structures, when private nuisance; RPAL 853;881;861;RPAPL 311;321

5   Proverb, self explanatory

6   NPS form 10-900 p.11 No.10. Wikipedia entries, and other web articles with reduced acreage entries.

7   Liber BH pp.471-472. dated 29 April 1847.Recorded 01 May 1847 at 5 o'clock PM

8   Liber BO pp.305-306. dated 22 March 1848.Recorded 21 August 1850 at 3 o'clock PM.

9   1843 Elnathan Ellis' wife is Mary M. Ellis refer to Liber AZ p.475

10   1836, Liber AO p.422-423; Elnathan & wife Mary M.;1843 Elnathan Ellis' wife is Mary M. Ellisrefer to Liber AZ p.475

11   1836 Zinah J. Moseley's wife, Mary Liber AN p. 474-475.

12   1836 Zinah J. Moseley's wife, Mary Liber AN p. 474- 475

13   1836, Liber AO p.422; Elnathan & Mary M.;1843 Elnathan Ellis & Mary M. Liber AZ p. 475

14   1883, May 05 Liber 156 pp. 329 - 331 one acre Congregational Church

15   1966, August 05 Liber 626 p. 306 presently the Georgetown Fire Dept., One rood 4 rods

16   1871,Oct. 28 Liber 125 p.283 ; 1966, August 05 Liber 626 p. 306: 40 feet square

17   Testament of love

18   Ch.3.p.104 paragraph 2.a Business & Property Law. Robert Stone. The Foundation Press.Chicago.1941

19   Madison County Leader and Observer Morrisville, NY Thursday Morning April 4, 1912 .Twenty – Seventh Year No. 43 : Georgetown. "Floyd Currier of Hamilton was in town Monday collecting the water rent for the Crystal Springs Water Company."

20   I am leaving her in a climactic shroud as she deserve more than just a mention in a footnote.

21   A blood relationship of the Currier's to Sarah H. Brown, a hearsay as of this writing.

22   Floyd to Chauncey deed of sale, 1898, Oct. 31 Liber 199 pp. 490-91 Rec. Dec. 5th 1898.3PM

23   A relation to John Currier: fact verification pending, still hearsay as of this writing.

24   Son of Albert Stevens. Wife Julia, daughter, Alice, son Elwin married to Bertha Spaulding infant daughter Frances.

25   Census

26   a relation on the Stevens side of the family

27   Liber 278 p.27

28   Madison County Leader and Observer Morrisville, NY Thursday Morning April 4, 1912. Twenty- Seventh Year No. 43;

29   Madison County Leader and Observer Morrisville, NY Thursday Morning May 16, 1912. Twenty- Seventh Year No. 49

30   refer to Liber 883 pp. 190-191 first paragraph

31   A buyout move, a legal strategy; a very ballsy decision, from a Woman of great courage.

32   1946, March 31 Liber 363 pp.56-57 Recorded: 15 April 1946.

33   1946, September 19 Liber 375 pp. 131-137 Recorded:

34   The reader have to compare both documents to appreciate the records.

35   Both the biblical Story & the best- selling book of the same title by a very famous author. Check it out.

36   www.NYIRS.gov

37   www.NYPARKS.gov

Here's a few of the documents that show how the problem for this Site to move forward

has been choreographed, directed and executed by design. Take a look yourselves:

(Page 1 of 15)

NPS Form 10-900
(Oct. 1990)

OMB No. 10024-0018

United States Department of the Interior
National Park Service

National Register of Historic Places
Registration Form

This form is for use in nominating or requesting determinations for individual properties and districts. See instructions in *How to Complete the National Register of Historic Places Registration Form* (National Register Bulletin 16A). Complete each item by marking 'x' in the appropriate box or by entering the information requested. If an item does not apply to the property being documented, enter "N/A" for "not applicable." For functions, architectural classification, materials, and areas of significance, enter only categories and subcategories from the instructions. Place additional entries and narrative items on continuation sheets (NPS Form 10-900a). Use a typewriter, word processor, or computer, to complete all items.

1. Name of Property

historic name ___Spirit House___

other name/site number ___Timothy Brown House, Brown Hall___

2. Location

street & number ___NY 26___   ☐ not for publication

city or town ___Georgetown___   vicinity

state ___New York___ code ___NY___ county ___Madison___ code ___053___ zip code ___13072___

3. State/Federal Agency Certification

As the designated authority under the National Historic Preservation Act, as amended, I hereby certify that this ☒ nomination ☐ request for determination of eligibility meets the documentation standards for registering properties in the National Register of Historic Places and meets the procedural and professional requirements set forth in 36 CFR Part 60. In my opinion, the property ☒ meets ☐ does not meet the National Register criteria. I recommend that this property be considered significant ☐ nationally ☒ statewide ☐ locally. (☐ See continuation sheet for additional comments.)

Signature of certifying official/Title   Date

___New York State Office of Parks, Recreation and Historic Preservation___
State or Federal agency and bureau

In my opinion, the property ☐ meets ☐ does not meet the National Register criteria. (☐ See continuation sheet for additional comments.)

Signature of certifying official/Title   Date

State or Federal agency and bureau

4. National Park Service Certification

I hereby certify that the property is: Signature of the Keeper   Date of Action

☐ entered in the National Register.
  ☐ See continuation sheet.
☐ determined eligible for the
  National Register.
  ☐ See continuation sheet.
☐ determined not eligible for the
  National Register.
☐ removed from the National
  Register.
☐ other, (explain:) _____

Plate 93 NRHP Application for Historic Landmarking form Page 1

Resurreccion Dimaculangan

(Page 2 of 15)

Spirit House (Timothy Brown House)   Georgetown, Madison County, New York
Name of Property   County and State

5. Classification

Ownership of Property   **Category of Property**   **Number of Resources within Property**
(check as many boxes as apply)   (check only one box)   (Do not include previously listed resources in the count.)

☐ public-local   ☐ district   Contributing   Noncontributing
☒ private   ☒ building(s)   1   buildings
☐ public-State   ☐ site   _____   sites
☐ public-Federal   ☐ structure   _____   structures
                                   ☐ object   _____   objects
                                                                   1   Total

Name of related multiple property listing   **Number of contributing resources previously listed**
(Enter "N/A" if property is not part of a multiple property listing.)   **in the National Register**

N/A   0

6. Function or Use

Historic Function   **Current Function**
(Enter categories from instructions)   (Enter categories from instructions)

DOMESTIC: Single dwelling   DOMESTIC: vacant

7. Description

Architectural Classification   **Materials**
(Enter categories from instructions)   (Enter categories from instructions)

OTHER   foundation _____ stone
_____   walls   wood

                                                           roof   asphalt
                                                           other

Narrative Description
(Describe the historic and current condition of the property on one or more continuation sheets.)

Plate 94 Application for Historic Landmarking Page 2

317

United States Department of the Interior
National Park Service

OMB No. 1024-0018, NPS Form

Spirit House (Timothy Brown House)
Georgetown, Madison County, New York

NATIONAL REGISTER OF HISTORIC PLACES
CONTINUATION SHEET

Section number 7 Page 1

NARATIVE DESCRIPTION

The Spirit House, also known as the Timothy Brown House, sits about 20 feet back from the road on the east side of New York Route 26 near the center of the hamlet of Georgetown in southern Madison County. The hamlet, which once boasted two hotels and various commercial activities typical of the center of a large agricultural area in the nineteenth century, is now primarily residential in character with a general store, churches and a few other services available to the local residents. The building is situated on a parcel of less than one acre with mature trees behind a picket fence in front and a wooded area in the rear. To either side and across the road from the Spirit House are other nineteenth-century buildings and just north of it is the intersection of New York Route 80, the center of Georgetown.

The main block of the house is essentially square, measuring 34'8" by 33'6", and is two stories in height. The Spirit House is constructed of wood and the front and side faces of the building are divided into three parts. On the front (west) is a center door flanked by single windows. The areas above and below the openings are sheathed in flush-board siding laid vertically but in the spaces between the openings and at the corners of the building are one of the features that make the building unique. Rather than conventional pilasters and corner boards, the Spirit House features two-by-fours arranged vertically and scalloped at regular intervals. In the center of each face of the corner elements, the boards are staggered so that the scalloped sections overlap each other, whereas at the corners they are laid with the scalloped areas adjacent to each other. The use of the scallop pattern gives the Spirit House a highly textured surface and it is almost impossible to discern how it is constructed without close inspection. At the corners, 26 two-by-fours are so arranged and separating the bays on the front and two side elevations are 13 two-by-fours.

Above the second story is a three-tiered cornice that features downward-pointing "keys." Each plane of the cornice projects slightly farther than the one below it, and above the third range is a corbelling that resembles a brick corbelled cornice, except that it is executed in wood. Originally, the building had a shallow pyramidal roof, but that was reconstructed in the 1930s to pitch into the center of the building. In either case, the roof was not visible from the ground.

Windows are double-hung with four-over-four sash and retain their original louvered blinds, painted green. In the front (west) center bay is a door, and another one has been added to the north side, east bay.

The east, or rear, of the building does not have the same decorative elements as the other three faces and part of the south face has been altered as well. The reason for this is that the Spirit House once had an entire church building moved from another location in the hamlet and attached to the east side, and after it was removed around 1906, a small addition was built across the rear and part of the south side. It is not clear whether the rear was always more plain than the other three sides of the building or whether this condition only came about after the other part of the building was demolished.

Plate 95 Application for Historic Landmarking Page 3

Resurreccion Dimaculangan

United States Department of the Interior
National Park Service

OMB No. 1024-0018, NPS Form

Spirit House (Timothy Brown House)
Georgetown, Madison County, New York

**NATIONAL REGISTER OF HISTORIC PLACES
CONTINUATION SHEET**

Section number 7 Page 2

On the interior, the Spirit House retains some of its original architectural elements. On the first floor, the openings in the front of the house have decorative woodwork resembling that of the exterior. The center entrance now opens into a living room that occupies the two north bays of the house, but this room originally stretched across the entire front of the building. South of the living room is a room last used as a bedroom. The entry, three window openings in this room, two in the adjacent room to the south that was originally part of this room, and two doors at the rear (east) side of the room are trimmed with two-by-four decorative architraves reminiscent of the corners and "pilasters" of the exterior. A wall pierced by a wide double doorway now separates this former space into two rooms, thought to have been constructed late in the nineteenth century when the use of the building changed.

Behind the living room and adjacent bedroom in the original building is a dining room and kitchen. Along the south wall of the original Spirit House is a one-story addition that houses a bathroom and sun parlor, and behind the east wall of the original house is a utility room, wood shed, pantry and enclosed porch. Entered from the dining room and hugging the original east wall of the house is a narrow enclosed stairway to the second floor. According to one former owner of the house, whose family purchased it from Brown's widow, the first floor behind the present-day living room and bedroom had been occupied by a miscellaneous room where the present-day dining room is located and two "dark rooms" where communication with the spirits took place, along with a hall, in the present-day kitchen.

Access to the second story is now gained via the narrow staircase where one of the darkrooms had been; it is not known where the original staircase was located. When the church was attached to the rear of the Spirit House, the back wall of the second story of the house was removed and an interior second story was added to the church, connecting to the Spirit House's second story, thereby creating a large room where séances were held. By the late-nineteenth century, interest in Spiritualism had waned, but the building continued to be used for public meetings, not related to Spiritualism. In 1906, after the use of the house for public meetings was discontinued, the former church was removed, the back wall of the house was reconstructed, and the second story was reconfigured into smaller bedrooms and later a bathroom was added. That is the present condition of the building. The original four-over-four windows are present but woodwork is plain and doors contain two panels, suggesting an early-twentieth-century origin. Throughout the house, narrow-board hardwood floors were installed, covering original wide-plank floors.

The house has been vacant for approximately twenty years, but it has not suffered any physical deterioration or vandalism and is in good condition. It has a historic marker in front of it but only the exterior has been accessible to the public since the 1980s.

Plate 96 Application for Historic Landmarking Page 4

Spirit House (Timothy Brown House)
Name of Property

Georgetown, Madison County, New York
County and State

8. Significance

Applicable National Register Criteria
(Mark "x" in one or more boxes for the criteria qualifying the property for National Register listing.)

Areas of Significance
(enter categories from instructions)

☒ A Property is associated with events that have made a significant contribution to the broad patterns of our history.

RELIGION

☐ B Property is associated with the lives of persons significant in our past.

ARCHITECTURE

☒ C Property embodies the distinctive characteristics of a type, period, or method of construction or represents the work of a master, or possesses high artistic values, or represents a significant and distinguishable entity whose components lack individual distinction.

☐ D Property has yielded, or is likely to yield, information important in prehistory or history.

Period of Significance
c.1865-1885

Criteria Considerations
(Mark "x" in all the boxes that apply.)

Property is:

Significant Dates
c.1865, 1885

☐ A owned by a religious institution or used for religious purposes.

☐ B removed from its original location.

Significant Persons
(Complete if Criterion B is marked above)

☐ C a birthplace or grave.

☐ D a cemetery.

Cultural Affiliation

☐ E a reconstructed building, object, or structure.

☐ F a commemorative property.

Architect/Builder
Timothy Brown

☐ G less than 50 years of age or achieved significance within the past 50 years.

Narrative Statement of Significance
(Explain the significance of the property on one or more continuation sheets.)

9. Major Bibliographical References

Bibliography
(Cite the books, articles, and other sources used in preparing this form on one or more continuation sheets.

Previous documentation on file (NPS):

☐ preliminary determination of individual listing (36 CFR 67) has been requested
☐ previously listed in the National Register
☐ previously determined eligible by the National Register
☐ designated a National Historic Landmark
☐ recorded by Historic American Buildings Survey #
☐ recorded by Historic American Engineering Record #

Primary location of additional data:

☒ State Historic Preservation Office
☐ Other State agency
☐ Federal agency
☐ Local government
☐ University
☐ Other Name of repository:

Plate 97 Application for Historic Landmarking Page 5

Resurreccion Dimaculangan

United States Department of the Interior
National Park Service

OMB No. 1024-0018, NPS Form

Spirit House (Timothy Brown House)
Georgetown, Madison County, New York

NATIONAL REGISTER OF HISTORIC PLACES
CONTINUATION SHEET

Section number 8 Page 1

SIGNIFICANCE:

The Spirit House, also known as the Timothy Brown House or Brown's Hall, is significant under Criterion A as a property related to the rise of Spiritualism in Central New York State in the 1850s. It was built in the 1860s by Timothy Brown for his residence and for meetings of Spiritualists in a large hall on the second floor. At the height of popularity of the movement, Brown attracted hundreds of people to the small hamlet of Georgetown for meetings. By the late 1870s, interest in Spiritualism in Georgetown declined but Brown retained the building as his residence until his death in 1885. His wife occupied the house for many years after that, finally leaving the property in 1899.

The property is also significant under Criterion C as an unusual example of the eclecticism that characterized architecture in the middle of the nineteenth century. The house defies stylistic classification and is a unique and very personal expression of one man's religious fervor at a time and in a place where many religious currents were consuming the local population.

Georgetown is a large town on the southern boundary of Madison County, and the county is nearly, at the center of New York State. Prior to the settlement of the area by European-Americans after the close of the American Revolution, present-day Madison County was the home of the Oneida Indians of the Iroquois Six Nations. By the time of the survey of the state after 1789, the entire northern half of the county was part of the Oneida Reservation while most of the southern part had been divided into rectangular townships within the large County of Herkimer. These "Twenty Towns" had been purchased by Governor George Clinton for the State of New York from the Indians in 1788, and Georgetown is Township #6.

European-American settlement of the area had begun to the north of Georgetown along the road laid out in 1790 by James and William Wadsworth, on their way to the Genesee Valley at present-day Rochester, 100 miles to the west. This road went from present-day Utica to Oneida Castle, the center of the Oneida Reservation.

At the beginning of the nineteenth century, the large counties in what is now Central New York were broken up into smaller entities, and in 1806, Madison County was formed by the breakup of Chenango County, which itself had earlier been part of the much larger Herkimer County. The name Chenango was retained for the county to the south of the new Madison County, while Madison was named for the United States president at the time of its formation.

Georgetown was incorporated in 1815 and among its most important early industries were dairy farming and hop growing, the latter of which declined in the later nineteenth century. Dairying gave rise to cheese making, an occupation that remained important for the balance of the nineteenth century. Sawmills were established in the very early nineteenth century on the many creeks that

Plate 98 Application for Historic Landmarking Page 6

United States Department of the Interior
National Park Service

OMB No. 1024-0018, NPS Form

Spirit House (Timothy Brown House)
Georgetown, Madison County, New York

**NATIONAL REGISTER OF HISTORIC PLACES
CONTINUATION SHEET**

Section number 8 Page 2

traversed the town, and as areas were cleared of forest growth, more substantial frame dwellings replaced the earlier log cabins. Georgetown grew slowly in the early years, as settlers from New England began to populate Central New York. The hamlet at the center of the town attracted merchants, doctors, and other types of workers that would logically serve the center of a large agricultural area.

In the first half of the nineteenth century, a number of religious upheavals took place in Central New York. Northwest of Georgetown, in Seneca or Ontario County, Joseph Smith founded the Mormon religion, later departing for Ohio. In the northern sector of Madison County, John Humphrey Noyes began the Oneida Community in 1848 with the following precepts: "the right of man to be governed by God and to live in the social state of heaven;...the right of woman to dispose of her sexual nature by attraction instead of by law and routine and to bear children only when she chooses; [and] the right of all to diminish the labors and increase the advantages of life by association." The Oneida Community lasted for almost 40 years.

In the early 1840s, William Miller preached that the world would come to an end in 1843 and attracted a large following for a short time during that decade. When nothing happened, interest in his movement declined.

A new religious excitement in the 1850s was Spiritualism. This faith attracted liberals who had drifted far from a literal interpretation of the Bible and became interested in the ideas of Swedish philosopher Emanuel Swedenborg. His writings "combined many of the liberal religious doctrines with the new sociological ideas of the time." In 1848, the two daughters of John Fox of Hydeville, Wayne County, claimed they heard strange tapping sounds at night and that they had communicated with spirits who answered their questions. Thus was born the Spiritualist movement, which, by 1855, claimed over a million converts throughout the world, more than one third of whom were in New York State.

Into the small hamlet of Georgetown, Timothy Brown arrived in 1845 and his wife Sarah and son joined him three years later. Brown was born in Vermont in 1815 and it is not clear whether he was an adherent of Spiritualism before he arrived in Georgetown or only became interested in the phenomenon after he took up residence in the community. Either way, soon after his arrival, he constructed a house south of the hamlet that was described in a newspaper article as having a "double cornice, with two rows of hand made balls." In the upstairs rooms, under the eaves, he built secret dark closets, where he claimed the spirits were kept. This house, which bears some resemblance to a Gothic-inspired cottage typical of the mid-nineteenth century, still exists.

Soon after, Brown began construction on his second residence in the center of the hamlet, the subject of this nomination. Conflicting sources say it took Brown five, ten, or fourteen years to construct the building, but it is assumed to have been completed by 1868 because an invitation to a public gathering at the house has been discovered.

Plate 99 Application for Historic Landmarking Page 7

322

United States Department of the Interior
National Park Service

OMB No. 1024-0018, NPS Form

Spirit House (Timothy Brown House)
Georgetown, Madison County, New York

**NATIONAL REGISTER OF HISTORIC PLACES
CONTINUATION SHEET**

Section number 8 Page 3

In 1879, in the *Banner of Light*, a Spiritualist periodical, the house and its construction were described as follows:

> Along with this [clairvoyant phenomena] was borne in upon him [Brown] the conviction that *this house must be built*, and consecrated to Spiritualism and to free speech in the service of humanity. He could not resist the conviction, and it became the aim and enthusiasm of his life. He bought a wood-lot, got out his own logs and hewed his timber for the frame, which he began to build himself. Not a carpenter, and all unused to tools, he found that if he put his chisel in the wrong place his arm had no power to use the mallet or strike a blow, but when the chisel was rightly placed the blows were freely dealt. So, amidst the doubt or ridicule of his neighbors, the frame of a front building, thirty-five feet square, was finished. A master carpenter took charge of its raising, and when it stood complete he said to the people, 'This is as good and perfect a frame as I ever saw,' and they went home astonished. All this time, and through all the ten years which he took to finish his task, he was obliged to make a living and go on as he best could, on simplest fare and with constant labor, up to sixteen hours a day. His brave wife could not share his enthusiasm, but wrought as a skilled cheese-maker in the factories near by, and so won good wages and kept the house in order.
>
> With the frame raised he still toiled on, and all the building, save doors and window-sashes—everything, from cellar floor and foundation stones to the quaintly beautiful and unique carving of the cornice, is the work of his own hands—not a week's work to help him, and that of common laborers. All these years he wrought after the spiritual model, ever clear in his mind and felt that he was guided by supernal intelligence and skill.
>
> The upper floor was a hall thirty-five feet square, the lower part of the home of his wife and himself. He then (in 1874) bought at small cost a second-hand Presbyterian church, put it in the rear on the north side, built a piazza, and laid a floor to divide it into two stories, threw all the upper floor, front and rear, together, and his free hall is now seventy feet by thirty-five, plainly but neatly fitted up to seat some six hundred people or more, and the whole perfected building is the architectural ornament of the town. The singular yet beautiful carving on the front would attract attention anywhere. Good judges say that the work is substantial and thorough, the skill in its finer parts remarkable.

Soon, the novelty of Spiritualism soon wore off. According to a local newspaper,

> The derision of local residents turned to irritability, especially when a visiting spiritualist left a notebook in the home of one of the townspeople. It was found by the landlady and curiosity prompted her to examine it. A few days later its contents were published in a local newspaper. The notebook contained names, dates, and epitaphs gleaned from old country

Plate 100 Application for Historic Landmarking Page 8

United States Department of the Interior
National Park Service

OMB No. 1024-0018, NPS Form

Spirit House (Timothy Brown House)
Georgetown, Madison County, New York

NATIONAL REGISTER OF HISTORIC PLACES
CONTINUATION SHEET

Section number 8 Page 4

records and the area's graveyards. This was so offensive to the good citizens' tastes that the meetings in Brown's Hall were brought to an end.

While Spiritualism in Georgetown declined, the Browns remained in the house. Timothy Brown died in 1885 and according to his wife's obituary of 1908, Sarah Brown remained in the house. Their son and daughter-in-law, who had moved to Chicago, returned to Georgetown in 1887 to take care of Sarah. However, both younger people died within a year and Mrs. Brown remained in the house alone until 1899 when she entered the Old Ladies' Home in Oneida. In 1908 she died at age 93.

Even after Spiritualism lost favor with the local population, Brown's Hall continued to be a gathering place for the residents of Georgetown. The interior of the house was altered to reflect its changing use, but the exterior remains very little changed from its original construction date.

The house went through a series of owners in the twentieth century. It was the subject of a history research paper by a State University of New York at Cortland student, Milton Chapin, in 1965, and was documented by the Historic American Buildings Survey (HABS) in 1966, using Chapin's research for the data pages of the HABS report.

Since the late 1960s, there have been numerous false starts in listing the property in the National Register, but presently, the Town of Georgetown, with cooperation of the present owner, is sponsoring the nomination of this worthy property to the Register so it can gain the recognition it deserves.

Sarah - 1908
Mrs Cossin - 1985
Mr Karble - HABS 20 — ?
Mr Wilson - and Mr
Rene

Plate 101 Application for Historic Landmarking Page 9

United States Department of the Interior
National Park Service

OMB No. 1024-0018, NPS Form

Spirit House (Timothy Brown House)
Georgetown, Madison County, New York

**NATIONAL REGISTER OF HISTORIC PLACES
CONTINUATION SHEET**

Section number 9 Page 1

BIBLIOGRAPHY

BOOKS

Ellis, David M., Frost, James A., Syrett, Harold C., & Carman, Harry J., A History of New York
State., Ithaca, New York: Cornell University Press., 1967.

Hammond, Louisa M., History of Madison County. Syracuse, NY: Truair, Smith & Co., Book and Job
Printers. 1872.

Smith, James H., History of Chenango and Madison County. Syracuse, NY: Mason and Company.
1880.

OTHER

Miscellaneous newspaper clippings, notes, photographs from files provided by previous nomination
sponsors.

Historic American Buildings Survey materials, 1963-1966.

Plate 102 Application for Historic Landmarking Page 10

Points to PONDER:

Look at the resourced Resources here. This is where this singular narrow context of Historical

Landmarking was based on and upon. WHY?

The above writings are narratives written by individuals other than the owners of the property.

WHY was the accepted proofs of ownerships not consulted? Or if consulted Ignored?

If between 1963-1966 this HABS survey materials were sanctioned and approved by MRS. Alice

Stevens Cossitt, why was this Landmarking effort not realized then?

Documentation is also about reliable resources, authentic, true, scholarly, scientific.

Spirit House (Timothy Brown House)	Georgetown, Madison County, New York
Name of Property	County and State

10. Geographical Data

Acreage of Property   less than 1 acre

UTM References
(Place additional boundaries of the property on a continuation sheet.)

1 18   439568 4734832
Zone Easting Northing

2 18
Zone Easting Northing

3 18
Zone Easting Northing

4 18
Zone Easting Northing

☐ See continuation sheet

Verbal Boundary Description
(Describe the boundaries of the property on a continuation sheet.)

Boundary Justification
(Explain why the boundaries were selected on a continuation sheet.)

11. Form Prepared By

name/title   Anthony Opalka, Historic Preservation Program Analyst

organization NYS Office of Parks, Recreation & Historic Preservation   date December 7, 2005

street & number PO Box 189   telephone 518-237-8643

city or town   Waterford   state NY   zip code 12188-0189

Additional Documentation
Submit the following items with the completed form:

Continuation Sheets

Maps

> A **USGS map** (7.5 or 15 minute series) indicating the property's location.
> A **Sketch map** for historic districts and properties having large acreage or numerous resources.

Photographs

> Representative black and white photographs of the property.

Additional items
(Check with the SHPO or FPO for any additional items)

Property Owner
(Complete this item at the request of SHPO or FPO.)

name/title

street & number   telephone

city or town   state   zip code

Paperwork Reduction Act Statement: This information is being collected for applications to the National Register of Historic Places to nominate properties for listing or determine eligibility for listing, to list properties, and to amend existing listings. Response to this request is required to obtain a benefit in accordance with the National Historic Preservation Act, as amended (16 U.S.C. 470 et seq.).

Estimated Burden Statement: Public reporting burden for this form is estimated to average 18.1 hours per response including time for reviewing instructions, gathering and maintaining data, and completing and reviewing the form. Direct comments regarding this burden estimate or any aspect of this form to the Chief, Administrative Services Division, National Park Service, P.O. Box 37127, Washington, DC 20013-7127; and the Office of Management and Budget, Paperwork Reductions Projects (1024-0018), Washington, DC 20503.

Plate 103 Application for Historic Landmarking Page 11

Resurreccion Dimaculangan

United States Department of the Interior
National Park Service

OMB No. 1024-0018, NPS Form

Spirit House (Timothy Brown House)
Georgetown, Madison County, New York

NATIONAL REGISTER OF HISTORIC PLACES
CONTINUATION SHEET

Photographs

Photograph key

Pictures taken July 2005
Photographer: Anthony Opalka
Negatives: NYSHPO, Waterford, NY 12188

1. View of front and north elevations
2. Close-up of cornice
3. Close-up of exterior wall treatments
4. Close-up of cornice
5. Close-up of corner treatment
6. View of rear elevation/addition
7. Interior first floor front room
8. Interior first floor front room (later 19th-century doorway on right)
9. Interior first floor front room
10. Interior second floor room

Plate 104 Application for Historic Landmarking Page 12

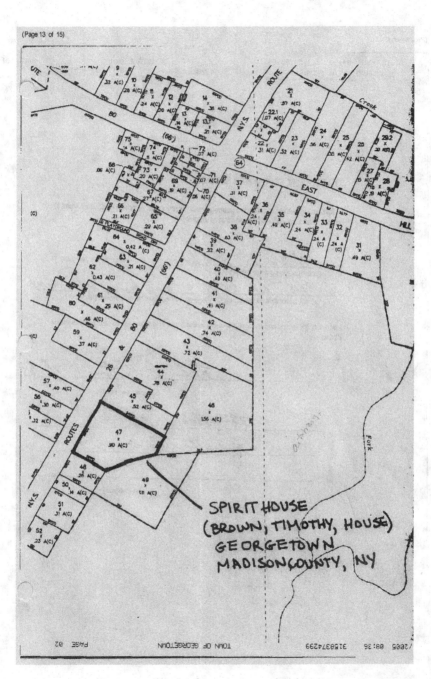

SPIRIT HOUSE
(BROWN, TIMOTHY, HOUSE)
GEORGETOWN
MADISON COUNTY, NY

Plate 105 Application for Historic Landmarking Page 13

Resurreccion Dimaculangan

STATEMENT OF OWNER SUPPORT

Before an individual nomination proposal will be reviewed or nominated, the owner(s) of record must sign and date the following statement:

I, _Helen B. Kartorie_, am the owner of the property at
(print or type owner name)

916 Rt. 26 S. Georgetown NY 13072
(street number and name, city, village or town, state of nominated property)

I support its consideration and inclusion in the State and National Registers of Historic Places.

Helen B. Kartorie 7/13/05
(signature and date)

333 Bevec Rd.

Aikville, Pa 17302

(mailing address)

Plate 106 Application for Historic Landmarking Page 14

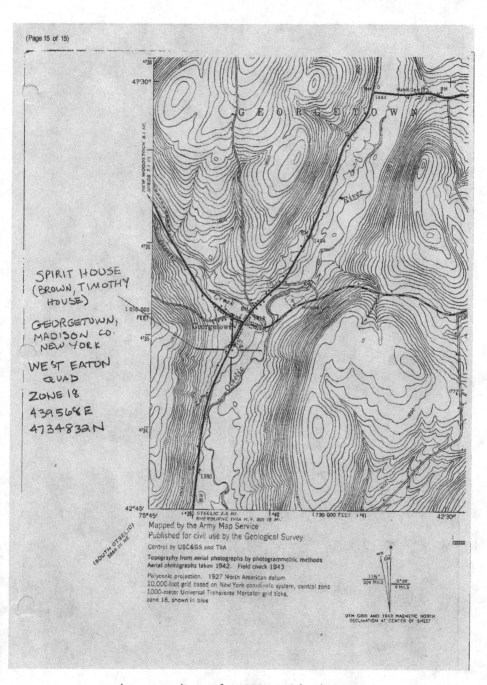

SPIRIT HOUSE
(BROWN, TIMOTHY
HOUSE.)

GEORGETOWN,
MADISON CO.
NEW YORK

WEST EATON
QUAD

ZONE 18

439568 E

4734832 N

Mapped by the Army Map Service
Published for civil use by the Geological Survey

Control by USC&GS and TVA

Topography from aerial photographs by photogrammetric methods
Aerial photographs taken 1942. Field check 1943

Polyconic projection. 1927 North American datum
10,000-foot grid based on New York coordinate system, central zone
1000-meter Universal Transverse Mercator grid ticks,
zone 18, shown in blue

UTM GRID AND 1943 MAGNETIC NORTH
DECLINATION AT CENTER OF SHEET

Plate 107 Application for Historic Landmarking Page 15

Timothy Brown House   HABS No. NY-3602
    (known as Brown's Temple or the Spirit House)
South Main Street, on Route 26, 600 feet south of the intersection
    of Routes 80 and 26   HABS
Georgetown   NY,
Madison County   27-GEO,
New York   1-

PHOTOGRAPHS
WRITTEN HISTORICAL AND DESCRIPTIVE DATA

Historic American Buildings Survey
Office of Archeology and Historic Preservation
National Park Service
Department of the Interior
Washington, D.C. 20240

Plate 108 Habs1

HABS
NY,
27-GEO,
1-
(Page 1)

HISTORIC AMERICAN BUILDINGS SURVEY   HABS No. NY-5602

TIMOTHY BROWN HOUSE

(known as BROWN'S TEMPLE or the SPIRIT HOUSE)

Location: South Main Street, on Route 26, 600 feet south
                       of the intersection of Routes 80 and 26,
                       Georgetown, Madison County, New York

Present Owner: Mrs. Alice Stevens Cossitt

Present Occupant: Mr. and Mrs. (Alice) Leemon R. Cossitt

Present Use: Residence

Brief Statement
of Significance: Unique "folk" architecture and center for
                       Spiritualist group from 1864 to 1885.

PART I. HISTORICAL INFORMATION

A. Physical History:

    1. Original and subsequent owners:
        1864, Nov. 21   - Samuel Clark and Ellania, his wife,
                           sell to Timothy Brown three-quarters
                           of an acre (Madison County Deeds,
                           Ledger 102, p. 434).
        1872, April 15   - Brown buys an additional 12 acres
                           from Winonthro Ellis (Madison County
                           Deeds, Ledger 126, p. 70) upon which
                           he put the back of his building and
                           out buildings.
        1885, May 5   - Property transferred to Sarah Brown,
                           wife of Timothy (Madison County
                           Deeds, Ledger 163, p. 155).
        1898   - Property sold by Mrs. Brown's
                           great-nephew, Floyd Currier and wife,
                           who had received it from Sarah Brown,
                           to Chauncey Stevens (Madison County
                           Deeds, Ledger 199, p. 490). Mrs.
                           Brown entered the Old Ladies' Home
                           in Oneida, August 3, 1899 and died
                           there July 6, 1908.
        1902   - Stevens died and property in estate.
        1920   - Property recorded in Alice Stevens'
                           name, now Mrs. Leemon R. Cossitt.

Plate 109 Habs2

332

TIMOTHY BROWN HOUSE
(known as BROWN'S TEMPLE or the SPIRIT HOUSE)
HABS No. NY-5602 (Page 2)

NY,
27-GEO,
1-

2. Date of erection: After 1864 and before 1868, when tickets
were sold for a Thanksgiving dance at the house.

3. Architect: Unknown.

4. Original plans, construction, etc.: The exterior of the
house is little altered and still has rounded corners
created by a series of scalloped 2" x 4" vertical planks
arranged in a semi-circle, similarly constructed
pilaster-like forms between each bay, and a mammoth
cornice of overhanging fascias decorated by symmetrical
brackets. Interior spaces once used for meeting halls
and darkrooms for spirits have been converted into use
as a house.

5. Builder, suppliers, etc.: Lumber probably came from
Brown's surrounding woodlots.

6. Alterations and additions:
1874 - rear portion of house removed and the former
Presbyterian Church building added to the rear.
1906 - Church addition torn down and present addition
built, porches added, and second floor divided into bedrooms.
1938-40 - second floor ceilings lowered; new roof installed
over old one.
1946 - bathroom, sun parlor, and sun porch on south side
added and the upstairs "den" enlarged.

B. Historical Events and Persons Connected with the Structure:
Timothy Brown was born in Vermont in 1815 and moved from the
town of Newburn, in Orange County, Vermont, to Georgetown, N.Y.
in 1847 with his wife, Sarah, and their children. Apparently
he was trained as a carpenter by the "spirits", which he
kept in dark closets, assisted him in all his work. The
present "Spirit House" was the second house he built in
Georgetown. The Browns lived in part of the house and used the
rest for meetings and allowed theatrical and touring groups to
entertain there. Brown died in 1885 and his widow in 1906.

C. Sources of Information:

1. Old Views: Clippings in scrapbook owned by Mrs. Cossitt.

2. Bibliography:

Alvord, Reed. "Designed by Spirits", The Ford Times.
Dearborn, Mich.: Ford Motor Company, 1957. pp. 57-58.

Child, Hamilton. Gazeteer and Business Directory of
Madison County, New York. Syracuse, N.Y.: Journal
Office, 1868. p. 147.

Plate 110 Habs 3

TIMOTHY BROWN HOUSE
(known as BROWN'S TEMPLE or the SPIRIT HOUSE) NY,
HABS No. NY-5602   (Page 3)

Courtright, John. *Georgetown Illustrated.* South Otselic:
    R. M. Reynolds and Son, 1906. Section marked "Churches."

Cross, Whitney R. *Burned-Over District.* Ithaca, New York:
    Cornell University Press, 1950. p. 1 and section
    on spiritualism.

Current, Richard N., T. Harry Williams, and Frank Friedel.
    American History Survey. New York: Alfred A.
    Knopf, 1963. p. 39.

Ellis, David M., James A. Frost, Harold C. Syrett, and
    Harry F. Carman. *Short History of New York State.*
    Ithaca, New York: Cornell University Press, 1957.
    pp. 307-308.

Smith, James Hadden. *History of Chenango and Madison
    Counties.* Syracuse, N.Y.: D. Mason and Company
    1880. pp. 591-592.

Smith, John B. *History of Madison County.* Boston History
    Company, 1899. p. 354.

Whitney, Mrs. L. M. Hammond. *History of Madison County,
    State of New York.* Syracuse, N.Y.: Truair, Smith
    & Co., 1872. p. 404.

Prepared by Milton Chapin
Georgetown, N.Y.
January, 1965.

PART II. ARCHITECTURAL INFORMATION

A. General Statement:

    1. Architectural character: Unique decorative work on the
       interior and exterior of the house built as a center for
       spiritualism.

    2. Condition of fabric: Good.

B. Description of Exterior:

    1. Dimensions: Two stories, original three bay front
       34'8", plus 11' addition, by 33'6", plus 16'2"addition.

    2. Foundations: Dry stone wall, half plastered.

    3. Wall construction: Painted (white) planking on north
       and west elevations, white clapboards on south and east
       elevations.

Plate III Habs 4

Resurreccion Dimaculangan

NY,
27-680,
t

TIMOTHY BROWN HOUSE
(known as BROWN'S TEMPLE or the SPIRIT HOUSE)
HABS No. NY-5602 (Page 4)

4. Structural system, framing: Mostly 10" x 14" beams and
   timbers, 9" x 14" posts. Dimensions of sills unknown but
   undoubtedly very large; mortise and tenon joints and
   square nails.

5. Porches, etc: Two entrance porches, west and north sides;
   back porch at rear of addition; stoop at east end of
   enclosed porch. Entrance porches each have two scalloped
   columns and jigsaw brackets in same design as on cornice.

6. Chimneys: Three at present; original ones no longer
   remain; brick construction.

7. Openings:

   a. Doorways and doors: All doorways simple single
      plank casing.

   b. Windows and shutters: Mostly four-over-four original
      windows. Storm windows one-over-one are on first
      floor only. Exterior green wooden louvred shutters
      are original.

8. Roof:

   a. Shape, covering: Prior to 1938, the roof peaked at
      the center and was covered with metal roofing. After
      1938 a new asphalt roof, that also peaked at the
      center, was put on over the original roof.

   b. Cornice: See photos. Extremely deep cornice on
      original house with three scalloped bands around the
      top on all sides; a greatly expanded architrave with
      jigsaw brackets hanging from the under edge of the
      three fascias on the north, west and south sides;
      average of seven brackets in each row.

C. Description of Interior:

   1. Floor plans:

      a. First floor: Present entrance on north into dining
         room (door originally a window); 14'9" x 14'11";
         entrance to present stairs opposite door on south
         wall; entrance to kitchen (formerly darkroom for
         spirits) on south wall; entrance to living room on
         west wall. Present living room 15'6" x 17'5";
         doorway from dining room, window frames, and west
         exterior door all have scalloped frames; living

Plate 112 Habs5

335

TIMOTHY BROWN HOUSE
(known as BROWN'S TEMPLE or the SPIRIT HOUSE)
HABS No. NY-5602 (Page 5)

NY,
27-GEO,
1-

room and bedroom to south originally one room.
Present bedroom in southwest corner, 15'6" x 12'11";
door into bathroom addition originally a window, door
into kitchen originally into hall. Present kitchen,
15'5" x 15'5"; beyond kitchen to east is storage area
(rear of original hall) and staircase (occupying space
of second former darkroom for spirits). Addition to
south of bathroom (at west end), 7'8" x 10'3"; sun
parlor, 15' x 10'3", and enclosed porch (at east end),
15'9" x 10'6". Addition to east of original house,
utility room (adjacent to enclosed porch) 15'7" x 9'4";
pantry (north west side) 3'6" x 10'; and, woodshed
(northeast side) 12' x 10'.

b. Second floor: Present second floor (originally one
large hall combined with church added by Brown at
rear): staircase and stairhall run north-south at
rear of original house on south side; hall to bedrooms runs east-west in center of house, termination
at closet (8'11" x 3'6") on west wall. Three bedrooms
along north wall; northeast room 8'11" x 14'5"; north
room 12' x 14'5"; northwest room 8'11" x 17'11" Den
in southwest corner 17'2" x 8'7"; bathroom (4'2" x 9'6")
adjacent between den and stairhall. In addition at
east end, one unfinished room 15' x 19'7".

c. Attic: Outside entrance through the cornice at rear
of house; new roof about 15' high in center over
original roof; evidence of fire c. 1922; originally
a drain from center to cellar.

d. Cellar: Inside entrance; contains storage shelves,
furnace, floor cemented c. 1940 and reinforcing steel
beams placed in center of ceiling to support first
floor.

2. Stairways: Stairway constructed c. 1908 along interior
east wall of original house in space of former spirit
darkroom.

3. Flooring: Original was maple planks, modern floor is oak.

4. Wall and ceiling finish: Originally walls plastered and
ceiling lathed; wainscoting on first floor is from
church pew doors. Present finish is knotty pine paneling
or plastered and wallpapered.

Plate 113 Habs6

TIMOTHY BROWN HOUSE
(known as BROWN'S TEMPLE or the SPIRIT HOUSE)
HABS No. NY-5602 (Page 6)

NY,
27-620,
1-

5. Doorways and doors: Three original doors remain with
   scallop trim; door to sun porch from utility room may
   have been from church.

6. Decorative features and trim: On original first floor
   doorways and windows are scalloped (1" x 2"); wainscoting
   in first floor dining room of three half round moldings.

7. Lighting: All electric lighting, most installed in 1930's.

8. Heating: Central oil furnace; one fireplace in sun parlor. According to the present owner, the house was
   formerly heated by stoves, except for second floor hall
   which was heated with a 15' x 5' iron heater. It sat
   up on bricks and was attached at one end to the chimney
   and at the other end could be opened for the insertion
   of long planks for fuel.

D. Site and Surroundings:

1. Orientation: House faces west (Route 26), but present
   entrance off driveway on north side.

2. Outbuildings: One shop and one garage located northeast
   of the house.

3. Landscaping: House surrounded by spruce, maples, and
   cedars. A picket fence runs north and south and east
   and west on west side and north side of the property.
   There is a driveway to the garage from Routes 26 and
   80 on the north side of house.

                    Prepared by Milton Chapin
                                 December, 1964

PART III. PROJECT INFORMATION

These records were part of the documentation of structures in the
Southern Tier of New York State undertaken by the Historic American
Buildings Survey in cooperation with the Cortland County Historical
Society and the Valley Development Foundation, Inc.

The project was under the general supervision of John Poppeliers,
Chief, Historic American Buildings Survey. Architectural information
was prepared in December, 1964, by Milton Chapin, at that time a
student at Cortland State College, University of the State of New
York. Historical information was prepared by Mr. Chapin in January,
1965. Photographs are by Jack E. Boucher and were taken in April,
1966. The material was edited for deposit in the Library of Congress
by Constance Werner Ramirez, March, 1974.

Plate 114 Habs7

337

WAS THIS COMPILED REPORT EVER EVEN CONSIDERED?

The Spirit House
Georgetown, New York

(Also referred to as
Brown's Free Hall)

Compiled by:

Georgetown Historical Society
1991

Copyright 1991
The Georgetown Historical Society

7/3

To Rep
from Estella Evans

Plate 115 GHSI

The Spirit House, Georgetown, New York
(Also referred to as *Brown's Free Hall*)

This house known as the *Spirit House*, located in the town of Georgetown about 600' south of the intersections of Routes 26 and 80, is a significant Madison County landmark. In fact, its' vernacular architecture is one-of-a-kind. It's architectural integrity should be respected because of its uniqueness and because of its significant role in the wave of the spiritualism movement that swept the country during the 1850's.

By 1855 spiritualists claimed over a million converts throughout the world, with perhaps a third of them in New York State. Several centers were established in New York, one of the centers being Georgetown, about 35 miles southeast of Syracuse. The "Burned-Over District" was a term applied to the region of central New York where revivalism was eagerly received. The Spirit House, which was constructed during this period, is an example of profusely eclectic decoration upon a relatively simple, vernacular house.

On March 31, 1848, American Spiritualism was born in the tiny hamlet of Hydesville in Western New York when the Fox Sisters first communicated with the spirit of a murdered peddler by means of mysterious rappings. In 1888 Margaret Fox revealed that her spirit rappings had been produced by snapping her big toe, but in those intervening 40 years, Spiritualism had become a widespread movement, involving thousands of people and producing much literature, particularly the many newspapers such as *Banner of Light*, *The Spirit Messenger* and *Spirit World*.

The town of Georgetown is pleasantly situated in the valley of Otselic Creek. The first name given to the settlement was Slab City at the time of the raising of the frame for the first saw mill in town. Georgetown was formed from the town of DeRuyter in 1815. The first settlement involved the building of a home by Ezra Sexton who came from Litchfield, Connecticut in 1804. He was a man of some local distinction having been a justice of the peace and captain of a militia company. During the next few years the county of Madison was rapidly filled, principally with people from New England.

Plate 116 GHS2

Merchants set up businesses in Georgetown at or near the intersection of Routes 26 and 80. The first merchants in the village were Dudley and Bemis who began trading across from the established Methodist Church. Soon thereafter, in 1817, a store opened on the north–west village corner. There was a tavern on the opposite corner operated by Mr. Fairchild who was there a good many years. In 1840 a Mr. Stanton built up a business trading in flour and feed. A post office was then established. In 1810 a doctor had come to town and remained until 1851. School sessions were first held in the various homes of the village with many taking advantage of the early education. A tannery was built which contained thirty vats and tanned about 40 sides a week. Businesses included saw mills, grist mills, cheese factories, a blacksmith shop and several stores.

It was during this period of the town's growth that eccentric mystics thrived in Upstate New York. This was fertile ground for all forms of eccentricity. At this time another New Englander, Mr. Timothy Brown, moved to Georgetown from Ryegate, Vermont, and purchased a small parcel of land south of town. Here he built a home for his family.

By 1855 Spiritualists claimed over a million converts throughout the world, and Mr. Timothy Brown was one of them. One day he announced that he had been called upon to build a house—a temple of spiritualism. Mr. Brown then purchased a piece of property near the town's center. He made no secret of the fact that the structure was to be built under spirit direction. The state of New York hosted more than twice as many converts as any other state and nowhere was the manifestation stronger than in Georgetown, a small village in Madison County, south of Cazenovia.

This was a more popular than intellectual movement—more rural than urban, and the enthusiasm persisted in mature, stabilized neighborhoods rather than those newly established. Therefore, this town was open to such a movement.

The entire community knew that Tim Brown was no carpenter, but in about 10 years time, after declaring his intent to build—the house was completed. The timbers came from local forests and he worked along with uncanny accuracy. With dogged determination he struggled on until he at last completed the frame. He engaged the assistance of a master carpenter for the raising of the frame. The carpenter surprised those who had been skeptical about Brown's workmanship when he told

Plate 117 GHS3

them it was the best frame he had ever seen.

With the completion of the house, members of the spiritualist sect from far and near came to 'Brown's Hall' in Georgetown. More space was needed for meetings, so in 1874 Brown bought a vacant Presbyterian church, moved it to the rear of the structure to provide living space downstairs and a 35' x 75' public hall on the second floor for meetings and entertainments.

On December 17, 1880, it is known that *Uncle Tom's Cabin* was performed there, with Miss Lizzie Pennock in her original rendition of Topsy with Song and Dance and little Minnie Wilbur, as Eva, supported by a magnificent cast of artists!

At times the village would be filled with people to feed and sleep for the night. Sometimes the town was hard-put to care for the multitudes. The horses would be tied to every tree and post in the village. The good citizens were willing to tolerate the unusual presentations at the Hall as long as the visitors were paying for room and board in the village.

The seances were held in a dark room in the "temple" and many were converted to spiritualism. The present kitchen of the home was, at that time, a seance room with no windows.

Much of the movement was based on the theory that mediums could communicate with the dead and was kept within the bounds of credulity. Spiritualists, it is reported, do not believe in "ghosts", but in spirits who have powers of communication unknown to mundane folks.

The town worked along with this movement, providing space and support for years, until finally the novelty 'wore off' for the Georgetown folks. Then came whispered words of fraud, first heard behind closed doors, and then openly in the streets and at gatherings. A notebook, left behind under a pillow by a visiting spiritualist, was discovered in the home of one of the hosts. Upon examination the notebook was found to contain names, dates and epitaphs gleaned from old county records and the area's graveyards. This was so offensive to the good citizens of the town that the meetings in Brown's Hall were brought to and end.

The town records of Georgetown date back to 1887. Newspapers record Brown's death to have been April or May 1885 at the age of 70, so his death record is not available.

Mrs. Brown worked hard to support the family during the 'Brown's Hall' period. She made and

Plate 118 GHS4

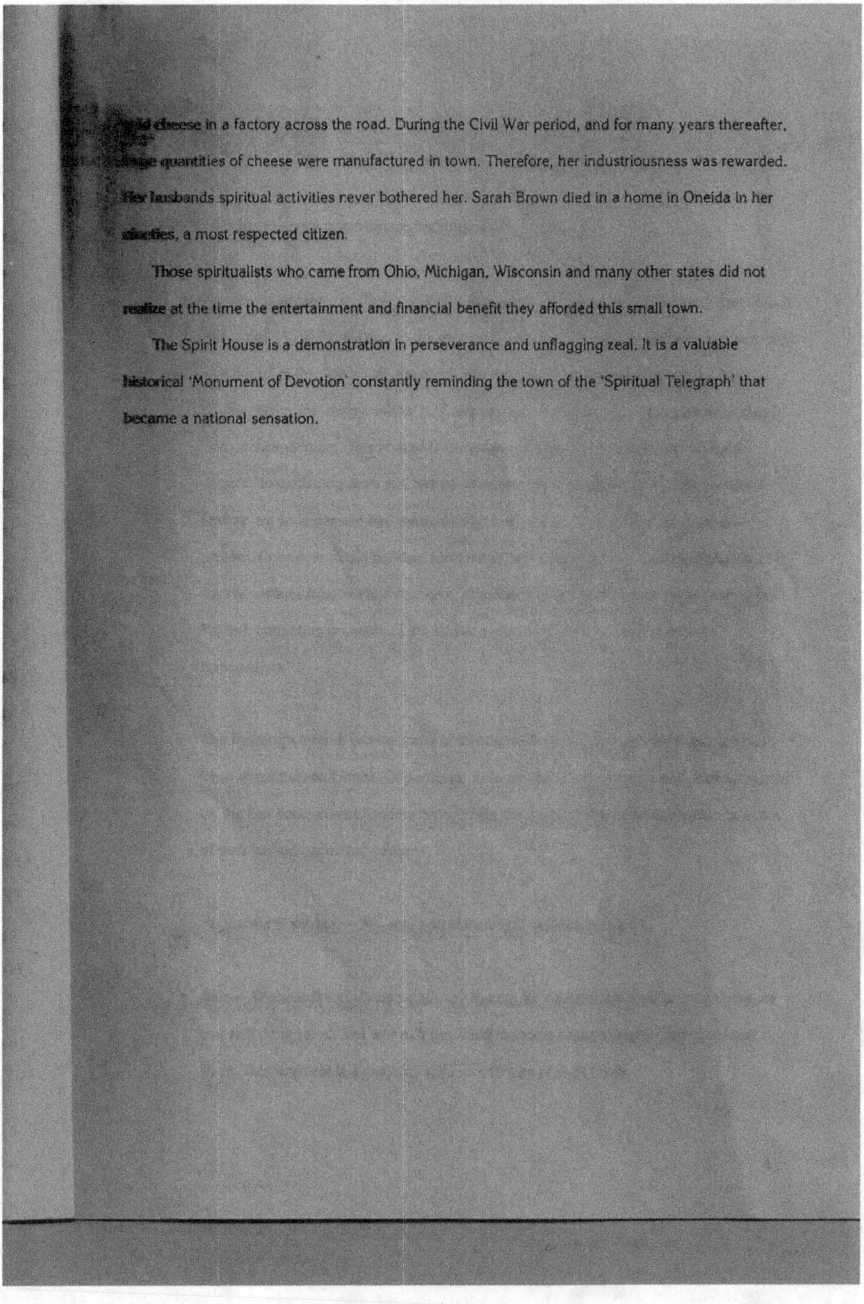

cheese in a factory across the road. During the Civil War period, and for many years thereafter, large quantities of cheese were manufactured in town. Therefore, her industriousness was rewarded. Her husbands spiritual activities never bothered her. Sarah Brown died in a home in Oneida in her nineties, a most respected citizen.

Those spiritualists who came from Ohio, Michigan, Wisconsin and many other states did not realize at the time the entertainment and financial benefit they afforded this small town.

The Spirit House is a demonstration in perseverance and unflagging zeal. It is a valuable historical 'Monument of Devotion' constantly reminding the town of the 'Spiritual Telegraph' that became a national sensation.

Plate 119 GHS5

Resurreccion Dimaculangan

Notice the Inconsistencies right on the acreage.

scription:

- *Buildings*— three (main house, barn and storage building)

- *House*— is situated on .09 acres. The building consists of a modest $2\frac{1}{2}$ story main block with small $1\frac{1}{2}$ story addition to the east/rear elevation; a second 1 story sun room/porch was added at the side/south elevation. The main body of the building is three bays square with a shallow pyramidal roof and crowned by an unusual elaborate entablature and cornice element. This feature is comprised of a series of staged tiers of wood decoration exhibiting sawn and turned ornamentation; complementing this dominant feature are wide pilaster-like elements which exhibit an intricate carved geometric pattern. Entrances to the building sport small pedimented porticos with decorative carved vertical supports and brackets. Alterations to the building's exterior have been limited, consisting primarily of the addition and/or removal of various minor appendages.

  The building's interior retains some of its original features although the floor plan has been altered several times. Of particular note are the carved window and door surrounds on the first floor; these elements compliment the building's exterior decoration in terms of their carved geometric patterns.

- *Suggested Boundary*—$3\frac{1}{2}$ acre parcel including woodlot in rear.

- *Sites*— The woodlot contains a pathway system for walks and a view of area where the saw mill once stood. The saw mill was used to process maple lumber from the local trees. This was sent to Boston for the manufacture of shoe heels.

Plate 120 GHS6

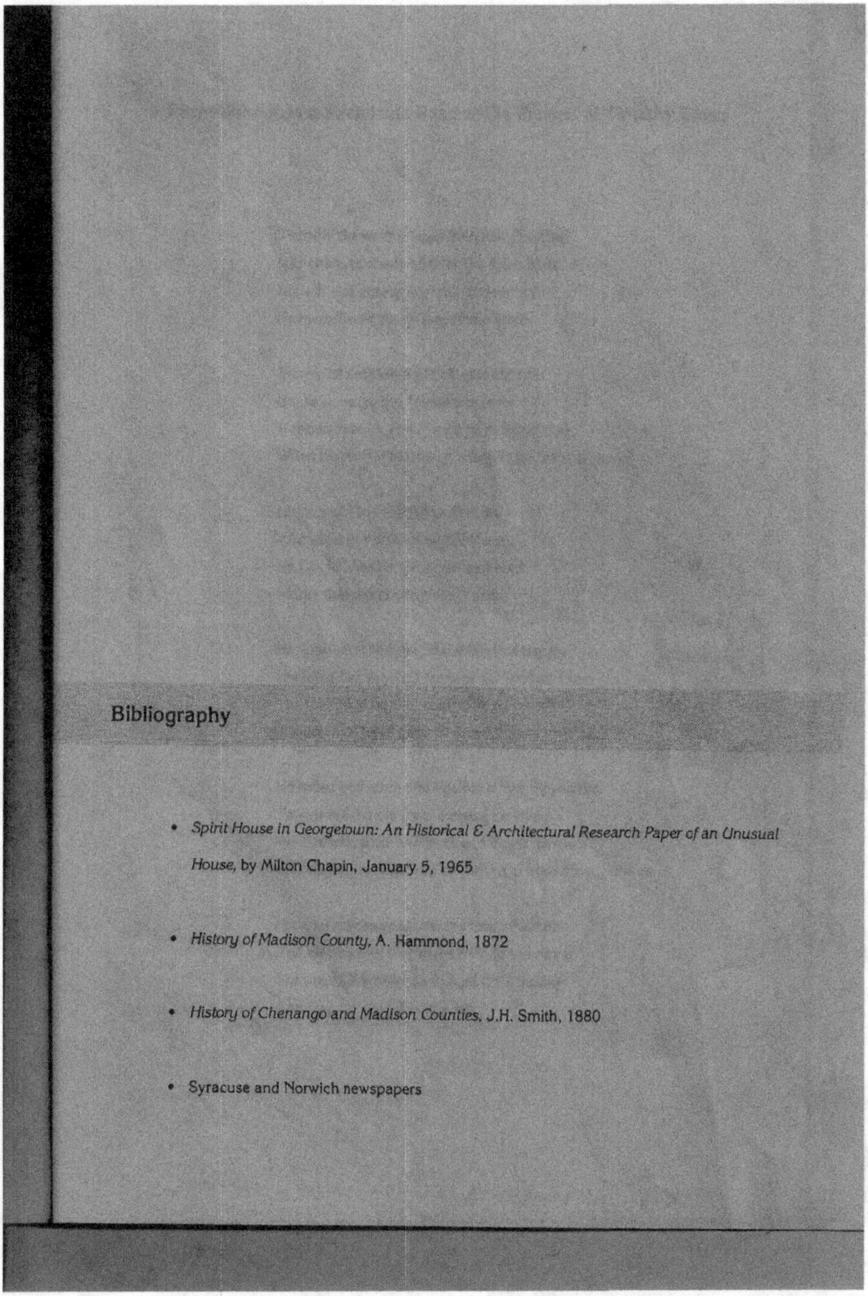

Bibliography

- *Spirit House in Georgetown: An Historical & Architectural Research Paper of an Unusual House*, by Milton Chapin, January 5, 1965

- *History of Madison County*, A. Hammond, 1872

- *History of Chenango and Madison Counties*, J.H. Smith, 1880

- Syracuse and Norwich newspapers

Plate 121 GHS7

Poem Written by a Friend and Read at the Funeral of Timothy Brown

Timothy Brown our aged friend and brother
Has changed the mortal for the spirit form
His will was strong, his soul undaunted
Has weathered many a scathing storm.

Storms of derision have oft assailed him
Because he sought to place in sight
A monument by which he'd be remembered
When his mortal form was changed for form of light.

His mortal life attained perfection
And while our brother had his faults
He has left behind to be remembered
Works that the poorest soul exalts.

He wrought with hand and brain this temple
His fame has reached far over the land and sea
The work that he has done lives on forever
Though moldered back to dust his form may be.

He toiled and struggled against strong opposition
To rear his temple for the cause he loved
He met with scoff and jeers and much derision
But still his work moved on with help from friends above.

His soul reached out into the land of spirits
And oft he knew that angel friends were near
They gave his strength to fight life's battles
And face the foe without a fear.

Plate 122 GHS8

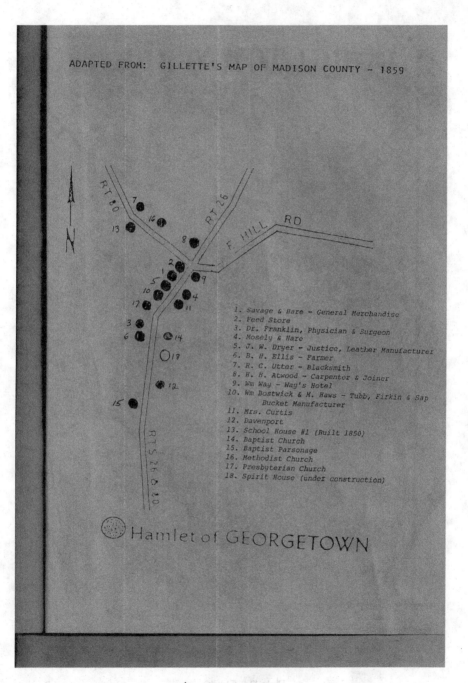

ADAPTED FROM: GILLETTE'S MAP OF MADISON COUNTY - 1859

1. Savage & Hare - General Merchandise
2. Feed Store
3. Dr. Franklin, Physician & Surgeon
4. Mosely & Hare
5. J. W. Dryer - Justice, Leather Manufacturer
6. B. H. Ellis - Farmer
7. R. C. Utter - Blacksmith
8. H. H. Atwood - Carpenter & Joiner
9. Wm Way - Way's Hotel
10. Wm Bostwick & M. Haws - Tubb, Firkin & Sap
       Bucket Manufacturer
11. Mrs. Curtis
12. Davenport
13. School House #1 (Built 1850)
14. Baptist Church
15. Baptist Parsonage
16. Methodist Church
17. Presbyterian Church
18. Spirit House (under construction)

Hamlet of GEORGETOWN

Plate 123 GHS9

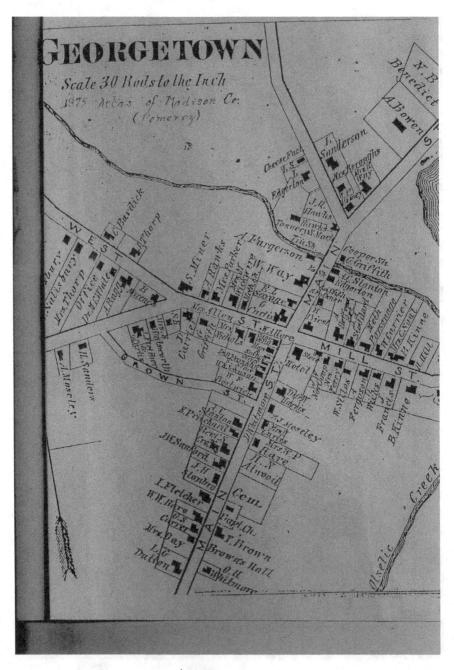

Plate 124 GHS10

"The trail of Evidence left by any single work of history becomes a key starting point for subsequent investigation of the same subject, and thus makes a critical contribution to our collective capacity to ask and answer new questions about the past."
[a direct quote from the AHA Statement on Standards of Professional Conduct no. 2 Shared Values]

As of this writing, the Wikipedia account for this Landmark entry had quoted and cited the source of information as the National Register and the Library of Congress. That information being proliferated around the world contain all the errors that come in these documents that had been stamped legitimate and allowed to have been filed; thus continuously being referred to. Does any body now gets the point being conveyed here, on the grave importance of competent fact checking; and that Preservation of Culture was intended to be serious business - even codified; yet can fall prey to this kind of ugly travesty!

The Short end of this History's Real Story.

The abridged Story would always start with the Deeded accounts of Timothy & Sarah H. Brown Estates, that included the following: 3/4 acres, 9' x 60', 2 & 1/4 acres, and 1/3 undivided rights to a Spring. Why so? There would not have been a structure if there was not a site to stand it on, is it not so? It should be common knowledge of the importance of securing the land first, to account for what to improve and be liable with. These packaged landholding was exactly what was passed on to Chauncey G. Stevens' & Family. The Period where the Buy - Out move of Alice Stevens occurred is the era of Historic Peak.

Another crucial moment of her life that rendered this history come full circle was when she got married to MR. Leemon Ray Cossitt; an entrepreneur widower from Hamilton NY. This gentleman had the heart to venture out to Georgetown, be it figuratively or in the literal, NY to meet Alice. I see this union to be as romantic even in today's standards.

Looking back, what would have been the chances of the land parcel Alice's brother Elwin Stevens sold to MR. William Trass in 1917 be bought by MR. Cositt in 1939?. Then, be handed back to Alice in 1955, together with the second parcel procured from Mr. Harold J. Evans in 1947, which was the so called Whitmore Farm. That was how these two parcels of land: 2 acres, and the 1 &1/2 acres, happened to be added to the first four deeded properties of Timothy & Sarah H. Brown that Alice Stevens bought - out from her mom Julia, Sister - in - Law Bertha & niece Frances. That was the story of what really happened. How do we confirm all these? The Deeds tell us. That's how we know.

First rate, brilliant. Even in a peanut shell, stripped of all Social Causes. The Characters herewith had contributed lovingly towards the economics, and improvement of human day to day lives. Is this Story so loathsome, that it had to be erased, Or be sanitized? From what? I wonder WHY? What happened to the People in this Town? In this Region? In this State? Please Wake Up.

Acknowledgements

There were numerous situations, and circumstances that swirled their way in the process of collecting, collating, cross referencing of the data presented here. While many of them left some not so sweet memories to recall, the sweet ones would not have been treasured the most, were it not for those that are just a little bit saltier.

For those Libraries that had been operating as such, Repositories of Knowledge, to Inspire Interests in the Pursue of Understanding:

Thank You.

Hamilton Library * Kellogg Library * Carnegie Library * Manlius Library
Oneida Library * DeRuyter Library * Oswego Main Library

Of course, these facilities would not have been named here without the Staff:
front, center, and behind the scenes, while everything had to go on.

Immeasurable

Thank you for Keeping the exemplar Mission of making the light to gain insights, and better understanding through free information, burn brighter.

To the following Family and the Love they Shared, the Times Spent Brain - storming:

Eppie & Reymie M & H Kinsley The Bliss's M Dixon George
L.Sprague Pastor Darling Mamie Josie Ate Lee M Winder
Geyser Allan Mr. Miller Kevin O. Kathleen
ManongM AteGisela AteEdna MS.Nola
Sidney Sam Graham
John T. PaulN

To the naysayers and the silent supporters, the kindnesses of many people that cannot be measured and better left unsaid to protect them from retaliation and undue attention; the offices and the public spaces that I have had the privilege of using: fxkkz,ofcdpt,wgms,themansion and to those that should remain anonymous.

My sincerest Gratitude.

I received the unsigned ziplocked coal for 2014 Christmas, the New Year of 2015 hanging by the South door candleholder. T.Y. The message is taken in the best context by its chemical composition and properties.
My apologies if my very best efforts for this Work may not have come up to your the standards; there would always be room for improvement and growth.

To the People that have made this Truth be Told, a Possibility,

To the Dead we Owe the Truth, that they may now Forever Rest in Peace, and for the Living to pay Homage to; in Honor, to Honor and Respect - in order to move Positively Forward without Fear.

Complex Simplified

The Short Story of the Story

of Narrating this History's Real Story,

and the attempt to have a Story

of Sustainable Conservation & Preservation Story,

In the manner that a Smithsonian Institution became a Story.

This story of the author 's journey can be likened to the animated movie about Ratatouille viewed instead from the satirical genre of a rat wanting to cook his way into joining Humankind. The Magnificent House comes alive in this story, is humanized, and given the character of Oliver Twist, the orphan boy and the hardships he had been subjected in today's Society and Culture so adeptly depicted in the story of Zorba, the Greek. The story is hoped to end in the manner that James Smith of Smithsonian Institute came about, before we know it today. Overall, the four borrowed characters are four individual stories of David[s] against Goliath[s] odds.

Ratatouille

With

Oliver Twist

in the cultural & social setting of

Zorba the Greek,

with the high hopes of a happier ending in

what the Story of

James Smithson

gave the World with the start up funds that took the form of the Smithsonian Institution.

MADISON COUNTY – STATE OF NEW YORK
KENNETH J. KUNKEL JR, COUNTY CLERK
138 NORTH COURT ST, WAMPSVILLE, NY 13163

COUNTY CLERK'S RECORDING PAGE
THIS PAGE IS PART OF THE DOCUMENT – DO NOT DETACH

```
RECEIPT NO. : 2011165877

Clerk:    TS
Instr #:  2011-6312
Rec Date: 11/04/2011 09:36:04 AM
Doc Grp:  D
Descrip:  DEED
Num Pgs:  5
Rec'd Frm: ALLIED LORENA

Party1:   WILSON VALERIE K
Party2:   RESURRECCION DIMACULANGAN
Town:     GEORGETOWN
```

```
Recording:

Cover Page                           5.00
Recording Fee                       40.00
Cultural Ed                         14.25
Records Management - Coun            1.00
Records Management - Stat            4.75
TP584                                5.00
RP5217 Residential/Agricu          116.00
RP5217 - County                      9.00
                                   _____
Sub Total:                         195.00

Transfer Tax
Transfer Tax                       260.00
                                   _____
Sub Total:                         260.00
                                   _____
Total:                             455.00
**** NOTICE: THIS IS NOT A BILL ****


*****  Transfer Tax  *****

Transfer Tax# :     776

Consideration:      65000.00
Transfer Tax:         260.00
```

I hereby certify that the within and foregoing was
recorded in the Clerk's Office for Madison County, NY

Kenneth J Kunkel Jr.

Madison County Clerk

Record and Return To:

PAUL V NOYES (ALLIED)
131 SHERRILL RD
SHERRILL NY 13461

EXECUTOR'S DEED

THIS INDENTURE made the 3rd day of November, Two Thousand eleven

BETWEEN

Valerie K. Wilson,
Individually, and as Executrix of the Estate
of Helen B. Kartorie, deceased
4485 E. Lake Rd.
Cazenovia, NY 13035

Grantor,

    and

Resurreccion Dimaculangan
170 Kenwood Ave.
Oneida, NY 13421

Grantee,

WITNESSETH, that whereas Letters Testamentary were issued to the party of the first part by the Orphans' Court Division, Court of Common Pleas, State of Pennsylvania on October 31, 2008 and also by Ancillary Letters Testamentary on May 12, 2009 and by virtue of the power and authority given in by Article 11 of the Estate, Powers and Trusts Law, or any amendment thereof from time to time made, and in consideration of Sixty Five Thousand and 00/100 ($65,000.00) Dollars, lawful money of the United States, paid by the party of the second part, the receipt whereof is hereby acknowledged, and other good and valuable consideration paid by the Grantee, does hereby grant and release unto the Grantee, the heirs or successors and assigns of the Grantee, forever,

ALL THAT TRACT OR PARCEL OF LAND, situate in the Town of Georgetown, County of Madison and State of New York, and being all of the premises deeded to Sarah H. Brown by Timothy Brown, May 5 1885 and recorded in the Madison County Clerk's Office May 14th at 9 o'clock a.m. in Liber 163 page 155 described and bounded as follows, viz: On the north by lands owned by the Baptist Church & Society; east by lands formerly owned by Mary M. Ellis; on the south by land formerly owned by Russell Whitmore; on the west by the center of the highway; being a part of Lot No. 91 of said town, CONTAINING ¾ of an acre more or less.

ALSO ALL THAT TRACT OR PARCEL OF LAND   DEEDED BY THE Trustees of the First Baptist Society of said town to Timothy Brown on the 15th day of August, 1882, and recorded in the Clerk's Office of the County of Madison on the 5th day of August, 1884 at 11 o'clock a.m. in Liber 161, page 20.

samja2

ALSO ALL THAT OTHER PIECE OR PARCEL OF LAND deeded by Zinah J. Mosely, Milton D. Allen and Mary his wife, Isaac Fletcher and Mercy, his wife to said Sarah H. Brown on the 22nd day of March 1871 and recorded in the Clerk's Office of the County of Madison on the 30th day of March 1871 at 11 o'clock a.m. in Book No. 123 of Deeds, page 347.

ALSO THE RIGHTS AND PRIVELEGES in and to a certain spring of water which was conveyed to the said Sarah H. Brown by a deed from Hiram N. Atwood and wife and George Curtis and wife and recorded in the Clerk's Office of the County of Madison on the 14th day of May, 1885 at 9 o'clock a.m. in Liber 162 of Deeds at page 140, to which said deed reference is hereby made for a more particular description of said water rights.

PARCEL II

ALL THAT TRACT, PIECE OR PARCEL OF LAND, situate in the Town of Georgetown, County of Madison, and State of New York, described as follows: BEING a part of Lot 91 of said town and bounded as follows: BEGINNING at a stake on the northwest corner of the lot now or formerly owned by Mrs. Fred Currier (formerly Ross) south line; running thence eaterly along said Currier south line about 199 ½ feet to a stake; thence in a southerly direction about 276feet to the corner of lands formerly owned by H. H. Whitmore; thence in a westerly direction about 323 feet to a stake; thence in a northerly direction 309 feet on the eat line of the old Cemetery to the northeast corner of said Cemetery; thence west about 9 feet; thence northerly about 97 feet to the place of beginning, CONTAINING about two acres of land, be the same more or less.

RESERVING THEREFROM a strip of land on the northerly end 65 feet wide on west line and tapering to 58 feet wide on east line.

PARCELL III

All that tract or parcel of land LYING AND BEING IN THE Town of Georgetown, County of Madison, State of New York and described as follows: Intending to convey that portion of the lands owned by the party of the first part (formerly) purchased from Gordon F. and Theresa B. Burgess on March 30, 1947 and known as the Whitmore Farm, described as follows: Said plot begins at the southeast corner of the Baptist Parsonage lot and continues easterly on the same course 241 feet to an iron post; thence in a northerly direction parallel with highway No. 26 for 267 feet to the line between the said Whitmore Farm and properties owned by Leemon R. Cossitt. The northerly boundary of this plot is the line of property now or formerly owned by Leemon R. Cossitt and the westerly line is the Baptist Parsonage lot.

samja3

Subject to covenants, easements and restrictions of record, if any.

The above described property consists of three separate tax parcels:
194.19-1-46
194.19-1-47
194.19-1-49

The property is on the east side of N.Y.S. Route 26S. Its postal address is 916 Route 26S, Georgetown, New York 13072.

The building on this property is registered on the U.S. National Register of Historic Places as the "Spirit House." [2006-06000160]

Being the same premises conveyed to Valentine T. and Helen B. Kartorie by Quit Claim Deed dated October 2, 1989 and recorded in the Madison County Clerk's Office on October 2, 1989 in Liber 895 of Deeds at Page 316.

TOGETHER with the appurtenances and all the estate and rights which the said Decedent had at the time of death, in said premises and also the estate therein, which the party of the first part has or has power to convey or dispose of, whether individually, or by virtue of said Estate or statute or otherwise.

TO HAVE AND TO HOLD the premises herein granted unto the Grantee, the heirs or successors and assigns of the Grantee forever.

AND the Grantor covenants as follows:

FIRST, the Grantee shall quietly enjoy the said premises;
SECOND, that the said premises are free from encumbrances;
THIRD, that the Grantor will execute or procure any further necessary assurance of the title to said premises.

This deed is subject to the trust provisions of Section 13 of the Lien Law.

IN WITNESS WHEREOF, the Grantor has executed this deed the day and year first above written.

In presence of:

Valerie K. Wilson

Intentionally left blank

samja4

355

NOTE:

STATE OF NEW YORK)
COUNTY OF ONONDAGA) ss.:

On the 3rd day of November, 2010, before me, the undersigned, personally appeared Valerie K. Wilson, personally known to me or proved to me on the basis of satisfactory evidence to be the individual whose name is subscribed to the within instrument, and she acknowledged to me that she executed the same in her capacity, and that by her signature on the instrument, the individual, or the person upon behalf of which the individual acted, executed the instrument.

_____
Notary Public

GREGORY A. SCICCHITANO
Notary Public, State of New York
No. 02SC5081204
Qualified in Onondaga County
Commission Expires June 30, 20___

Samja5

Plates & Illustrations Index

Plates & Illustrations Index

Plates & Illustrations Index

INDEX

This page is a miniaturized Guide formatted to fit not the Institutional Guidelines of Indexing, but to highlight some of the auxiliary data not markedly listed in the Table of Contents.

ART LOG

Timothy, Migrant
Black synthetic glossy leatherette verso Top – Hat.
½ x ½ in [1 x 1.2 cm]
White Double breasted four buttoned Long Jacket: white tulle on paper; black synthetic glossy leatherette lapels; matching black formal slacks: black synthetic glossy leatherette black toed white, lace shoes, on flat print Paper Backing.
5 ½ + 1.2 in. [14.2 x 3 cm]

Timothy, devoted husband
Black leatherette verso sporty hat.
Sport Matching Riding Outfit in wax paper and satin collar. Stockings are of striped gray paper. One white gloved hand akimbo.
6 x 1 ¾ x 1 ½ in [15 x 4 ¼ x 3 ¼ cm]

Sarah H. beloved wife
Pink purple-organza hat with black cotton underlay and black cotton asterisk accent on top.
1.1 x 1 ½+ [3 x 4 cm]
Matching pink-purple organza puffed long sleeved long gown with white tulle rippling effect with black V- shaped serrated shawl
6 ½ x 2 x 4.2 in. [16 ½ x 5 shoulders x 10 ½ cm]

Sarah H. in Love
Burgundy taffeta circular beret-inspired hat with circular white and burgundy accent on top.
¾ x .6 in [2 x 1 ½ cm]
High necked white tulle & burgundy taffeta bodice in Black & white paper printed puffed long sleeved gown with burgundy taffeta striped over white paper and white satin hemline horizontal accents
5 ½ x 1.3 x 3 ¾ in [14 x 3.6 x 9 ½ cm]

Sarah H., Widow
Black sheen side-up sateen hat.
¾ x 1 ½ in [2 x 3 ½ cm]
Black cotton puffed long sleeved top over full balloon scalloped gown length skirt of black satin and white papered little bows.
7 x 1 ½ x 4 ½ in [17 ½ x 4 11 ½ cm]

Cora V. Marvin
Mongolian black and burgundy with a beige stripped formal Hat.
1 x 1 ¾ in [2 x 4 cm]
Old rose- colored cape with beige serrated implied long dress, black- toed shoes.
6 x ½ in [15 x 3 5 cm]

William Trass
Straw colored formal sport Hat.
¾ x 1 in [2 x 2 ½ cm]
Matching black netted- tulle vest with straw colored cardstock lapel, straw colored cardstock shoes and gray inside shirt with netted tulle.
5 ½ x 1 ½ x 1 ½ in [14 x ¾ x 4 cm]

Alice Stevens, Orphan
Rhombic headgear on black satin verso.
½ x 1 ½ in [1 x 3 cm]
High necked short sleeved flared black sheen side satin over white cardstock button down below the knee black dress bedecked with black satin verso ribbon over white tulle right side hip, matching high heeled closed formal shoes, satin sheen side- up.
6 ½ x 1 x 4 in. [15 ½ x 3 x 10 cm]

Julia, Widow
Matching Black cotton tie over beribboned head gear; and matching black cotton slip on closed toe shoes.
1 x ½ in [2 x 1 ½ cm]
Square halter inspired ¾ sleeved black cotton rippled gown over white print paper; and paper printed elbow length left hand glove, showing.
6 x 1 ½ x 2 ¾ in [15 x 4 x 7 cm]

Bertha, Widow
Matching Black satin verso 6 projections stylized Hat
1 x 1 ¼ in [2 ½ x 3 cm]
Chino collared black cotton long sleeved blazer over pleated black slacks under white net tulle and white satin formal pumps.
6 x 1 ½ x 1 ¼ in [15 x 3 x 3 cm]

Frances, Orphan
Matching beribboned, white over black head- gear satin, sheen side up.
¼ x ¼ in [1 x 1 cm]
Baby collared long sleeved pleated black satin dress sheen side up with black paper shoes and white paper print stockings.
3 x ¾ x 1 ½ in [8 x 2 x 4 cm]

Leemon Ray Cossitt
Matching sheen deprived black hat with white satin accent strip.
½ x 1 in [I x 2 cm]
Black cotton blazer with white satin lapels over black satin long pants sheen deprived; white satin formal shoes with one horizontal strip of glitter accent each.
6 x 1 ½ x 1 in [15 x 4 x 3 cm]

Alice in Love
Matching Blue on Brown wax paper with silver white tulle with 4 flowered purple bottom- lined hat.
1 x 1 ½ in [2 ½ x 4 cm]
Square collared pink purple long sleeved, button down long dress with flowered shimmering silvery white tulle
5 ½ x ¾ x 2 ½ in [14 x 2 x 6 ½ cm]

Baby Frances
Beribboned burgundy, and pink tulle headgear as hat.
¾ x ¾ in [2 x 2 cm]
Baby collared long sleeved, hip belted dress wit pleated skirt; paper printed shoes and socks.
2 ½ x ¾ x 1 in [6 x 1 ½ x 2 ¼ cm]

Bertha
Textured black flop hat with orange silk accent on top.
½ x ¾ in [1 x 2 cm]
V-collared short sleeved dress of orange silk sheen side up, mid leg length skirt with pocket. Black high heeled leatherette glossy shoes. Paper printed short white glove.
6 x 1 ¼ x 1 ¾ in [15 x 3 x 4 ½ cm]

Elwin
Jet- black flop hat.
½ x ¾ in [1 x 2 cm]
Matching jet- black, camiso- chino styled dinner jacket; matching jet black pants and formal shoes.
6 x 1 ½ x 1 in [15 x 4 3 cm]

LR Cossitt / Chauncey Stevens/ Floyd Currier
Light Tan wax paper hat.
¼ x ¾ in [1 x 2 cm]
Robin blue cardstock with silver white et tulle; royal blue card stock lapel, tangerine tie and matching one tangerine hand cuff. Light tan wax paper formal shoes.
6 x 1 ¼ x 1 in [15 x 3 x 3 cm]

John Currier / Laverne C. Marvin
Light tan wax paper sport beret styled hat.
½ x 1 in [1 x 3 cm]
Matching light tan wax paper formal dinner jacket and black cravat; black sheen side silk formal pants; light tan wax paper formal sport shoes.
6 x 1 ½ x 1 ¼ in [15 x 3 ½ x 3 ½ cm]

Valerie Wilson
Light tan wax paper hat with net tulle.
½ x ½ in [1 ½ x 1 ½ cm]
Matching light tan wax paper long sleeved short jacket with tangerine lapels that matches the pleated pants over high heeled light tan wax paper shoes.
5 ½ x 1 ½ x ¼ in [14 x 3 x 3 ½ cm]

James Wilson
Jet- black sport hat.
¼ x ¾ in [1 x 2 cm]
Black silky jacket with tan wax paper lapel, and matching light tan wax paper pants over burgundy taffeta shoes.
5 ¾ x 1 ½ x 1 ¼ in [15 x 3 ½ x 3 cm]

Mrs. Kartorie
Matching Elegant black sheen side up Hat with tulle.
½ x 1 ½ in [1 x 4 cm]
Strapless little black dress with a black bow on the bodice and formal closed shoes.
5 ½ x ¾ x 1 ¼ I [14 x 2 x3 cm]

Atty. John Marshall
Matching black over burgundy colored hat.
¾ x 1 in [2 x 2 ½ cm]
Sheen side up black satin jacket with burgundy lapels, black pants and matching burgundy colored shoes.
6 x 1 ½ x 1 ½ in [16 x 3 ½ x 4 cm]

Mrs. Dorothy McLean
Black cotton Hat with extra long netted tulle cover
½ x 1 ½ in [1 x 3 cm]
Black sleeveless, haltered serrated hipline long gown with heeled black pumps. One wrist flower.
5 ½ x 1 x 1 in [14 x 2 ½ x 2 cm]

Mr. Richard McLean
Matching Black leatherette glossy Hat.
½ x ¾ in [1 x 2 cm]
Gray- black satin, sheen side up dinner jacket, with black leatherette glossy lapels. Gray-black tailored pants sheen side up; black leatherette gloss shoes.
6 ¼ x 1 ½ x 1 ½ in [16 x 4 x 4 cm]

Mrs. Alice Stevens - Cossitt, Widow
Matching black silk verso Hat with tulle net.
¾ x 1 ¼ in [2 x 3 cm]
Standing collared long sleeved, sleek oriental silk long dress with matching silk verso heeled- shoes.
6 x 1 x 1 in [15 cm x 2 ½ x 2 ½ cm]

rexie
Orient inspired light tan wax paper hat over blood- red shiny backdrop accent.
½ x 1 ½ in [1 x 4 cm]
Little blood-red shiny paper little body forming tailored dress, tapered below the knee length. Matching shiny blood-red, paper high heels. A reddish white, tiny tulle flower on each wrist.
5 ¾ x 1 ¼ x ¾ in [14 ½ x 3 ½ x 1 ½ cm]

Page Finder for the Keywords of the Message Being Conveyed:

Provenance
p.___
I
p.___
YOU
p.___
Me   together   Us
p.___   p.___   p.___
Responsible   Stewardship
p.___   p.___
Trust   Righteous   Individuality
p.___   p.___   p.___
Honesty   Integrity   Accountability   Respect
p.___   p.___   p.___
Respectful   Respectability   RESPECT   Respectable
p.___   p.___   p.___   p.___
Discourses   Empirical method   Conscientious   Reliable
p.___   p.___   p.___   p.___
Open Communication   Nurturing   Welcoming   Diversified
p.___   p.___   p.___   p.___
Inclusive   Trustworthy   Helpful   Cooperative   Peaceful
p.___   p.___   p.___   p.___   p.___
Kindness   Comforting   Transparency   Open-minded
p.___   p.___   p.___   p.___
Scientific   Accurate   LOVE   Unified   Precision
p.___   p.___   p.___   p.___
Repeatable   Measurable   Humane   Sincere
p.___   p.___   p.___   p.___
Learned   Refinement   High Culture
p.___   p.___   p.___
Positive   Mindset   Courtesy
p.___   p.___
Inquiry   Selflessness
p.___   p.___
Brotherly
p.___
Class
p.___

Yes, you find them. Thank You.

No matter how dreary and hopeless a situation seemed to be; it is LOVE that is the Universal Neutralizer to Negativity.

i
yOu
Hurtful
Narrow – minded
Greed Jealousy Covetous
Common Thief Disrespectful
Undermine Dishonest Stealing
Stolen Parasitic Unreliable Oppressive
Prejudice Take Something Not One's Own
Grab what you can Opportunistic Selfishness

LOVEloveLOVEloveLOVEloveLOVEloveLOVEloveLOVEloveLOVEloveLOVE

Grab what you can Opportunistic Selfishness
Prejudice Take Something Not One's Own
Stolen Parasitic Unreliable Oppressive
Undermine Dishonest Stealing
Common Thief Disrespectful
Greed Jealousy Covetous
Narrow – minded
Hurtful
yOu
US
I

One Person at a Time. One Person at a Time. One Person at a Time. One Person at a Time. The CHOICE has Always been Yours.

Fill it with LOVE. Replace with action words that mean Love and See the difference.

I
r._
yOu
r._
Hurtful
r._
Narrow – minded
r._
Greed Jealousy Covetous
r._   r._   r._
Common Thief Disrespectful
r._   r._   r._
Undermine Dishonest Stealing
r._   r._   r._
Stolen Parasitic Unreliable Oppressive
r._   r._   r._   r._
Prejudice Take Something Not One's Own
r._   r._
Grab what you can Opportunistic Selfishness
r._   r._   r._
LOVEloveLOVEloveLOVEloveLOVEloveLOVEloveLOVEloveLOVEloveLOVE

Grab what you can Opportunistic Selfishness
Prejudice Take Something Not One's Own
Stolen Parasitic Unreliable Oppressive
Undermine Dishonest Stealing
Common Thief Disrespectful
Greed Jealousy Covetous
Narrow – minded
Hurtful
yOu
US
I

See any difference in what positive words can do? Let us all try positive actions on these positive words.

Find the page in your heart to neutralize these words with positive words of Love.

I
r._
yOu
r._
Hurtful
r._
Narrow – minded
r._
Greed Jealousy Covetous
r._   r._   r._
Common Thief Disrespectful
r._   r._   r._
Undermine Dishonest Stealing
r._   r._   r._
Stolen Parasitic Unreliable Oppressive
r._   r._   r._   r._
Prejudice Take Something Not One's Own
r._   r._
Grab what you can Opportunistic Selfishness
r._   r._
LOVEloveLOVEloveLOVEloveLOVEloveLOVEloveLOVEloveLOVEloveLOVE

Grab what you can Opportunistic Selfishness
r._   r._   r._
Prejudice Take Something Not One's Own
r._   r._
Stolen Parasitic Unreliable Oppressive
r._   r._   r._   r._
Undermine Dishonest Stealing
r._   r._   r._
Common Thief Disrespectful
r._   r._   r._
Greed Jealousy Covetous
r._   r._   r._
Narrow – minded
r._
Hurtful
r._
yOu
r._
US
r.-
I

AMORETTO

367

Resurreccion Dimaculangan is the Owner of US National Register Historic Site # 06000160. Rexie earned a Master's Degree in Museum Studies from Syracuse University, New York; a Bachelor of Science Degree in Medical Technology, from Manila Central University; a Certificate in Teaching Degree, from Philippine Normal University. While pursuing her Master of Arts in Education Degree at PNU, the International Travel Bug caught up on her so bad, she was a Semester short from it. With the use of combined integration of literal, practical life experiences, hands - on applications of multi - disciplinary viewpoints, both perspectives as an Educator, and as a Life - long Student, Rexie is currently trying to debunk the notion that:

A. Historical Conservation & Preservation is all about the millions & the last name.

B. History when altered to custom fit vested Interests cannot be re - routed back on the Fact Track.

While big, deep pockets make achieving goals easier: Passion, Dedication, a Conscientious Work - Ethic coupled with the Tenacity to Stay with the Facts can make huge dents, in Achieving the Goal of Making a Positive Difference One Person at a Time, Possible - Plausible. The Presentation of Authentic Facts, and conscientious ideas founded on parity, acted upon sincerely, make moving forward a reality, one minute step at a time, but that which are hinged to a basic human trait: Unbiased collaborations of Real Diverse Professionals of the same Values.

"Spirited Deed Revelations"

06000160 The Factual Quest for the Truth & Accuracy
In The Authenticity of The Spirit House Story

Resurreccion Dimaculangan

Printed in the United States
By Bookmasters

Printed in the United States
By Bookmasters